The Sound of
Two Hands Clapping

Kenneth Tynan

The Sound of
Two Hands Clapping

Holt, Rinehart and Winston
New York

'Lenny Bruce' first appeared as the Introduction to *How to
Talk Dirty and Influence People*, copyright © 1965 by *Playboy*.

Acknowledgments

For permission to reprint most of what follows, the author is
grateful to the editors of seven publications, three of them
English — the *Observer*, the *New Statesman* and *Punch* — and four
American — the *New Yorker*, *Playboy*, *Esquire* and the *Atlantic
Monthly*. The author's thanks are also due to Rupert Hart-Davis
for permission to reprint the essays on *The Recruiting Officer* and
Othello.

Library of Congress Catalog Card Number: 75-27194

ISBN: 0-03-016726-4

First published in the United States in 1976

Printed in Great Britain

Contents

To Kathleen

Preface

With one exception (to which I'll return), the pieces collected
in these pages have a common theme. They represent enthu-
siasms. They are celebrations of people, places and ideas that
have excited me. To some readers this may seem out of character, because when I was operating as a drama critic in the '50s
and early '60s I was generally reputed to be a congenital
knocker. The fact, as any critic will confirm, is that most
theatrical productions, like most books and most television
shows, are extremely dreary; and whereas a book reviewer or
TV critic is not expected to cover everything that floods into
the bookshops or flickers out of the tube, a drama critic is
compelled to report on every production that hits the stage,
with however sickening a thud.

So although I always enjoyed praising shows, it was not a
pleasure in which I could often indulge without incurring
suspicions of bribery or brain damage. In 1963, however, I gave
up regular reviewing, and since then I have been free to focus
on what fascinated me, as opposed to what happened to be set
before me. The result is this harvest of preferences and predilections, an armful of bouquets tossed at some of the talents
by which I have been awed and exhilarated in the course of
the past decade. It also commemorates places I have visited,
causes I have supported, and hobby-horses I have ridden.
Two of the pieces were written as introductory essays to picture-
books dealing with the National Theatre's productions of
The Recruiting Officer and *Othello*; and a third was anthologized
in an American compilation called *The New Eroticism*. The
remaining dozen are making their first appearance between
hard covers.

Section One consists of tributes to great individualists in the
arts. I once coined a phrase — High Definition Performance —

to sum up what I liked most about authentic stars. In a nutshell (and many of the people who have this quality could fairly be described as nutcases), H.D.P. means the ability—shared by great athletes, sportsmen, bullfighters and conversationalists as well as stage performers—to communicate the essence of one's talent to an audience with economy, grace, no apparent effort, and absolute, hard-edged clarity of outline. My selection from this category includes two comedians (Lenny Bruce and Eric Morecambe), two legendary ladies (Ethel Merman and Marlene Dietrich), a matador (Antonio Ordoñez), a movie director (Roman Polanski, as much for his personality as for his movies), an actor (Nicol Williamson, as much for his personality as for his acting), and an all-round man of the theatre (Noël Coward). I am told that Mr Williamson was not best pleased by my account of his journey to give a solo performance for Richard Nixon at the White House: at all events, he has not spoken to me since I wrote it. A pity: it was admiringly intended, and I still think it reads that way.

Section Two is devoted to *The Recruiting Officer* and Laurence Olivier's *Othello*. And here I must declare an interest. I spent ten years (1963–73) as Literary Manager and alleged *éminence grise* of the National Theatre, which was responsible for both productions. The former, with a cast led by Maggie Smith, Robert Stephens, Colin Blakely and Olivier, was quite simply the best production of a Restoration comedy I have ever seen; and the latter gave me a unique chance of observing, at close quarters, the greatest stage actor of his time at work on one of his greatest roles. Like Polanski, with whom I collaborated on the screenplay of *Macbeth*, Olivier was my employer; but I don't think sycophancy enters into my judgment of either man. I do not admire them because I worked for them: I worked for them because I admired them.

In Section Three there appears, for the first time in print, a personal credo in the form of a *Playboy* interview, which was tape-recorded in 1970. My interlocutor on this occasion was Alan Coren, a brilliant journalist who stubbornly declined to let me off any of the hooks he had baited for me. The resulting dialogue never reached the magazine's pages, possibly because it was thought too dull, possibly because I was too obscure a figure to justify such V.I.P. treatment, but mainly because it had not been intended for publication in the first place. To fill in the background: *Playboy* had advanced me money for a couple of articles they subsequently rejected (one of which, on pornography, was later accepted by *Esquire* and is reprinted elsewhere in this book); and their Literary Editor, the late and much-missed Augie Spectorsky, generously offered to write off the debt in exchange for an interview. I am grateful to his successor and to Alan Coren for permission to publish it here.

Section Four plunges into sex and pornography, of both of which — when executed with the proper verve and elegance — I entirely approve, some would say to the point of obsession. Horace Walpole once wondered when the world would realize that 'peace and propagation' were the happiest and healthiest activities available to mankind — a sentiment I would wholly endorse, provided it could be rephrased to include sex with contraception.

The fifth and final section is concerned with foreign travel, mostly in a southerly direction. I do not find Northern Europe an ideal zone for human habitation. It is a fine place for industrial productivity, but its climate breeds puritans and the terrible dictates of the Protestant Work Ethic. The Romans were right to pull out when they did; and, for myself, I would rather be a sun-drenched peasant in Luxor than a miner in Merthyr Tydfil. This section includes a guided tour round four of the great European fiestas, and a heart-felt eulogy addressed to stinking Valencia, my favourite Mediterranean city. It also contains — a single thorn among the laurels — a bitter reminiscence of a weekend spent in a perfectly beastly Cairo hotel.

The rest is applause and affirmation — coupled with regret that I have no space in which to salute the other High Definition Performers, such as Lennon and McCartney, before they became Lennon versus McCartney; Gary Sobers, loping in to bowl or carving off-side boundaries; Jeff Thomson of Australia, catapulting the batsmen of England into flinching collapse; Peter Ustinov, incomparably talking; Johan Cruyff, dancing past the boots of a dozen countries in the 1974 World Cup; Rodnina and Zaitsev, world figure-skating champions, all but making love on ice; James Cagney, the spring-heeled imp with the velvet voice; Fred Astaire, the jaunty elf with the pleading knees; Dizzy Gillespie, most durable of trumpet virtuosi; Peter Brook, until he exiled himself; Mel Brooks, *le vrai* Superjew and unrivalled comic improviser; Peter Cook, our funniest educated comedian; Eduardo de Filippo, subtlest of great Italian actors and doyen of living Italian playwrights; Muhammad Ali, who regained in Zaïre what he should never, rightfully, have lost ...

And many (but not, now I come to think of it, all *that* many) more.

KENNETH TYNAN

Section One

Nicol Williamson: the Road to the White House

On February 24th, 1969, Richard Nixon arrived in London at the end of a European tour. He dined that evening at Chequers, the Buckinghamshire mansion that is the official country home of Britain's Prime Ministers. After dinner, his host, Harold Wilson, drew him over to a sofa, where (as Nixon tells it) 'he engaged me in a very extended and animated conversation'. The other guests assumed that some international problem had grabbed the two men's attention, and wondered busily what it was. In reality, they were talking about an actor. An infrequent and normally unenthusiastic playgoer, Wilson had recently attended the first night of a new production of *Hamlet*, staged at the Roundhouse—a converted Victorian railway shed in north London—by Tony Richardson, and what he was now so urgently saying was that the President must make a point of seeing Nicol Williamson, whose performance in the title role had been highly praised by the London critics. Williamson, said Wilson grandly, was the best Hamlet of his generation, perhaps of the century. Nixon explained that he had no free evenings, and this seemed to be the end of the matter. But the name clearly stuck in his mind, because later in the year items began to appear in the American press about the President's interest in Williamson's work.

These clippings reached the desk of Abe Schneider, the chairman of Columbia Pictures, which is the company responsible for distributing the movie version of Williamson's *Hamlet*. Schneider called Raymond Bell, his man in Washington, and instructed him to find out from the White House whether the President would like to see the film. It seemed that he didn't have time. Too bad, said Bell. In that case, how would it be if Williamson came out to Washington and gave the President an hour or so of *Hamlet* in person? It was now late in January,

1970. Red Skelton had just inaugurated a series of so-called Evenings at the White House, which would subsequently include the Broadway cast of *1776* and a *tour de chant* by Peggy Lee. A fair, square sampling of popular culture—but a touch of *Hamlet* in the night could do the Nixons' intellectual status nothing but good, and the Columbia proposal was referred to the President for a decision.

At about this time, a London newspaperman telephoned Oscar Beuselinck, a stocky, outspoken London solicitor, who acts as Williamson's agent in England, and asked him to confirm or deny reports that his client was going to Washington to entertain the President. Beuselinck replied, with that bluntness of manner and delicacy of grammar which characterize him, 'Who's kidding whom?' He scented a hoax and, knowing Williamson to be of a mischievous nature, suspected that he might have started the rumours himself. A few days later, Columbia got the answer it was hoping for: Nixon whole-heartedly approved of its suggestion and would be happy to devote an Evening to Nicol Williamson, who thus became, at the age of thirty-two, the only legitimate actor ever to be invited to give a solo performance at the White House.

I first met Williamson about seven years ago—fleetingly, at theatrical parties in London. Not that he relished parties as such: he was rightly reputed to be a solitary, and lived alone in a cramped ground-floor flat in Notting Hill Gate. From time to time, there were girl friends (or so one heard), intensely cherished until some long-ticking emotional time bomb exploded, after which all would be over, but what he mainly needed was 'mates to stay up with' (as one mate put it)— companions to see him through the dark hours when extreme dismay might strike. Among people he trusted, he could be excellent party value. I think of him at John Osborne's house, one night in 1965, singing jazz standards of the '20s and '30s and accompanying himself on an eighteenth-century keyboard in a style you might describe as stride spinet. Already he was a figure of some mystery and consequence, his work admired by his fellow-actors as well as by the critics and the public, his general demeanour a boon to the show-biz columns, where epithets like 'wild man' and 'hell-raiser' were ritually dusted off in his honour. He was known to have talked back

to noisy late-comers, to have walked offstage in more than one
fit of self-hating rage, and even to have slugged David Merrick
backstage in Philadelphia. (Oscar Beuselinck, a stickler for the
proprieties, had repeatedly warned him, 'You're in the public
eye, cock, and you've bloody well got to learn how to behave.')
He had made his first London success in 1962, at the age of
twenty-four, when he joined the Royal Shakespeare Company
and appeared—within a single season—as a thieving aircraft-
man in Henry Livings' *Nil Carborundum*, a penniless Russian
gambler in Gorky's *The Lower Depths*, and a seedy Jacobean
cuckold in Middleton's *Women Beware Women*. At the Royal
Court Theatre, he had gone on to play the inordinate hero of
J. P. Donleavy's *The Ginger Man* and (quite indelibly) Bill
Maitland, the cynical, defeated lawyer in John Osborne's
Inadmissible Evidence.

From a few encounters in the mid-1960s I learned that he
was savagely observant. He had a disconcerting ear and eye for
one's weaknesses, for the tricks of gesture, accent and inflexion
that expose and define one too vividly for comfort. Even today,
I cannot think of Tony Richardson or John Osborne without
recalling Nicol's rendering of their voices: the impersonation
has usurped the original. His physical presence was immediately
potent—the tall, stooping, tapering silhouette, the receding
ginger hair, the worn forehead, the bemused blue eyes, and the
smile that was all tired commiseration, suggesting an ex-champ
making a dubious comeback rather than a young contender
for the title of best actor in the world. The lower lip protruded
Hapsburg-fashion, as in a Velázquez portrait of Philip IV.
Now and then, there would be a winning flash of a grin,
crooked and raffish, accompanied by an upward flick of the
eyebrows, which he shrugs as others shrug their shoulders—a
grin of wicked complicity. At the same time, his eyes would roll,
making him look slightly desperate. I remember talking to
him about *Inadmissible Evidence*. He said he used to sit onstage
'with the stench of death in my nostrils'. He acted best, he told
me, when he was contemplating death—'not the character's
death but my own'. He added, 'You must go to the edge; you
must look over the brink into the abyss.' He did not sound in
the least pretentious.

He has a sly but well-organized urge to dominate whatever
group he finds himself in. When listening to a substandard

anecdote, I normally manage to stay poker-faced, no matter how eminent the raconteur, but if it is Nicol, my lips automatically crease into a smile. He makes you feel that not to respond, not to complete the emotional circuit, would be an act of betrayal. By seeming to be always vulnerable, he succeeds in being always one up. He is fond of quoting a phrase that was brayed at him by a young Birmingham intellectual when he was in his teens: 'Dear Nick—*yet* so hesitant, *yet* so sure!' He is at once hypersensitive and supremely self-confident, and it can be difficult to tell, from one moment to the next, which is the kernel and which the shell. A girl named Pauline Peters, who recently interviewed him for the magazine *Nova*, has shrewdly remarked, 'You feel that whatever you say you're putting the boot in.'

I tentatively reached the same conclusion some four years ago, when he came to dinner with me for the first time. He behaved like a king stag transported to an alien domain and exercising the territorial imperative as if it were a divine right. To begin with, he turned up an hour early—a masterly ploy that caught my wife and me unwashed and unchanged. Full of apologies, he volunteered to pass the time by Hoovering the living-room, on the mildly annoying tacit assumption that the carpet was dirty. Before we could dissuade him, he had dragged the machine down from an upstairs closet and was passionately mowing away. 'Who else is coming?' he asked when I returned in a clean shirt to prise the Hoover from his grasp. I told him that one of the guests was Jonathan Miller, the director, writer and former comedian. 'Biggest phony in London,' Nicol said crisply. 'Who else?' I said that, apart from the Millers, there would be a pretty girl named Yvonne Stacpoole, who had been having a lengthy affair with the celebrated Italian director Piero Ghiberti. (Both Stacpoole and Ghiberti are pseudonyms.) Nicol stored up this information for later use. No sooner had the other guests arrived than he strangled conversation almost at birth by producing an L.P. of the Mamas and the Papas and playing it at full volume on the stereo. It takes a lot to silence Dr Miller, who had already launched into a vivacious chat about Byzantine art, but even he had no answer to tactics so blatantly anti-social. When we moved downstairs to the dining-room, Nicol munched for several minutes in silence before addressing his first remark to Miss Stacpoole. 'So you're the girl', he said engagingly, 'who was being fucked by Ghiberti?' He reinforced the remark by placing his left hand on his right biceps and making a swift upward jab with his clenched right fist. For the second time in the evening, everybody stopped talking. Miss Stacpoole, who had never met Nicol before, was exquisitely unfazed. 'I'm afraid you've got it wrong, Mr Williamson,' she said simply. 'I *am* being fucked by Ghiberti.' Nicol grinned and nodded, but he was obviously affronted by her cool, and a few minutes later he got up and left the room. We soon heard a deafening five-minute blast of the Mamas and the Papas, followed by a clatter of footsteps on the stairs and a slammed front door. 'I enjoy sacred monsters,' said Jonathan Miller, 'but preferably in zoos.' That night was Nicol at his worst, trapped among intellectuals, uncertain of the rules and therefore opting out of the game. Penelope Gilliatt, one of his closest friends, said to me on another occasion, 'Nick likes jousting with people, but he jousts to win. And, of course, he's a congenital no-sayer. He regards a lot of quite considerable men as vermin.'

For some time after that aborted dinner, my only contacts with him were professional. In the winter of 1967, I did a long filmed interview with him for an American TV programme on the art of acting. Leaning against his own mantelpiece, sipping his own champagne, he was fluent and secure. Among other things, we discussed the conventional wisdom that urges young actors to play as many parts as they can in order (so the cliché goes) 'to keep the instrument in tune'. I asked him why, since his success three years earlier in *Inadmissible Evidence*, he had played only three new parts, each for a strictly limited run.

His reply was an adroitly modulated tirade: 'Every man knows his own instrument, and I know mine. I know what it is capable of, and there are certain things I want to play. But I don't want to stand up there every night and do all the parts in the book. People say "Keep the instrument tuned," but there are a lot of hairy parts that you just have no time for, that it would bore the anus off you to play. So what—so you can do it, so you're the most technically accomplished actor in the world—but why? It's like that camera filming us. If you keep that machine running and running and running and running, it is going to have to be serviced, it is going to break down. Now, I've talked to actors who have played the same parts I have, and when I tell them I'm tired or I'm shattered or I'll go nuts if I do this any longer, they say, "Oh, but I played it for *x* number of performances and I didn't find it tiring at all." The simple answer to that is "No, because you don't work the way I do." Because I am playing it totally and absolutely, which means that I sink everything in it to make it the most marvellous, compelling, total thing you can see. And nobody will do that better than I will. They will do it differently, but they won't do it better. Now, you can't go on working like that all the time. I am going to die quite young anyway and move into the ashes department, but before I do I am going to *choose* what I do, and it's going to be the most exciting departments of drama and comedy that I can think of, and you can't do that indefinitely or you are going to thrash yourself into the grave, and for what? For "I did six hundred and thirty-two performances of *The Bells*"? *But how well did you do them, Henry Irving?* Or "I played *Othello* three hundred times"? *But how do we know, Edmund Kean, that you were really all that good?* If you are going to be the best at your job—if you feel that, which I do feel—then you have got to take it easy. Most audiences don't want to go under the skin, they don't want to get into the heart and bones of things, because it frightens them and they don't like it. But they have *got* to be frightened. They may not like what I do, but they won't fault me on it—at least, not much. I am going to do certain pieces of work in certain areas that actually mean my life, that are going to keep me alive by their value and excitement. And that is all. There is nothing else in my life. I've lost about three women that I was deeply in love with because I didn't pay enough attention to them. Look at all this, for Jesus' sake.' He indicated the little room. 'Not that it's all that much, but it *is* comfortable and it *is* happy, and we can smash out the odd bottle of Bollinger and it's lovely. *But . . . But* my whole life is circled and centred round the next piece of work, and I've got to take time over it because it's going to have you on the edge of your seat, and I want you to like it and be destroyed by it.'

I asked him what he would like to have engraved on his tombstone. He gave me the slanting grin and said, ' "Life isn't all you want, but it's all you've got, so stick a geranium in your hat and be happy." '

In January, 1970, I took him to lunch at his favourite London restaurant—the Etoile, in Soho—to find out whether he would like to work with Laurence Olivier's National Theatre Company, where I was employed as literary adviser and general idea man. I wasn't particularly sanguine: a notorious non-joiner, he had turned down many such invitations since quitting the Royal Shakespeare in 1962. All the same, the offer that Olivier had authorized me to make him was certainly better—as the Australians quaintly say—than a poke in the eye with a burnt stick. For his first season with the troupe, he could pick any three of the following roles: Rogozhin in an adaptation of Dostoevsky's *The Idiot*, Judge Brack in *Hedda Gabler* (directed by Ingmar Bergman), Danton in *Danton's Death*, Hildy Johnson in *The Front Page*, the elder son in *Long Day's Journey Into Night*, and the title part in *Macbeth*. If he chose the O'Neill, I added, I could promise him Olivier as his father and Mike Nichols to direct. Royal flushes like that are rarely dealt to young actors. Nicol gave me a sympathetic hearing, generously praised the bouquet of the La Tache '61 that we were drinking, and took just twenty hours to consider and reject the whole glittering package.

Nicol regards it as a weakness to answer the telephone. Moreover, when he is using it to call others, he never identifies himself; you have to guess who it is, and if you hesitate your uncertainty instantly puts him one up. On February 11th, 1970, his phone rang all morning, but he was in a non-answering mood, to the high annoyance of Oscar Beuselinck, who was fuming at the other end of the line. 'I might have been offering him a million dollars, but he still wouldn't have given a damn,' Beuselinck said later. 'If that client of mine doesn't take care, he's going to end up in the gutter. You can cry wolf just so often, and then the offers stop coming. He isn't really an actor at all. He's a bloody busker.' (Buskers are kerbside entertainers who perform for theatre queues, passing the hat round afterwards; when Nicol heard of Beuselinck's remark, he said that, if anything, he felt flattered.) He went out to lunch and came back to find a message from his charwoman: 'Ring Oscar B. He sounds very excited.' He dialled the number and learned that Columbia had confirmed the rumour: Nixon wanted him to give a Shakespeare recital at the White House on Thursday,

March 19th, just over five weeks away. Columbia would pay all expenses. Almost for the first time in his professional life, Nicol said yes without hesitation.

I heard about the project (and formed the idea of joining him on it) a few days later, when he called me up to discuss it. Already it was clear that his plans for the Evening were rather more ambitious than anyone in Washington imagined. 'I don't want to just read bits of Shakespeare, or even just read bits of other books, or even just read,' he said. 'I want to give them something breathtaking, something not many people can do.' He told me he had decided to sing as well as act. Knowing his taste in music, which was nurtured at Jimmy Ryan's under the tutelage of people like J. C. Higginbotham and the De Paris brothers, I wasn't surprised to hear that his accompanists would be a nine-man group called the World's Greatest Jazz Band, led by Yank Lawson and Bob Haggart, and dedicated to basic Dixieland. (The seven other members of the ensemble included such survivors from the pre-microgroove era as Billy Butterfield, Lou McGarity, Kai Winding and Bud Freeman.) I asked him whether, as a presumed liberal, he had any qualms about serving as court jester to Nixon. 'I wouldn't act in South Africa,' he replied after a pause, 'but otherwise anything goes.' This was the first entrance of a theme that was to be heard with several variations during the next few weeks.

While the Evening took shape in odd corners of his mind, he busied himself professionally by recording an L.P. for Columbia Records. (Entitled simply 'Nicol Williamson', it was released in the summer of 1971.) I turned up at the studio to watch the first session. It was 8 p.m., but work had only just begun: Nicol is a night creature. A large orchestra, twenty strings strong, was playing a ballad; the star murmured soulfully into a mike, his forehead a map of undulating furrows, his face resembling one of those sad but resilient saints you see carved on the portals of Romanesque churches. He was wearing a blue shirt with a silk scarf knotted inside it, and looked hairier (except on the thinning scalp) than I remembered him. Near-Dundrearies now flourished on his jowls, and the moustache drooped down to the chin in a thin reddish line. When he smiled, he put me in mind of Randle Patrick McMurphy, the obstreperous hero of Ken Kesey's *One Flew Over the Cuckoo's Nest*: 'This guy is red-headed with long red sideburns and a tangle of curls out from under his cap ... broad across the jaw and shoulders and chest, a broad white devilish grin, and he's hard ... kind of the way a baseball is hard under the scuffed leather.'

As the song built to a climax, he let rip with an amazingly rich and pungent tenor voice. It was obvious from his timing and breath control that he had not studied Sinatra for nothing. 'They can say what they like,' said a young sound-mixer in the control room, 'he's the best pop singer who ever played Hamlet.' The number ended, and Nicol came in to hear the playback. When it was over, he said, 'I'm a quarter-tone flat in the middle section, and I bet nobody noticed it.' Nobody had.

'Were you nervous at all?' asked the producer.

'What you think is nervousness is in fact my tremolo,' Nicol said. 'That's not what's wrong. Let's do another take.'

'Can you bear to?'

'Six times a week and twice on Sundays. But first, where's the thunderbox?'

While he was gone (thunderbox is archaic military slang for toilet), an engineer said incredulously, 'Is he really making his first L.P.?'

I gathered that from the beginning of the session Nicol had been commanding retakes, suggesting changes in instrumental entries, and generally running the show. He loves to be a pro among pros: to talk football to footballers, music to musicians; to be accepted by the inner circles of professions other than his own. When he got back, he had somehow acquired three bottles of champagne (Taittinger Blanc de Blancs), which he distributed in teacups to the crew. Someone asked him about the film of *Inadmissible Evidence*, which was the first he had ever made. 'I didn't see it,' Nicol said. 'But when it was finished I said to the cameraman, "Am I any good? Am I as good as Spencer Tracy at his best?" Because those are the boys who really know. And he said I was. So that was enough for me.'

'Shall we go on, Nick?' said the producer tentatively.

Nicol clapped him on the shoulder. 'You know us actors,' he said. 'A glass of champagne, a pat on the arse, and we'll eat fucking grass.'

In all, the session lasted three hours and yielded one fine track—a version of Jim Webb's 'Didn't We, Girl?'—of which I later obtained a test pressing. Guests at my house have

confidently identified the performer as (among others) Perry
Como, Dean Martin and Andy Williams. The trouble with
Nicol's singing voice may well be that it makes you think of
everyone but Nicol.

On February 24th, he phoned me to say that word of his
Washington gig had appeared in the *New York Times*, in an
article about Mrs Connie Stuart, director of Mrs Nixon's staff,
and 'producer-in-residence' (the *Times* said) of all White House
entertainment. Mrs Stuart was described as 'a tall, peppy
redhead' who liked moose-hunting and had taken a degree
in speech and drama at the University of Maryland. 'When you
come to the White House, it's a real cultural experience,' she
said, adding that future Evenings would 'run the whole gamut'.
(To illustrate where that might lead, she revealed that the
President 'would like to have good college choruses from the
Midwest'.) Nicol, she announced, would be doing scenes from
Shakespeare. Either the *Times* man wasn't listening very
closely or Mrs Stuart's speech was slurred (unlikely, in view of
that Maryland degree), because the piece went on to say that
Nicol's name had been proposed by 'Earl Wilson, the night-
club columnist'. 'So it's all fixed now,' Nicol said to me gloomily.
'That's when you start to panic.'

Another recording session took place on March 6th, with
more Taittinger out of teacups. This time, there were no violins;
the supporting group was a Chicago-style septet, bursting with
middle-aged pep, and featuring the veteran Max Kaminsky,
who had been flown in from New York at Nicol's request to
play lead trumpet. The star rehearsed and recorded 'I Ain't
Gonna Give Nobody None of My Jelly Roll', then paused to
pass out champagne to a bunch of theatre people who had
dropped in to listen. 'You look a bit wild tonight, Dad,' said a
dapper little actor, accepting a cup. 'You've been pulling at
your hair again.' Nicol was absorbed in argument about the
liquor intake of a celebrated jazzman: 'I tell you, before every
set he used to sink *two half-pint tumblers* of neat Courvoisier.'

Finishing his drink, he went off to run through 'I Wish I
Could Shimmy like My Sister Kate', and I chatted with John
McGrath, a handsome Scots playwright in his thirties, who had
written two of the films— *The Bofors Gun* and *The Reckoning*—
in which Nicol had starred. McGrath's version of *The Seagull*,
modernized and set in the Scottish Highlands, had been

directed by Anthony Page for the Dundee repertory company in 1960; Nicol had played Duncan, which was how McGrath renamed Chekhov's suicidal hero, Constantin. 'After the performance one night, Nick and I were drinking in a pub with some of the cast,' McGrath told me. 'Suddenly he said that, like Constantin, he was going to kill himself. He leaped up and ran out of the bar towards the Tay estuary. On the way, he stopped to take off his shoes and socks, which seemed a rather eccentric touch. Maybe he was just giving us a chance to catch up with him. Anyway, he actually did jump into the river, and we actually had to pull him out. Nick has some great spiritual discomfort. I mean, you can't go *on* chucking yourself off things.' On at least two other occasions, it seemed, Nicol had convinced McGrath that he was about to die. 'Once, in the pub next door to the Royal Court Theatre, he said he'd had an electro-cardiogram and his heart was going to pack up at any moment. I think he really believed it by the time he'd finished telling me. I certainly did. Another time, he conned me into driving him to Harley Street by saying he'd had some tests and the doctor was going to tell him that afternoon whether or not he had terminal cancer. Of course, there were no tests and no doctor. But he gave a great performance.'

We talked about Nicol's acting. 'In Dundee, he wasn't a star,' McGrath said. 'He was an actor the way other people are coal miners. Nowadays he's become something you might call the Actor as Existential Hero. You know the story of how he walked offstage halfway through *Hamlet*, saying he didn't feel good enough to act that night? That was a kind of Existential bravado. He had to show that you could do it and survive. Really he deserves a four-hundred-page preface by Sartre. As a matter of fact, there's a bit about acting in Camus's *Myth of Sisyphus* that comes pretty close to Nick.' (Consulting the Camus book later, I found the following passage, in which the author explains why the Catholic Church used to condemn actors: 'She repudiated in that art the heretical multiplication of souls, the emotional debauch, the scandalous presumption of a mind that objects to living but one life and hurls itself into all forms of excess.')

McGrath's first stage play, *Events While Guarding the Bofors Gun*, was filmed in 1968, with Nicol as the central character, a self-destructive psychopath: both play and part were written 'for and in some minute measure about Nick', McGrath told me. 'What I like about him as an actor is his ambiguity,' McGrath said. 'He's capable of thinking—and expressing—two different things at the same time. And what I like about him as a person is that he has no ultimate goal, no overriding ambition. You remember he appeared with Wilfrid Lawson in *The Lower Depths*?' Lawson, who died in 1966, at the age of sixty-six, was a performer of wayward genius—sometimes galvanic, never predictable, given to bouts of alcoholism, and venerated by many of his juniors in the profession. 'Nick reminds me of Lawson. He gives off the same sense of danger, and he doesn't give a damn. More than anything, I'd like to see him play Macbeth.' It seemed to me, I told McGrath, that Nicol the actor was dazzling in wild attacking vein ('Who the hell do they think they are?') and in moods of abject vulnerability ('They'll louse me up the way they always do'), but that he was sometimes less persuasive in more temperate emotional zones, such as tenderness and charity. 'Ah,' McGrath said, 'he can do *them* to music. Next to Macbeth, I'd like to see him in a musical.' As if to prove his point, Nicol's voice floated gently over the mike:

> Leave them laughing when you go—
> And if you care, don't let them know.

I should have recalled that Nicol had in fact appeared in a musical, though only for one night. He played the title role in T. S. Eliot's *Sweeney Agonistes*, set to music by John Dankworth and performed in London as part of a tribute to the poet shortly after his death. He had been hair-raisingly good, especially in a song beginning with Eliot's lines:

> I knew a man once did a girl in
> Any man might do a girl in
> Any man has to, needs to, wants to
> Once in a lifetime, do a girl in.

McGrath's most recent collaboration with Nicol had been on the film called *The Reckoning*. The role, again written with Nicol in mind, was that of a ruthless, thuggish company director from the slums of Liverpool. 'Nick's commitment to the character was total. He identified with it so much that he nearly overbalanced the picture. The thing about Nick is that he really likes the jungle. That's where he lives.'

On March 8th, the Variety Club of Great Britain held its annual luncheon, at which Nicol was presented with its award as the best film actor of 1969 for his performances in *Inadmissible Evidence*, *The Bofors Gun* and *The Reckoning*. He made a one-sentence speech of thanks and sat down. 'I didn't even feel patronizing,' he told me. 'I just felt nausea and self-disgust. But at least I resisted the temptation to just say "Bollocks".'

Despite the acclaim his film appearances have received, I haven't always found them convincing. In *The Bofors Gun*, directed by Jack Gold, he played a baleful Irish private, serving with the British Army in postwar Germany, who spends a long and increasingly drunken night on guard duty trying to provoke a saintly young bombardier (David Warner) into having him arrested. The bombardier is a decent liberal who believes in trusting people. Expecting the best of mankind, he meets the worst in Nicol, a symbolic Lucifer to his Christ. The rest of the cast assembles in true theatrical style, a cross-section of British society fully aware that it is taking part in a play and that a moral crisis must therefore be precipitated and duly resolved. The satanic Irishman is so bombastically overwritten, his madness and death wish are so heavily signalled ('I should not be at large,' 'I hate all goodness,' 'I am not long for this world'), that the part can hardly be played without being overplayed. Nicol did his best, and it was far more than enough.

Laughter in the Dark (1969), one of the numerous cinematic progeny of *The Blue Angel*, was directed by Tony Richardson and concerned a rich middle-aged art connoisseur who falls for a sexy little usherette (Anna Karina) and is destroyed by her. After losing his sight in a car crash, he retires to a Mediterranean villa, into which the girl smuggles her new boyfriend; together they mock the blind man by making love almost under his nose. Nicol seemed ill at ease playing a member of the ruling class, and in several early scenes he looked like a sheepish butler in his own house. The authority that should have gone with the character's wealth and rank just wasn't there: he was too easily flustered, too perceptibly dismayed, so that one began to suspect that Nicol's face might be too expressive for the movies. Moreover, he lacked the effortless confidence we associate with the '30s superstars (where did they get it, with the Depression at home and Hitler prowling abroad?), and it was only in his blindness that he showed his real class,

Defenceless and humiliated, he came into his own: it isn't easy to forget the scene in which he weeps, his fingers fumbling for a cigarette, as Karina describes the view of mountains and ocean that he cannot see.

The film that Tony Richardson made of Nicol's *Hamlet* was shot in the Roundhouse, where the production had been staged, but it was mostly big heads spotlit in the dark and seemed to be taking place in a sunless nowhere. Nicol was a sedulously anti-romantic prince, a Hamlet out of Grünewald or Dürer, superlative in moments of rancour, contempt and needling resentment, worrying the lines like a terrier worrying a bone. But he made some curious verbal slips, one of which killed outright the only surefire laugh in the play. This occurs when Polonius takes his leave and Hamlet comments, 'You cannot, sir, take from me any thing that I will more willingly part withal.' Nicol said, ' ... I would *not* more willingly part withal,' which is meaningless. The performance, for all its power in negation and its genuine pain, seemed unwilling or unable to convey any objective passion, by which I mean a passion for such things as ideas, ideals and causes. Something in the actor's temperament appeared to inhibit—even to exclude—strong feelings about anything outside himself. Quite often this was Hamlet at Hamlet's own lowest valuation ('a dull and muddy-mettled rascal ... a-cursing like a very drab, a scullion'); he could never have been as Ophelia describes him—'the courtier's, soldier's, scholar's eye, tongue, sword'. It is relevant to note that Roman Polanski at one time considered inviting Nicol to play the lead in his movie of *Macbeth* but finally decided against it. When I asked him why, he said, 'Nicol Williamson should not play geniuses or kings or princes. He should play ordinary men who are extraordinary.'

Sometimes, as *Variety* might put it, crix nix Nick's pix. 'I could go on for ever about how people have put the knife into me,' he once told me. 'It doesn't matter. Pull it out, turn round, move on.' While it's in, however, it hurts. Some of the worst perforations were inflicted in January, 1970, by Pauline Kael, who wrote in the *New Yorker*:

> Nicol Williamson is a violently self-conscious actor whose effect on the camera is like that of the singers who used to shatter crystal ... He goes from being gracelessly virile to

being repulsively masochistic, and, whichever it is, he's too much ... Williamson is always 'brilliant' and 'dazzling'. He *is* brilliant, he *is* dazzling—yet he's awful ... probably the worst major (and greatly gifted) actor on the English-speaking screen today.

'That review', Nicol said to me, 'was like POW!' He has buddies among the critics, but only after they have gone on record in his favour; he would never try to charm a good notice out of a stranger. Alan Brien, in the *Sunday Times*, called him 'this most versatile of our young actors', and said that his West End début in *Inadmissible Evidence* had 'probably not been matched since the first appearance of the youthful Charles Laughton'. Having listed a few of his physical characteristics— 'eyes like poached eggs, hair like treacle toffee, a truculent lower lip like a pink front step protruding from the long, pale doorway of his face' (Nicol breeds similes in critics like a god kissing carrion)—Brien summed him up thus:

However small the part or the theatre, however short the run or sparse the house, he plays for honesty and truth, callously unsympathetic towards the prejudices and senti-mentalities of his audience.

Although Brien is *persona grata* to Nicol, his favourite critic is unquestionably Ted Kalem, of *Time*. When the stage pro-duction of *Hamlet* reached New York, Kalem jumped in off the deep end:

His Hamlet is a seismograph of a soul in shock. Here is a Hamlet of spleen and sorrow, of fire and ice, of bantering sensuality, withering sarcasm, and soaring intelligence. He cuts through the music of the Shakespearian line to the marrow of its meaning ... Take him, all in all, for a great, mad, doomed, spine-shivering Hamlet, and anyone who fails to see Nicol Williamson during this limited engage-ment will not look upon his like again.

Later, drawing on his most incantatory prose, Kalem installed Nicol in his private pantheon of living great ones:

Some actors occupy the stage; a few rule it. Some actors hold an audience; a few possess it. Some actors light up a scene; a few ignite the play. These combustible few blaze with the *x* factors of acting—intensity, intelligence, and authority. There is a royalty apart from role, and when an Olivier, Gielgud, Nicol Williamson, or Irene Papas treads the stage, their fellow actors are as rapt as the audience.

If Kalem is Nicol's trusty pilot fish, there is no doubt about the identity of the Creature from the Black Lagoon. This role belongs, by right of devastation, to Walter Kerr. The *Time* eulogy of *Hamlet*, published on May 16th, 1969, was by way of being a counterblast to a scorching piece by Kerr that had appeared a few days earlier in the Sunday drama section of the *New York Times*. Kerr's general point was that Nicol played *Hamlet* in exactly the same manner that he had played *Inadmissible Evidence*. He granted the actor's intelligence. What he missed was, first of all, 'physical tension':

Mr Williamson's arms hang idly from shoulders already idle. His is a pale, flattened face, with kinky uncut hair billowing out so far behind him that it becomes his head, robbing his features of dimension. It is also a face that seems to have severed association with the listless members ⁺hat might have been expected to carry it anywhere ... His coming or going makes no emotional difference.

No ignition here, no shivered spine. Kerr's second, and major, objection was to 'the particular noise Mr Williamson makes':

The voice is a quick twang, the sort of sound a man might make if he spoke rapidly while carefully pinching the bridge of his nose ... The performance, as a whole, seems one given by a museum guide who obviously knows what he is talking about but is severely crippled by a blocked sinus.

The notice was headed 'Oliver Twist as Hamlet', and Nicol deeply resented it. 'He reviewed my voice, not my interpretation,' he said. 'Jesus Christ, I was trying to make an *interesting* noise, not a beautiful one. The trouble with people like Kerr is that they can't forgive me for making Hamlet someone who is *insufferably alive*.'

The name of Kerr recurred to haunt the next development in the White House project. On March 11th, Nicol and I were to fly from London to New York, where he planned to rehearse for a week before the big night. At two o'clock that morning, 1 was awakened by the phone. 'It's all off,' said Nicol, sounding insufferably alive. 'The whole thing is off. Forget it.' His New York agent, an expatriate Englishman named Lionel Larner, had just received a copy of the guest list for his Evening, and had called to tell Nicol that they had invited Walter Kerr. The star was in a state of near-paranoid fury: 'Why should I spend all this time and energy just to go and be savaged? It's diabolically immoral. I've told Lionel that either they cancel Kerr's invitation or they can forget the whole thing.' He hung up. Hoping to persuade Kerr to have a diplomatic illness, I called the *Times*, and learned that he was attending an opening at the Ethel Barrymore Theatre. By 3 a.m., I was through to the box office, leaving a message for Kerr to call me collect during the intermission. Soon Nicol was on the line again, with a short bulletin: 'Lionel has talked to the White House people. They said they couldn't withdraw an invitation. So the hell with them.' Around 4 a.m., a bewildered Walter Kerr spoke to me from the theatre lobby; he said he couldn't get to Washington anyway, because of a prior engagement, and had just mailed a letter expressing his regrets. I dialled Nicol's number, only to find out from the operator that, with characteristic elusiveness, he had changed it the day before (for the third time in a month), and that, in any case, it was ex-directory. I then went back to bed for roughly thirty minutes, after which the phone rang again. 'Listen to this,' said Nicol, chuckling richly. 'The White House has just called Lionel back. They finally got mad and said to him, "Who's running this show — Mr Williamson or Mr Nixon?" And Lionel said very coolly, "Mr Williamson is running the *show*. The President is running the *country*." ' I told him the news from the Ethel Barrymore, which appeared to mollify him: the trip was on again. In its uneasy blend of confusion, hysteria and exhaustion, this nocturnal episode encapsulated much that was to come.

Later that morning, on the plane to New York, Nicol orders champagne and tells me the story of his life. He was born on September 14th, 1938, in Hamilton, Scotland, a mining town eleven miles from Glasgow. His parents were poor. 'When they got married, they came out of the registry office with half a crown in their pockets. That was in the morning. Dad went back to work in the afternoon.' When he was eighteen months old, the family moved to Birmingham, where his father worked as a labourer in a foundry. 'I had the usual boring suburban childhood. I kept saying to myself, "I've got to get out of here or I'll *die*." I read a lot at first. By the time I was five, I knew all about the Macedonian phalanx and things like that. But when I was twelve or thirteen I stopped reading—or, at least, I stopped amassing useless knowledge.' Nicol's father (whom John McGrath had described to me as 'an imposing man, strong and gentle, very Scottish') looms up in his conversation as a powerfully reassuring figure. 'He came to London to see me in *Inadmissible* and afterwards I introduced him to George Devine, the director of the Royal Court. George said to him, "Your son's doing very well, isn't he?" 'Yes," he said, without a flicker. "That's what he's there for." ' In 1957, Williamson senior returned to Scotland; now in his late fifties, he owns a small factory that makes aluminium ingots. 'Typically, he hates the unions, but he pays his workers more than union rates.'

From 1947 to 1953, Nicol went to the Central Grammar School in Birmingham, where a man named Tom Reader taught him English and prophesied success for him as a classical actor. 'I still see Tom. One rainy day in 1963, when I was feeling miserable because of a bird, I got on a train and went to see him at his home in Staffordshire. We went out to a pub, but he insisted on buying the drinks, which meant beer when I was dying for vodka. I asked his advice about getting married, and he was all against it. "He that hath wife and children", he said, "hath given hostages to fortune." Peter Hall had just offered me a long-term contract with the Royal Shakespeare, and Tom said I should accept. He told me I should learn to "use the system". I said that wasn't possible for me—I wasn't patient enough. I went home and turned Peter Hall down.'

In 1953, he enrolled in the Birmingham School of Speech Training and Dramatic Art. He was there for three years, during the last of which he was lent to the celebrated Birmingham Repertory Theatre to play unpaid walk-ons. (One of the paid members of the company was the young Albert Finney,

then half-way through his first season as a professional.) Under
the false impression that Easter Monday was a holiday for
actors, Nicol missed a performance and was fired. The management gave him the option of playing one more night if he
would make a public apology to the cast, but he preferred to
leave on the spot. 'I told myself, "I'm after that mountain.
This little hill is nothing to trip over." ' After drama school, he
spent two years at Aldershot, doing compulsory military
service as a gunner in an airborne division. He made fourteen
parachute jumps, but he never gained promotion. He discovered, however, that he could impose himself on people and
become their leader by force of temperament. 'Somebody
told me I was very good at what he called "personality black-
mail".' The phrase means: Play ball with me or I shall exude
such a dislike of you that you will feel simply dreadful. Out of
the army, he went to Scotland and worked for a while with his
father. Growing restless, he wrote to the management of the
Dundee Repertory Theatre, which hired him to play a pirate
in *Sinbad the Sailor*. Three months of unemployment followed,
and, in desperation, he was about to audition for a job as a
crooner when a telegram arrived inviting him to return to
Dundee. 'There were actors there,' he says, 'who were definitely U.F.P.' (under false pretences), and it wasn't difficult
for him to distinguish himself. During the next seventeen
months, he appeared in thirty-three productions, most of them
staged by Anthony Page, the company's resident director.
Word of Page's discovery filtered south, and in 1961 Nicol
made his London début at the Royal Court Theatre in *That's
Us*, a colourless piece of social realism by Henry Chapman. It
was at the Court that he met (and soon afterward worked with)
Tony Richardson, who was then George Devine's second-in-
command.

Nicol demands and obtains extra caviare to augment our
B.O.A.C. lunch. He then launches into a dissertation on
loyalty, declaring that although he has been scrupulously loyal
to Richardson and Page, they have both betrayed him in their
time. 'When Tony Page wanted to cast me in *Inadmissible* in
1964, Tony Richardson sent him a cable saying Nicol Williamson very bad idea stop nothing more than good rep actor.'
Page none the less stuck to his guns. When the play reached
America after its London run, David Merrick wanted to fire

Page during the Philadelphia try-out. Nicol defended his director, and a noisy argument broke out backstage. 'As a rule, I detest people who get into fights. They are *thunderously* boring, and that kind of behaviour is *fantastically undesirable*. But Merrick had to be insulted, and insults must be delivered with style. I was holding a glass of Budweiser. Suddenly, I remembered how José Ferrer had thrown champagne over Fred MacMurray at the end of *The Caine Mutiny*. He didn't chuck it at him, he flicked it forward like this.' Gesture as of a man throwing a dart. 'So I said, "I won't stoop to spit in your eye," and let him have it with the beer. Then he sort of rushed at me, and I stuck out my fist and he was on the floor. The funny thing was that nobody in his entourage tried to attack *me* or help *him*.' Page stayed. It was shortly after the Broadway opening that his alleged act of treachery occurred. Merrick had asked Nicol to take a salary cut until the weekly gross improved. 'I refused. So he talked to Tony Page, and Tony Page came to see me and absolutely *begged* me to accept the cut. It was pathetic. I haven't forgiven him for that and I never will.' His relationship with Tony Richardson declined to a nadir of comparable bitterness. Just before the *Hamlet* production was due to go to America, Richardson returned from a Riviera holiday to see the last London performance. Not liking what he saw, he called a company meeting at which he singled out Nicol for particular blame. Describing the incident, Nicol leans towards me and speaks with venomous distaste: 'I said to him, "I'm not going to *ask* you not to talk to me like that again. *You. Will. Never. Talk. To. Me. Like. That. Again.*" '

Signalling for more B.O.A.C. champagne, he says, 'I'm not what they call a good company man.' Togetherness in any form has invariably been a hazard for him; it is a room that he enters warily and, more often than not, wrecks before quitting. Outraged by the faithlessness of women, he has been known to stub cigarettes out on the palm of his hand. 'He wounds and is wounded easily,' one of his female mates had told me, 'and he's always very courteous to other walking wounded. He gives them bottles of Dom Pérignon.' During the Broadway run of *Inadmissible Evidence*, he fell in love with a young actress who was appearing in the show; when it closed, she got a TV job in Hollywood. He followed her there, and she deserted him for a stunt man. 'I almost destroyed myself. I got extremely drunk

and drove a car at top speed down a hill full of hairpin bends.'
He crashed off the road into someone's patio; the accident cost
him a week in hospital. On his next trip to Hollywood, he dined
at Chasen's restaurant with Lionel Larner and Jenny Beuselinck,
a pretty, dark-haired young woman who is the wife of his
London agent. The bill, which included a selection of his
favourite wines ('*great* Moselles, Burgundies like La Tache
and Grands Echezeaux, and the very *best* champagne'), came to
more than three hundred dollars. After dinner, Nicol, who was
driving, insisted on re-enacting the zigzag jaunt he had so
narrowly survived a few years earlier. With his two agonized
passengers clutching each other and sobbing with fright in the
back seat, he carried out his threat, and finally swung safely into
the driveway of the Beverly Hills Hotel. Mrs Beuselinck retired,
trembling, to bed; Nicol and Larner unwound by consuming
more champagne, to the value of two hundred dollars. 'I have
the Jonah hangup,' Nicol says serenely. 'I seem to bring bad
luck on myself and my friends.' (On July 17th, 1971, he married
Jill Townsend, the actress whose defection had provoked that
first hell-bent excursion.)

We land at Kennedy Airport, with slight loss of focus on my
part. The alcoholic pace is beginning to tell, so I resolve to
rely on a journal, rather than my memory, for a record (or
fever chart) of the next eight days, which are now all that
stand between us and Nixon.

Wednesday, March 11th. Our flight is met by Lionel Larner,
brisk, dapper, soft-voiced, dark-haired, fur-collared, somewhere
in his thirties. Manner: expatriate showbiz British, or camp on
the verge of being struck. Has some trouble with his R's. In
addition to Nicol, he represents the music-hall singer Tessie
O'Shea. He has organized a limo to take us to New York. On
the way, Nicol shows us the official White House invitation, an
ornately printed card announcing the appearance of 'Nichol
Williamson in Five Hundred Years of Entertainment in Poetry,
Drama and Song.' Sounds like a longish evening. Nicol finds
the misspelling inoffensive but ominous.

Installed in the Cecil Beaton Suite at the St Regis, he rings
for cocktails and outlines what he intends to give the Pres. From
Hamlet: the speech to the players, the 'O what a rogue and
peasant slave' soliloquy, and possibly 'To be or not to be'.

2

Elsewhence in Shakespeare: Macbeth seeing the dagger, Malvolio finding the letter, Hotspur confronting Henry IV, and mainstream-jazz settings of 'Sigh No More', 'Blow, Blow, Thou Winter Wind', and 'When Icicles Hang by the Wall'. From the modern repertoire: Willy Loman's protest against the callousness of superannuation ('A man is not a piece of fruit'), from *Death of a Salesman*; Bill Maitland's attack on the uncaring coolness of the young, from *Inadmissible Evidence*; an extract from Eliot's 'Little Gidding'; an erotic poem by e.e. cummings, and the final pages of Samuel Beckett's novel *How It Is*. In addition, Nicol will sing 'Baby, Won't You Please Come Home?', 'Darktown Strutters' Ball', and a song by John Dankworth about Macbeth, called 'Dunsinane Blues'. To give the star pause for breath, the World's Greatest Jazz Band will play 'South Rampart Street Parade' and Kid Ory's 'Savoy Blues'.

We are silenced. The proposed range is enormous, even for Nicol. My mind races, wondering what the Nixons will make of the Beckett, which I recall as a prolonged nihilistic shriek of despair. Lionel coughs, and says the White House isn't expecting more than a 45-minute act. Penelope Gilliatt, who has shown up to greet her old pal, is worried by the anti-youth content of the *Inadmissible Evidence* bit; she feels that Nicol must avoid giving aid and comfort to Presidential prejudices. She therefore makes a few discreet cuts to soften the tone of conservative crustiness already audible in John Osborne as early as 1964, and much amplified since. I suggest adding a comic set piece — Robert Benchley's 'The Treasurer's Report' — and Nicol agrees. Muttering in a corner, Lionel and I debate the major problems. First, can Nicol prepare and learn all this material in a week? Second, even if he can, will he, with no director to keep him on schedule? The White House engagement is important for Lionel. After ten years with one of the big agencies, he struck out on his own only eighteen months ago, and Nicol is his most prominent client.

Evening: With Nicol to the Grill in the basement of the Roosevelt Hotel, where his backing group, the World's Greatest Jazz Band, is appearing. Champagne in bulk. The nine veterans on the stand (led by Yank Lawson on trumpet and Bob Haggart on bass) are tearing into 'Up, Up and Away' as if it were a Dixieland standard (though Kai Winding's trombone strikes a more modern note—early 1950s, say). You would think they were a board of jolly school trustees living out a childhood fantasy. They resemble those volatile silver-haired gentlemen who in old Hollywood musicals used to waggle their index fingers and start trucking on down when taught to jitterbug by Gloria de Haven or Madcap Michael Rooney. At the end of the set, members of the band swarm up to embrace Nicol: Bud Freeman (tenor), mistakable for a bank president or prosperous dentist; Yank Lawson, beefy and beaming; and the more studious-looking Bob Haggart, perhaps an early James Stewart part. They are as flattered by Nicol's respect as he is by theirs. He has known them for years; jazz clubs offer the only kind of nightlife he enjoys. During the next set, he joins them on the stand to sing 'Baby, Won't You Please Come Home?' He grows exuberant in their company—this shambling cultural missionary, with his long pink face hanging out.

In the taxi home, he is reminded that this trip is an expedition into anxious territory. Three midtown offices have been bombed today.

THE CABDRIVER: Know what they should do with any guy that plants a bomb? The *'lec*tric chair. Rapists and muggers? The *'lec*tric chair. Guys who kill cops? The *'lec*tric chair. Guys who beat up prison guards? The *'lec*tric chair. They killed six cabdrivers in the last three months. Show no mercy. They'll take your life, you take theirs.

NICOL: How fantastically undesirable.

I propose—and Nicol accepts the idea—that it would help to relate his programme to local reality if he were to add a few admonitory lines from Yeats' 'The Second Coming', beginning with 'Things fall apart. The centre cannot hold.'

I am staying at the Algonquin, and he drops me there at about 1 a.m. There is a wakeful light in his eyes.

Thursday, March 12th. By early-morning limo to LaGuardia with Nicol and Lionel: we are going to Washington to examine the White House—to check technical facilities, and, in general, to decide whether it rates as what the trade would call a class room. The star, swathed in overcoat and muffler, slumps in his seat, racked by bronchial paroxysms. He was out (whispers Lionel, rolling his eyes upward) until 4 a.m., none knows where.

LIONEL: If they don't like the look of us in Washington, they may cancel the whole thing. We have nothing in writing.

At the airport, the star sips a beer, obviously (in Dashiell Hammett's precise but repulsive phrase) to cut the phlegm. En route for the boarding gate, he treads with extreme wariness. Noticing that I have noticed this, he explains carefully, 'I walk on my heels, leaning backwards and slightly to the right. If I tilt two inches too far'—he indicates the concrete floor—'it's a cracked skull.'

Mrs Penny Adams, spruce and wholesomely pretty in her mid-twenties, who is a member of Mrs Nixon's eight-woman staff, meets the plane, and we drive to the White House. Here Mrs Adams introduces us to Mrs Connie Stuart, thirty-one, the First Lady's staff director and press secretary, also wholesomely pretty, and very gay with it. Over her desk there is a framed motto at which Nicol raises a startled, Alastair Sim eyebrow. It reads 'WHATEVER TURNS YOU ON'. Penny says that Connie is a magnificent actress, or was at college. The star responds by telling a long, obscure and totally irrelevant story about a misdemeanour he committed in the army, involving the burning of some boxes containing kippers. Smiling a little dutifully, Connie suggests that we take a quick tour round the building.

LIONEL (*chirpily, as Connie shows us the State Banqueting Chamber*):
It may not be much to look at, but it's home.

Faced with a portrait of Jefferson, Lionel observes that it doesn't look a bit like Howard da Silva. With something of a flourish, Connie escorts us into the East Room, long and rectangular, with windows at either end, where the Evening is to take place. The star at once reacts to the cavernous echo.

NICOL: The band will have a *hernia*.

LIONEL: Oh, Nicol, it could easily be—

NICOL (*flatly*): *Dreadful*.

After some debate with White House technicians, it's decided that a stage (for the band and Nicol) will be erected halfway down one of the long walls, with the audience in a shallow arc around it. Nicol and I are discussing lighting angles, with illustrative gestures, when we see two unintroduced men regarding us with heavy-lidded interest.

NICOL (*jerking his head towards them*): Secret Service. They think we're discussing angles of fire.

Back in her office, Connie invites us out to eat. As we leave,

Nicol unnerves her secretary (who wasn't present during his telling of the anecdote) by laying a hand on her shoulder and murmuring in her ear, 'Don't light any fires with kipper boxes.'

Lunch at the Sans Souci (at the taxpayers' expense, except for two bottles of Echezeaux '62, contributed by Nicol):

PENNY: How do you feel before you go onstage?

NICOL: Elated. There's always the chance of getting that extra ingredient, that jab of adrenalin. When that happens, you do things that can scare you stiff.

PENNY: Are you good at taking direction?

NICOL: I'm the ideal subject for a director. I work from subjective to objective. I start from here (*he indents a small circle on the tablecloth with a fork*) and move outwards to here (*he draws a large concentric circle round the first*). That's the object of the exercise — not my ego.

CONNIE: Do you find that diet affects your work?

NICOL: I never booze before acting. I tried it ten years ago in rep and said never again. Also, I can't eat food cooked in butter or with garlic. If I do, I'm likely to vomit all over the stage.

The girls are giggly by now and propose taking us back to the office, for some sherry. (*Sherry?*) Demurring, with thanks, we depart for the airport.

Cocktails at the St Regis: P. Gilliatt feels there should be something in Nicol's programme to dissociate him from Nixon. For an hour or so, he will have the ear of the most powerful man on earth. He should choose at least one item to indicate to the Pres why 'people like us' do not support him. Hamlet caused the players to enact 'something like the murder of my father' in front of Claudius while Horatio observed the King's looks. Similarly, Nicol should perform something referring to (though not directly about) Vietnam, police brutality or the Black Panther shootings before the President, presumably with me standing in for Horatio. But what is the something to be? Being the man's guest, Nicol cannot actually spit in his face: what is needed is something oblique, analogical, but none the less crystal clear to all present. I come up with an idea: Creon has a speech in Sophocles' *Antigone* extolling the merits of absolute subservience to authority. But the danger (and the likelihood) is that the President would miss the intended irony and take the speech straight.

Dinner at the Russian Tea Room: Several New York friends of Nicol's come up to our table and give him their reactions — in varying tones of shock and reproach — to the news that he is going to entertain Nixon. One of them calls him 'a collaborator'. Nicol is uneasy and starts to brood: 'I should never have accepted the invitation.' He is discovering the difference between being a hell-raiser and being a rebel. Because he knocks critics, uses rude words on TV talk shows, and generally goes his own way, he is regarded as an anti-system man. In reality, he is simply an anarchic individualist. But he projects individuality with such intensity that he has become, however inadvertently and in however peripheral a way, something of a symbol. It is this symbol that he is now being called on to live up to, and it upsets him.

LEONARD LYONS (*greeting Nicol, who looks distraught and barely registers his presence*) : The only good thing I can say about this Administration is that they've invited you to Washington.

MYSELF: Do you think he should have accepted?

LYONS: Why not? He's honouring the office, not the man.

Troubled by all this, Nicol suddenly rises and plunges out of the restaurant without a word. The experience of this evening is forcing him to make commitments, to declare himself, to *join*. Which he hates.

An hour later, guesswork leads me to seek him at Jimmy Ryan's. He is singing 'Sister Kate' with a band headed by Max Kaminsky. The number over, he walks through the middle-aged audience to join me at the bar, where he introduces me to two preposterously obese men called The Bookends, for whom he buys drinks. He tells me equably that he sees no good reason to go on living, since he isn't interested in praise or acceptance or public love: 'I know myself, but I don't understand myself.' The proprietor of the club approaches and shakes his hand. Nicol grips my arm.

NICOL: Listen. There will be a statement. I shall make a statement at the White House.

PROPRIETOR: You're going to meet a beautiful man in Mr Nixon. A really beautiful man.

NICOL (*paying the bill and staring at a wild-eyed, martyred-looking photo of himself by Lord Snowdon that hangs behind the bar*) : Christ never looked so *hopefully* sorrowful.

A Bookend, performing a grotesque solo dance, pauses to wave us goodbye.

Friday, March 13th. The star informs me by phone that, although he was in bed by 2 a.m., he has awakened with a throbbing pain in the liver and a strong feeling of terror: 'There's so much to learn, I'm paralysed.' He will spend the morning studying the script and try a run-through in the afternoon. The significance of the day and date has not escaped him.

After lunch, pacing up and down his living-room, 'like a great famished wolf' (Ellen Terry's description of Henry Irving as Macbeth), he rehearses the non-musical parts of the Evening. Accusation and complaint, disgust and self-disgust are the dominant moods. The *Hamlet* bits are unmelodious harangues, but they ache with real distress. He is as fine as I remember him in the Osborne, and there is genuine pathos in his straw-clutching Willy Loman. Best of all are the cummings poem, delicately wry, very nearly charming, and the Beckett, a staccato tirade of negation, taken at tracer-bullet speed. This latter, and the Benchley, he cannot possibly learn and will have to read. But even in the excerpts from plays he is appallingly shaky on words: unless he masters them, he will be lectern-bound and thus denied all mobility. Already, it's clear that the programme, including music, may top seventy minutes. More than the President bargains for, but, as Lionel says, 'what are they going to do—throw him off the rostrum?'

Working out a running order, Nicol discovers that he has no finale. He wants to make 'O what a rogue and peasant slave' his climax. Hereabouts, I suggest, a hint of self-deprecation wouldn't come amiss, so we add a few lines from Eliot's 'J. Alfred Prufrock':

> No! I am not Prince Hamlet, nor was meant to be;
> Am an attendant lord, one that will do
> To swell a progress, start a scene or two,
> Advise the prince; no doubt, an easy tool,
> Deferential, glad to be of use,
> Politic, cautious, and meticulous;
> Full of high sentence, but a bit obtuse;
> At times, indeed, almost ridiculous—
> Almost, at times, the Fool.

An ending is found by not shunning the obvious. Nicol settles for a bushel of evergreen corn. From the Eliot he will go straight into Prospero's 'Our revels now are ended ... '

Last night's conscience pangs seem to have abated. The individualist speaks only *for* himself; the egotist speaks only *of* himself. In Nicol there are elements of both, and they combine to precipitate a deep resistance to the idea of speaking for others.

Work is interrupted by an urgent phone call from Oscar Beuselinck, in London. A lucrative film offer has come up, requiring an immediate yes or no. His face contorted with boredom and impatience, Nicol turns it down. Somewhat wanly, Lionel remarks that his client is truly uninterested in money; if he were not, why would he come so far to do so much for nothing? He adds that Nicol recently rejected a bid of four hundred thousand dollars to play Enobarbus in Charlton Heston's film of *Antony and Cleopatra*. Possessions do not attract him. As long as his food, drink, shelter and transportation are paid for, he has no financial ambitions.

It is 4.30 p.m. Vodka sours begin to arrive; we have thus far been nipping at minor Burgundies and Valpolicella. Rehearsals are over for the day.

NICOL (*sunk in an armchair*) : Actually, I've got about two years left to live. (*Pause*) I think I'm the most boring man in the world. I really do. People say I'm lucky because I'm free, because I can do what I like. But they don't understand. And why should they? Who can analyse anguish?

This is said ruminatively, without rhetoric, though in full awareness of the effect it is producing. Nicol, I reflect, would be a superb Dostoevsky actor. And I remember how good he was as the hero of Gogol's *Diary of a Madman*.

NICOL (*saturnine smile*) : I believe I know how I shall end the show. (*He rises and declaims.*) ' ... and our little life—is rounded—with a sleep.' (*He mimes unscrewing a bottle cap and swallowing handful after handful of pills. Rolling his eyes, he clutches at his throat and collapses on the carpet.*)

He is never exultant or euphoric. His relaxed moods are respites—temporary, you feel—from an unassuageable melancholy.

Saturday, March 14th. The star has lost a morning. He was singing at Ryan's until 4.30 a.m. Telephoned at lunchtime, he claims to be learning lines: 'They'll get their money's worth.'

We meet for drinks at 5 p.m., and again the question comes up of the 'statement' he promised to make at the White House. He says he thought of a solution last night but has since forgotten the process by which he reached it. From here he steers the conversation towards safety.

NICOL: Some people can remember rational processes of argument. I can't. What I do remember, after ten or fifteen years, is exactly how a man fiddled with a matchbox while he was talking. Nervously. Tensely. I slot it away with lots of other details I pick up about him. Then later I take them out and mix in some of myself, and then I've got something separate that I've made.

6 p.m. First band rehearsal at the Roosevelt Grill. The star, who has a curiously stately wardrobe, arrives in a well-cut, sober check suit and a crisply laundered shirt by Turnbull & Asser of St James's. Lawson and Haggart (of 'St James's Infirmary') have written some gay and bouncy arrangements of the Shakespearean settings, and it's nice to hear the sound made by their ripping, rasping four-man front line of brass. Nicol is much intimidated by their expertise and preparedness.

He takes me to a dowdy bar on Third Avenue for whisky sours. A large elderly Irishman in a Homburg hat gravely embraces him—an ex-barman, it turns out, recently retired from another of the star's pet haunts. Nicol's best friends seem to be permanently dispersed on some kind of rota system in unfashionable bars throughout the major cities of Britain and the United States, patiently awaiting the off-chance of his arrival. I have entered many such places with him, seldom without running into an unsurprised lifelong chum. It is always a man, and the man is never an actor.

We dine at Lionel's bijou bachelor pad in the East Fifties. Nicol's frame of mind as he contemplates next Thursday veers abruptly between groundless optimism and extremely rational pessimism. Immediately after eating, he departs alone on some unspecified mission. Lionel shrugs helplessly and shakes his head.

Later. Johnny Carson's special TV guest (with tinted glasses and deep décolletage) is Richard Harris, whose career and personality in many ways parallel Nicol's. Both played the title role in productions of *The Ginger Man* (Harris in Dublin,

Nicol in London); both starred in (different) adaptations of *The Diary of a Madman*; both have reputations for tumultuous living and warlike imprudence; and both fancy themselves as pop singers. Following the traditional practice of such maniacs on talk shows, Harris says that seriously, Johnny, all kidding aside, he is a devout believer in discipline and professionalism. Tremulously, he sings a new Jim Webb song, looking almost as vulnerable as, and undeniably lovelier than, Nicol. He then announces that he's about to direct and star in *Hamlet*, but, Johnny, he says, although that's a hell of a big responsibility, he puts just as much of the old discipline and professionalism into singing one song on the 'Tonight' show. Applause. I can *just* imagine Nicol saying that, but (to his credit) it would not sound so sincere.

Sunday, March 15th. Lionel opens the door as I arrive at his apartment for lunch. He says nothing but looks alarmed. I walk past him and halt, seeing why. Standing before us is his client, regarding me with a bemused and rueful smile. On his forehead is an egg-sized bump surrounded by contusions. The injury proves to have been self-inflicted.

NICOL: I got back to the hotel at 5 a.m., pissed out of my mind. While I was taking off my trousers in the bathroom, I fell and knocked myself out. The moral is: If you are pissed out of your mind, keep your trousers on.

Over lunch:

NICOL: If I ever write an autobiography, it will be called *Waif and Astray*.

LIONEL: That sounds very sweet.

NICOL (*dangerously*): When I sound sweet, that's the time to avoid me.

In the afternoon, we drink Puligny-Montrachet while Lionel plays records for Nicol — camp collectors' items, nostalgic tracks from pre-war England featuring people like Evelyn Laye, Dorothy Dickson, and the crooner Al Bowlly. Nicol requests a novelty number called 'My Canary Has Circles Underneath Its Eyes' and says he hopes to record it with Yoko Ono and John Lennon. 'John was going to come to Washington with us, but he couldn't get an American visa.' The ban on Lennon is due to his criminal record: he was found guilty in London of possessing pot. Lionel puts on a series of Noël

Coward records. All thought of rehearsing evaporates. Nicol venerates Coward.

NICOL: That's the right way to sock it to them.

By 'them' he means guarded people, prudent people, anti-impulse people, those whom he sometimes calls simply 'the foe'. He listens raptly to the famous duologue between Coward and Gertrude Lawrence in *Private Lives* and then lets slip a remarkable pronouncement on his craft.

NICOL: Acting is nothing but reminding people. That's all it is. It's reminding people of things. (*Pause*) Sometimes, if it's very good, it can even remind them of themselves. (*Pause. More Puligny-Montrachet*) I don't think I shall ever act on stage again.

LIONEL: How about next Thursday?

NICOL: I mean after that. (*Pause. Then, portentously, as if imparting great news in strict confidence*) It's going to go over *very big*.

LIONEL: Of course it—

NICOL: Like the *biggest lead balloon ever*.

My impressions of Monday and Tuesday, March 16th and 17th, are blurred. The handwriting in which I kept my notes begins to lurch about, and sentences of glaring banality are inscribed in a large, childish hand and doubly underlined—an infallible sign of powerful alcoholic sedation. The reason is that during this period of our association I tried to 'drink for' Nicol, as I phrased it to myself. When he ordered wine, I would consume as much of it myself as I discreetly could, in order to keep his energies fresh for rehearsal. I do not know whether this unselfishness was of any real use to him. It nearly crippled me.

From these two days, then, I retain only fragments—a few meals *in toto*, certain courses of others, moments of elation and apprehension during rehearsals, self-questioning about what constitutes a fatal dose of Alka-Seltzer—the one constant factor being a steady drain on Manhattan's reserve supplies of wines imported from the communes of Vosne-Romanée and Flagey-Echezeaux. One clear memory is of part of a lunch at the St Regis, with Nicol, in the grip of a 'massive depression', telling me that more than anything else he needs a woman in his life, but 'I'm too destructive, I make too many demands'. He says he is sexually obsessed and states that throughout the run of one London production in which he appeared he made love to the leading lady twice every night in the dressing room *during the performance*. (His italics.) To alleviate gloom, he either gets smashed or takes tranquillizers (Valium for preference) to make him feel nonchalant and uncaring, so that the obligatory question — 'What's it all for?' — temporarily recedes.

Other flashes from the lost days: Nicol repeating, with unconvincing assurance, 'Don't worry, I'm going to wing it'; Nicol aware that he is terribly unready for Thurday, yet remaining stubbornly inert in the face of crisis, daring the lightning to strike; Nicol briefly coming to life, baring his teeth, and galvanizing everyone, even the band, with his delivery of the Osborne, the Miller and the Beckett. 'He really is a fabulously talented man,' breathes Lionel, and, after the Beckett, Bud Freeman walks up to shake his hand, saying, 'You're one hell of a tenor-sax player.' (I see what he means; it's like listening to the worrying, burrowing frenzy of Paul Gonsalves playing 'Crescendo and Diminuendo in Blue' on a good night several years ago.) Freeman continues, 'I thought I knew you pretty well, Nicol, but *man* — as the jazz people say — that was *something else.*'

Now, on D Day minus 2, it's discovered that Nicol has no technical staff, no one to light the act or cue the musicians. A dumbstruck Bob Haggart is told that he must compose and arrange a short overture and half a dozen mock-Elizabethan music bridges. Midnight phone calls produce a young stage manager, Warren Crane ('He's worked the White House before,' Lionel says. 'He was there with Helen Hayes during the Johnson Administration'); and Rosaleen (Ro) Diamond, Lionel's pretty 25-year-old secretary, who has bought her first mink coat for the Washington trip, is roped in to prompt and give music cues. In the early hours of Wednesday morning, the makeshift crew has its first conference with Nicol, at the St Regis. The Echezeaux intake becomes particularly onerous during this session. Voices emerge from the general clamour: 'I shall snarl Willy Loman right in the President's face.' 'Will Tricia be there? We have "balls" in the Beckett and "come" in the cummings.' And, summing it all up (Nicol): 'If this thing works, it will be like a Heath Robinson machine giving birth to a baby.'

Footnote. William Heath Robinson (1872–1944): English cartoonist who, like Rube Goldberg, designed elaborate mechanical devices for carrying out useless tasks.

Wednesday, March 18th. I awake at noon like a dwarf refreshed. To the Roosevelt Grill for a full rehearsal before an invited audience of band members' wives and friends. Nicol fluffs repeatedly, misses laughs, and sends line after line winging out into the dark only to fall (as Noël Coward said, in a comparable plight) wetly, like pennies into mud. Perversely, the star regards this disaster as propitious.

NICOL: Tomorrow night will be something disquieting, disturbing, *weird*.

I dine with him at the Ground Floor, on Sixth Avenue (all glass and black leather, the kind of place you'd expect to find in the Michelin guide to Alphaville), and bring along a guest: the beautiful black actress and writer Ellen Holly. During the meal (about half a crate of Echezeaux '61), Nicol proposes marriage to her, not wholly unseriously, and is gently turned down. Richard III's 'Now is the winter of our discontent' goes into the act, replacing Malvolio's letter scene, which had died an especially grisly death at the Roosevelt. A Columbia Pictures limo, with an elderly, battered-looking P.R. man in attendance, rushes the star and me to LaGuardia. On the way, a car rams into our rear fender ('My Jonah hangup again,' says Nicol breezily), and time is squandered on the rituals of recrimination and name-taking. We just make the last flight to Washington, passing through the departure lounge at a brisk trot.

Another P.R. man, physically indistinguishable from the first, awaits us at Washington with an identical limo. Nowadays, Nicol's life is upholstered throughout with such aids and easements, shock-absorbent cushions against the brute impact of reality. There will always be a limo, and someone will always pick up the hotel and restaurant bills. If America does this for an actor whose screen credits include no American movies and no box-office smashes, what on earth does it do for Jack Nicholson? It's approaching 2 a.m. when we pull up at the Mayflower Hotel. I blench to hear Nicol talking about nightcaps and asking (in the words of B. Brecht) the way to the next whisky bar. The P.R. man tells him that Washington goes to bed early and that the bars are all closed, and the star seems to have reconciled himself to sleep when suddenly, in pursuit of a hunch, he crosses the street, walks a few blocks, and finds the only bar in town that is still open. The P.R. man fades, leaving the night to Nicol and to me.

Inside the bar (which is underlit to the point of inducing disorientation), I begin to hallucinate. Brain damage of some rare kind appears to have set in. Not without panic, I point out to Nicol that the walls are covered with close-up colour transparencies of the female pudenda. From the middle of the room, where we are sitting, Nicol squints through the darkness, but to no purpose: he says there is nothing there. I hesitate to go over to the wall and check, in case he is right. I recall Laurence Olivier's warning to me before I left London: 'Be careful, or that man will magic you.' I had better believe it. He is looking straight at me, smiling curiously and nodding. At my urgent request, we finish our drinks and go. I am aware, as we do so, of all those flamboyant mirages shimmering obscenely away in the gloom, and I half-close my eyes. (On a subsequent trip to Washington, I retraced my steps and shyly revisited the bar. It is marvellous what tricks exhaustion and an overheated imagination can play with travel posters of the Canadian Rockies.)

Over at the hotel, Nicol sends out for hamburgers. We go up to his suite, where the food arrives thirty minutes later. There is Dom Pérignon on ice in his sitting-room, but I manage to restrict consumption to one bottle. At 3 a.m., I drag myself away. Outside in the corridor I see a little sign-post pointing to Nicol's door. It reads 'The Puerto Rican Hospitality Suite'. I hope to God it is there tomorrow.

Thursday, March 19th. Donne may have got it wrong. Perhaps some men are islands. Fuelled from within himself, responsible to nothing and no one outside himself, impervious to all social, moral and professional pressures that seek to influence or modify his behaviour, Nicol is at least a formidably isolated peninsula, a sort of human Mont Saint-Michel. Today will see him wind-swept and wave-battered.

I return to the Puerto Rican Hospitality Suite (sign still there) at 11 a.m. Stripped to the waist, the star is pacing up and down, villainously hung over. Inexplicably, Lionel and Ro have failed to turn up. This does not lighten his mood.

NICOL: Today I can be a monster. No more of this lovable crap.

A newpaper is delivered. Nicol peers at the front page, freezes, and passes it to me in silence. I read that the Cambodian government has collapsed; Sihanouk has been deposed while away in Peking. So Nixon has a crisis on his hands. There's nothing a man needs more than a cultural soirée when his South-East Asian policy is falling apart. I notice that I am cowering in a corner. Nicol broaches a bottle of champagne. I point out that I am disintegrating fast, but he cajoles me into taking a glass. I emerge a little way from my corner.

NICOL (*seriously*): Do you think I drink a lot?

MYSELF (*ever the plain speaker*): On the whole, yes

NICOL (*struck by this new idea*): Funny, I always thought I drank less than most people. (*Pause. He muses.*) You see, I have low blood pressure and a low blood-sugar count. Sometimes I get terribly dizzy. I drink to prevent myself from collapsing. (*The thought entertains him.*) Listen, if you ever see me staggering about on the verge of collapse, just *rush* the alcohol to me. Preferably champagne — it has a high sugar content. I have to have it to avoid passing out.

The phone rings. Lionel and Ro have arrived, and I go down to join them in the coffee shop. They missed the early flight because (Jonah strikes again) the car in front of theirs crashed on the way to the airport, holding up traffic. Lionel is in a state of petulant fatalism, bitching about everything to cover up specific forebodings about the hours ahead.

LIONEL: The rooms here are *too crucial*. You ought to see mine. I walked in so quickly I nearly fell out of the window. The only way to enter that room is blindfold, with a sleeping pill in one hand.

He reminisces about Nicol, dwelling morbidly on examples of erratic behaviour.

LIONEL: I was there when he walked offstage in the middle of the first night of *Hamlet* in Boston. It was incredible. He flung a goblet clear across the stage and marched off. The management argued with him for twenty minutes, and then he came back and told the audience he didn't feel at his best and he thought they were being cheated. He said they could have their money back if they wanted. As it happened, they didn't, so he went on with the show.

In the minds of both of us, I can see, there is a fear that

something of the sort may happen tonight. Accompanied by Ro and the star—all four of us thickly wrapped against the bitter spring weather—we limo off to the White House for a final rehearsal.

LIONEL (*airily, glancing out of the window*) : Wonderful to be back in Philadelphia.

A White House guard stops us as we enter.

GUARD : Are you the entertainment?

NICOL : I beg your pardon?

GUARD : I said, are you the entertainment?

NICOL (*utterly dulcet*) : Yes. To be exact, *I* am the entertainment. In just one moment, a dove will escape from my hip pocket and I shall pull the flags of all nations out of my mouth.

We are admitted to the building, which today suggests a large Swiss hotel in the off season—all uniformed flunkeys and no guests. Another guard takes us to the East Room, where the band and the stage manager (whom we greet thankfully) have just arrived. Security men are searching their instrument cases. One of Connie Stuart's assistants brightly points out to Nicol that the East Room was where Lincoln's body lay in state. He thanks her for the information. After one look at the stage, he says it must be enlarged. While this is being done, we move into the adjoining (and aptly named) Green Room for a word rehearsal.

LIONEL : Take your coat off, Nicol.

NICOL : No, thanks, I'm not staying.

He wanders over to the wall and stares at it for a moment, hands deep in pockets.

NICOL : Lend me a pen, will you?

LIONEL : What for?

NICOL : I want to write up here, 'For a good time, call TE 8-4622.'

I sit in for the President. Nicol makes a sweeping entrance, bows, mimes pulling a pin from a hand grenade with his teeth, and blithely tosses it into my lap. Soon his flipness fades and the rehearsal stops. He says he wishes he were with his parents in Scotland—'anywhere but here'. There is a great lack of yeast in his spirit; sadness weighs him down. (What is he mourning?) Lionel chatters on, wondering what Nicol is going to wear tonight. The answer is grey slacks, a blue sweater and a silk scarf. By now, it is 3 p.m.; he goes on at eight, and still the stage and the lighting aren't ready. A further nerve-scraping half hour passes before the run-through can begin.

It goes smoothly enough and lasts sixty-four minutes. The star, rightly, performs at no more than half pressure. He is unsmiling but as relaxed as only the profoundly hung over can be. The first quarter hour is filmed for television.

'And now', says Lionel, 'for the female Mafia.' Nicol, who has not eaten all day, has agreed to be interviewed for the social columns by lady members of the Washington press corps.

The first question is so outlandish that it stuns him into silence. 'Would you say', asks a grey-haired woman, 'that Shakespeare was the James Bond of his day?' Lionel bustles over to help him out.

GREY-HAIRED WOMAN: What was that first song that Mr Williamson sang?

LIONEL: 'Sigh No More.'

GREY-HAIRED WOMAN: What show is it from?

LIONEL: *Much Ado About Nothing.*

GREY-HAIRED WOMAN: Is that a musical?

SECOND GREY-HAIRED WOMAN: I'm going to London next week, Mr Williamson. Is it possible to get Chinese food in London?

NICOL: Oh, yes. Quite good Chinese food.

SECOND GREY-HAIRED WOMAN: Where would you recommend me to go?

NICOL: Well, my favourite place is the Wan King.

SECOND GREY-HAIRED WOMAN: Have you the address?

NICOL: Oh, you won't need an address. Just go up to anyone in the street and say, 'Can you direct me to the Wan King?' or 'Where is the Wan King?'

Nicol's face is glowing with sincerity. To understand why Lionel is compelled to move away, his lips compressed and his shoulders shaking, it is necessary to know that the verb 'to wank' is British demotic usage for the act of self-abuse.

Five-thirty. We rush back to the hotel to change. Lionel and Ro cravenly disappear to their rooms, leaving me to keep watch over Nicol. Up in Little Puerto Rico, the phone rings. It is Lionel, hissing, 'Force him to eat something.' I call room service. While I am ordering deep-fried butterfly shrimps, a cork pops and Nicol offers me champagne. Taking a selfless decision, I bring up the name of Tony Richardson, which I count on to provoke a monologue and/or an impersonation. It provokes both ('Tony Richardson', he begins, 'symbolizes power without love'), thereby diverting the star's attention from what he is drinking to what he is saying, and enabling me to dispose of all but one glass of the bottle. Room service is not at its most appetizing, and when we depart for the White House at seven-forty (Ro in her mink, Lionel and I in dinner jackets), Nicol's stomach is vacant apart from a glass of champagne and two bites of shrimp encased in congealed fat.

This time, the man on the door recognizes us.

GUARD (*beaming*) : Good to see you again, Mr Nicholson.

Lionel winces. Nicol's eyes are beady, but his smile does not flicker. We deposit him backstage, with much patting on the back and gripping of the upper arm. Braided guards escort us into the East Room, where most of the audience—two hundred and seventy in all—has already arrived. The band sits red-faced and black-tied on the rostrum. Lionel turns to me with a fixed grin and says, 'I am petrified.' We slump in the second row and consult his guest list. Many of the names are those of campaign contributors, here to receive their social reward. John Chapman, the damson-complexioned drama critic of the *Daily News*, is among the journalists present; so, exuding loyalty, is Ted Kalem, of *Time*. John Freeman, the British ambassador (and former editor of the *New Statesman*), has a ringside seat. Top Columbia Pictures brass is represented by Leo Jaffe, the president, and Abe Schneider, the chairman of the board. Other notabilities include the daughter of the Australian Prime Minister, a granddaughter of President Cleveland, Vice-Admiral Rickover, Henry Cabot Lodge, David Eisenhower, and, of course, Henry Kissinger, bleeper no doubt in pocket. Also Dick Cavett, the actor Lee Bowman, and Harold Smith, of Harold's Club, Reno.

To prolonged applause, Mr and Mrs Nixon (he in tuxedo, she in something long and pink) enter and seat themselves front centre. The President rises and tells the story of how he heard about Nicol from Harold Wilson more than a year ago.

NIXON (*hands clasped before him*) : ... So because I couldn't stay to see that star in London, that star is here tonight—the man the Prime Minister says is the greatest Hamlet!

The President returns to his chair. Nicol ambles on, takes a bow, and launches into the address to the players.

NICOL: Speak the speech, I pray you, as I pronounced it to
   you ...

Silence. He has dried. Five long seconds pass before he
completes the sentence, with a phrase that could hardly be less
appropriate.

NICOL: ... trippingly on the tongue.

He covers up well, making it look as if it were Hamlet, and
not he, who was groping for the right words, and he finishes the
piece without further problems. The band now contributes to
the tension by wrecking the first musical bridge. Two howling
clinkers are blown, and I can see Bob Haggart's face, bug-eyed
with shock. The first song ('Blow, Blow, Thou Winter Wind')
finds Nicol still uneasy. But in the Osborne and the cummings
he starts to hit his stride. Command enters his voice. There is
still, in his stance vis-à-vis the audience, a nonchalance that
seems to border on contempt, but it is electric, corrosive
contempt, a passion not to be tamed or ignored. (Nobody can
complain that he doesn't follow Hamlet's instruction to 'show
scorn her own image'.) 'To be or not to be' is first-rate: the
morose, familiar lines bite into the mind like acid into metal.
The songs—especially 'Dunsinane Blues' and the 'Winter'
lyric from *Love's Labour's Lost*—are warming the audience up.
The President is seen to smile, and rounds of applause are
coming, still faintly, but frequently. Lionel and I are going
with the flow, even enjoying ourselves.

Then we both jerk forward, hearing Nicol say, 'Things fall
apart.' They certainly do. He has jumped straight from *Love's
Labour's* to Yeats, omitting the Miller, the Benchley, and two
whole songs. The band is baffled. We are sweating, realizing
that at this rate he will end twenty-five minutes early. The
champagne churns within me. When he gets to the end of the
Yeats, there is a frozen pause, after which he says, 'Howard, all
I need to set my table is fifty dollars a week.'—and we relax.
He has spotted his error, gone into *Death of a Salesman*, and put
the derailed Evening back on its tracks. From here, everything
builds superbly. The Miller extract—Willy's lament for the
heroic days of salesmanship and his old pal Dave Singleman
('And by the way he died the death of a salesman, in his green
velvet carpet slippers in the smoker of the New York, New
Haven & Hartford, going into Boston'), and his bewildered
rage at a business ethic that discards spent human beings like

garbage—comes fervently across. I'm surprised what a punch Miller still packs for an audience like this, especially when the part is played, as now, entirely without sentimentality.

Nicol finds the right note of insanely jovial pedantry for Benchley's bumbling Treasurer. 'O what a rogue and peasant slave' is given in a splendid tempest of self-laceration. But it's with the Beckett that he and his material really fuse. The sound we hear is that of a man (or at least a being) in his last extremity, living on the very margin of existence:

> ... alone in the mud yes the dark yes sure yes panting yes someone hears me no no one hears me no murmuring sometimes yes when the panting stops yes not at other times no in the mud yes to the mud yes my voice yes mine yes not another's no mine alone yes sure yes when the panting stops yes on and off yes a few words yes a few scraps yes that no one hears no but less and less no answer LESS AND LESS yes
>
> so things may change no answer end no answer I may choke no answer sink no answer sully the mud no more no answer the dark no answer trouble the peace no more no answer the silence no answer DIE screams I MAY DIE screams I SHALL DIE screams good ...

The way Nicol punctuates this into lucidity is a technical *tour de force*. I have never heard his voice more hypnotic: as it rises from a wintry monotone to a high, urgent, terrified whinny, you would think he was a medium, possessed and shaken by an unquiet demon. Nixon's face is rigid and expressionless, but he is staring straight into Nicol's eyes. I don't think he has ever heard anything quite like this before.

Finally, the star gives us his dying fall—'Alfred Prufrock', followed by Prospero's farewell to the revels—and bows. Applause crashes over him, wave upon wave. He withdraws, returns to cheers and bravos, shares them with the band, withdraws again. Lionel stops clapping for a second to give me the thumbs-up sign. Against all the auguries, his wayward client has pulled it off. He is the Entertainment.

The audience moves into the next room, where there is a hot buffet. Dick Cavett sniffs as we enter.

CAVETT: Something's burning.

MYSELF: Someone's let Agnew into the library again.

A big Williamson fan, Cavett enjoyed the show immensely; so did Kissinger. Like many others, John Freeman was particularly knocked out by the Beckett. Outside in the hall, the guests are shuffling along in line to shake the Nixons and Nicol by the hand. I receive an exceptionally slow and searching wink from the Entertainment. The President — his face like a leather brief-case that has seen long service: you expect to find a pocket for ballpoint refills behind one ear — says he thought the Miller and the Osborne outstandingly memorable:

NIXON (*with the admiration of one pro for another*): It's so wonderful the way he changes so quickly. One thing ends, something completely different begins. And to think that your Prime Minister started it all.

Passing on, I hear Mrs Nixon whisper to Nicol, 'Stand on the carpet, not the stone floor. It's easier on the feet.' In the State Banqueting Chamber, the Marine Corps Band is playing the score of *Hair* in strict ballroom tempo. Careless of tomorrow, Lionel, Ro and I drink champagne while the fiscal caryatids of the Republican Party swing and sway. After a few minutes, the Marines quit the stand, to be replaced (at Nicol's request, we learn) by the W.G.J.B. The Chamber livens up; some portly jitter-bugging is observed. The Nixons smile briefly in at the door, then retire. No slight intended — they are notoriously quick off the mark to Blanket Bay. And tonight, no doubt, the President will be anxious to know who is minding the store in Phnom Penh. Nicol, looking ten years younger, grabs the microphone.

NICOL: This should be an evening that swings. We should all have fun and get boozed. And I hope to God we don't wake the people upstairs.

He dances fancifully with Ro, Mrs Ted Kalem and others, sings 'Darktown Strutters' and 'I Can't Give You Anything but Love, Baby', and even borrows Yank Lawson's trumpet to blow a stammering but heartfelt chorus of 'Tin Roof Blues'. The whole place begins to vibrate like a Hamburg dance palace on Saturday night. An astonishing amount of affectionate goosing is going on. It is half past midnight before Nicol is ready to move. His departing gait is regal.

NICOL: We leave with dignity. With our own dignity. (*He stands on the steps of the White House and contemplates the sky.*) Tonight this is our town, Thornton Wilder! Do you hear? Our town!

A private bus takes us and the musicians to a jazz club called Blues Alley, where Charlie Shavers is playing. The W.G.J.B. sit in, and for two hours Nicol blows, sings, drinks, and spreads himself. Chewing a cigar, sardonically grinning, rolling his rheumy eyes, he looks like a Mississippi gambler on a winning streak. I reflect: How limited is the range of things he wants to do with these moments of riot. All he asks of triumph, all he means by relaxation and release, is the opportunity to drink a few great wines from the Champagne district and the Côte de Nuits, and to go to places where small-group mainstream jazz is played late at night.

At 3.30 a.m., Nicol, Lionel, Ro and I bring hamburgers back to the Puerto Rican Hospitality Suite and eat them with more champagne. Nicol's hair clings to his skull like damp ginger worms.

NICOL (*holding up a half-eaten hamburger*): So this is what it was all for.

RO (*ecstatically phoning a friend in California*): Listen, I just spilled Dom Pérignon over my mink coat!

NICOL: Nixon said he could take the programme twice over. 'You must come and do it again,' he said.

LIONEL: Why did you do it in the first place?

NICOL (*with mock-heroic shrug*): A challenge.

He has come three thousand miles to please and impress a man who was not, perhaps, all that interested in what he was doing, or all that capable of being pleased and impressed in those regions of human response where Nicol's talent is best equipped to strike. All one can say is that by his unpaid exertions Nicol has enabled Nixon to keep a diplomatic promise.

A fortnight later, the following letter arrived in Nicol's mail:

Dear Mr Williamson,

Your magnificent performance in the White House on March 19th surpassed even the exceptionally favorable advance notice which I had received, and I want to express my thanks to you once more for your generous gift of your time and talent. Your presence made a spectacularly successful evening deeply memorable as well.

With best wishes,

RICHARD M. NIXON

Friday, March 20th. Press reactions are good. The *New York Times* says that Nicol 'shifted mood, pace and tone with seeming ease', and Richard Coe, of the *Washington Post*, reviews the act in the style of *Variety*:

> Known for mod treatment of classics as well as savvy way with smart stuff (T. S. Eliot and Samuel Beckett, Nobel '69), thesp cooked up novel touch ... Williamson, using characteristic North Country nasal twang, feels for and finds total meaning of excerpts from *Hamlet*, *Richard III* and modern material ... Construction of act is ingenious, nicely fitting counterparts of today with classic stuff ... Sock hits, finding star wholly at home as singer, include *Macbeth* follow-piece, 'Dunsinane Blues', and encored 'Blow, Blow, Thou Winter Wind' ...

Nicol celebrates by giving lunch at the Jockey Club to Lionel, Ro, me, and a couple of Washington friends of mine. The occasion is pleasantly hysterical (Taittinger Blanc de Blancs, Château Margaux '61), with the Entertainment at his most ebullient. Just before going on last night, he tells us, he contemplated chickening out by pretending to be under the impression that the invitation was to entertain the Nixons *and nobody else*. Most of the restaurant is watching as he mimes what he planned to do: stride in beaming at the President; come to an affronted halt as his eyes register the presence of *other people*; sniff querulously; raise eyebrows; turn on heel; march straight off stage and out of the building. He meditates on what he actually did.

NICOL: I don't know why it happened, but it happened, and I stand by it. Why they asked for it, Christ only knows. Why they got it, Christ only knows. But they got it.

Together with Ro and Lionel, he has to leave for the airport. They are returning to New York; I am booked on a later flight direct to London. As he gets into the limo, one of my friends, a young woman who has never met him before, shakes his hand and says, 'You're a very extraordinary man, Mr Williamson.'

NICOL: Lady, the mome rath isn't born that could outgrabe me.

That evening, I sit with a beer at Dulles Airport, trying to exorcize Nicol from my consciousness. I have been too close for too long. But there is no escape. In a corner of the bar, on a TV set badly in need of adjustment, he comes looming through a snowstorm of videotape to sing 'Dunsinane Blues':

> Now's the time for you to be —
> A wary 'un:
> I wasn't really born, it was a —
> Caesarean ...

No, the barman says, he isn't allowed to switch off the set, which now adds a slow rolling-frame effect to its repertoire. Dozens of Nicols float before my eyes: Will the line stretch out to the crack of doom? He looks supremely buoyant in his blizzard; I, on the other hand, feel drained and enfeebled, a mere husk of a man. How much (I wonder) of Nicol's neurosis is a deliberate, expertly adopted pose? On the whole, actors are not the compulsive neurotics we take them for. Many of them come from idyllic and unbroken homes, where they were idolized by their parents. They seek (and will go to any lengths to obtain) the same central position, the same applause, the same devout attention in adult life. These things, to use be-haviourist language, are their reinforcers. No, actors are not crazy, nor are they compensating for emotional neglect. They are simply re-enacting golden childhoods. Remove the rein-forcers, however, even temporarily, and what one gets is that other Nicol, sunk in accidie, of whom I've had so many glimpses this past week.

I buy a paperback by Simon Raven (*Friends in Low Places*) to read on the plane. Just as I am settling down, with my usual sense of pleasurable loathing, into Captain Raven's archaically structured world, a sentence brings Nicol vividly back to my mind: 'Mark had an acute sense of self-preservation (an attri-bute which is often very strong in second-rate performers and does much to explain their mediocrity) ... '

Whatever else he is, Nicol is not a second-rater.

The last time I saw him was in May, 1971, when we had another of our lunches at the Étoile in London. On this occasion, the part I had to offer him was King Lear. The answer was no, as it had been when I approached him with an assortment of other roles sixteen months earlier. He said he was no longer interested in being 'the greatest actor of my generation, and all that jazz'. Although he had made a film, he had not appeared before a live audience since the White House date, more than a year before.

'The individualist', says B. F. Skinner, in *Beyond Freedom and Dignity*, 'can find no solace in reflecting upon any contribution which will survive him. He has refused to act for the good of others and is therefore not reinforced by the fact that others whom he has helped will outlive him. He has refused to be concerned for the survival of his culture and is not reinforced by the fact that the culture will long survive him. In the defence of his own freedom and dignity, he has denied the contributions of the past and must therefore relinquish all claim upon the future.'

In Memory of Mr Coward

One night in the spring of 1959 I sat down to dine at Sardi's, the New York theatrical restaurant. Crowded before the Broadway curtains rise and after they fall, it is usually empty in between, and was on this occasion. Suddenly I looked up from the menu and froze. Noël Coward, also alone, had come in; and that very morning the *New Yorker* had printed a demolishing review by me of his latest show, an adaptation of Feydeau called *Look After Lulu*.

I knew him too well to ignore his presence, and not well enough to pass the whole thing off with a genial quip. No sooner had he taken his seat than he spotted me. He rose at once and came padding across the room to the table behind which I was cringing. With eyebrows quizzically arched and upper lip raised to unveil his teeth, he leaned towards me. 'Mr T.,' he said crisply, 'you are a cunt. Come and have dinner with me.'

Limp with relief, I joined him, and for over an hour this generous man talked with vivacious concern about the perils of modishness ('There's nothing more old-fashioned than being up to date'), the nature of the writer's ego ('I am bursting with pride, which is why I have absolutely no vanity'), the state of the theatre in general and of my career in particular. Not once did he mention my notice or the play. It would have been easy to cut or to crush me. It was typical of Coward that he chose, with an almost certain flop on his hands, to amuse and advise me instead.

As a writer, this was one of his bad times, and there had been many since the war—since, indeed, the high period from 1925 to 1941, which produced the five plays by which he will be remembered: *Hay Fever, Private Lives, Design for Living, Blithe Spirit* and *Present Laughter*. *Sigh No More*, the revue he wrote in 1945 to celebrate the return to peace, was an especially low point, although it contained some marvellous things: the title song, for example, at once joyful and elegiac, and 'Nina from Argentina', a model of intricate rhyming on which Cole Porter at his best could hardly have improved. Lowest of all was *Pacific 1860*, Coward's Drury Lane musical of 1946, of which I remember little except Graham Payn singing about his awe-struck affection for a South Sea volcano by the name of Fum-Fum-Bolo. But even if we agree that Coward the post-war writer was past his prime, it's impossible to accept the judgment laid down by Cyril Connolly in 1937:

> One can't read any of Noël Coward's plays now ... they are written in the most topical and perishable way imagin-able, the cream in them turns sour overnight.

In fact his best work has not dated, by which I mean his most devotedly ephemeral. One feels the same about many movies of the 1930s: with the passage of time, the profundities peel away and only the basic trivialities remain to enchant us. They have certainly enchanted John Osborne, who learned from Coward the disparaging use of 'little' (as in 'nasty little', 'repulsive little', 'disgusting little', etc.), and Harold Pinter, whose spare, allusive dialogue owes a great deal to Coward's sense of verbal tact. Consider *Shadow Play*, a haunting one-act piece that Coward wrote in 1935. A couple whose marriage has gone sour attempt to reconstruct their halcyon days, correcting each other as they misremember. The parts were originally played by Coward and Gertrude Lawrence. 'Small talk,' Miss Lawrence says at one point, 'a lot of small talk, with other thoughts going on behind.' What could be more Pinterish, or for that matter more Chekhovian? And what more subtly sexy than the four brief declarative sentences that Miss Lawrence addresses to Coward at their first meeting:

> You're nice and thin. Your eyes are funny. You move easily. I'm afraid you're terribly attractive.

An exquisite bone-dry lyric precedes the marital flashbacks:

> Here in the light
> Of this unkind, familiar now,
> Every gesture is clear and cold for us,
> Even yesterday's growing old for us.
> Everything's changed somehow ...

Coward took the fat off English comic dialogue: he was the Turkish bath in which it slimmed. Nothing could be more elliptical than the country-house conversation in which Coward and Miss Lawrence (Simon and Victoria) discover between the lines that they are mad about each other:

VICTORIA: Are you good at gardens?
SIMON: Not very, but I'm persevering ... I can tell a Dorothy Perkins a mile off.
VICTORIA: That hedge over there is called *Cupressus macrocarpa*.
SIMON: Do you swear it?
VICTORIA: It grows terribly quickly, but they do say it gets a little thin underneath in about twenty years.
SIMON: How beastly of them to say that. It's slander ...

I first met Coward in the early 1950s, during his cabaret seasons at the Café de Paris, and heard him exploding with mock-outrage when he found in 1954 that the place had been completely redecorated in honour of Marlene Dietrich's impending début. 'For Marlene', he said, 'it's cloth of gold on the walls and purple marmosets swinging from the chandeliers. But for me—sweet fuck all!' To describe his own cabaret appearances, I went back to his boyhood and wrote: 'In 1913 he was Slightly in *Peter Pan*, and you might say that he has been wholly in *Peter Pan* ever since.' The young blade of the 1920s had matured into an old rip, but he was as brisk and energetic as ever; and if his face suggested an old boot, it was unquestionably hand-made. The qualities that stood out were precision of timing and economy of gesture—in a phrase, high definition performance. After a lifetime of concentration, he gave us relaxed, fastidious ease.

I once said of an uxorious writer that he had put his talent into his work, and his genius into his wife. Coward did not make that mistake. The style he embodied—as writer and performer alike—was the essence of high camp. He was one of the brightest stars in the homosexual constellation that did so much to enliven the theatre between the wars. Coward invented the concept of cool, and may have had emotional reasons for doing so. At all events, he made camp elegant, and wore a mask of amused indifference—'Grin and rise above it'—to disguise any emotions he preferred not to reveal. From the beginning of his career he was a shrugger-off of passion and a master of understatement—queerdom's answer (you might say) to Gerald du Maurier, the matinée idol of his day. It was du Maurier who led the attack on Coward's first hit, *The Vortex*, on the grounds that it was a dustbin drama.

In later years Coward himself was not above knocking his juniors, especially if they wrote plays of ideas. 'Political and social propaganda in the theatre,' he wrote, 'as a general rule, is a cracking bore.' Many of his own post-war works (presumably the exceptions) show him to be a convinced reactionary. In *Peace in Our Time*, which deals with London if Germany had won the war, the first Englishman to collaborate with the Nazis is a left-wing intellectual. And *Relative Values* (1951) ends with a toast to 'the final inglorious disintegration of the most unlikely dream that ever troubled the foolish heart of man— Social Equality.' But more often his objection to contemporary drama was simply that it was drab. After he saw David Storey's *The Changing Room*, his companion said that the rugby players, when stripped in the bath scene, were not physically very impressive. 'No,' said Coward, 'fifteen acorns are hardly worth the price of admission.'

In 1964 we decided to put *Hay Fever* into the repertoire of the National Theatre and to ask Coward to direct it. Nobody alive knew more about sophisticated comedy, and I remembered Coward's remark to Rex Harrison: 'If you weren't the finest light-comedy actor in the world next to me, you'd be good for only one thing—selling cars in Great Portland Street.' Coward himself was astonished by the invitation. Soon after it was issued, I was walking along a Mayfair street when a Rolls pulled up at the kerb. The electric window zoomed down and Coward peered out. 'Bless you,' he said, 'for admitting that I'm a classic. I thought you were going to do nothing but Brecht, Brecht, Brecht.' When he arrived to start rehearsals with a company led by Edith Evans and Maggie Smith, he made a little speech that began, 'I'm thrilled and flattered and frankly a little flabbergasted that the National Theatre should have had the curious perceptiveness to choose a very early play of mine and to give it a cast that could play the Albanian telephone directory.'

The rehearsals yielded a classic *mot*. Dame Edith persisted in upsetting Coward's rhythm by saying 'On a very clear day you can see Marlow,' instead of 'On a clear day you can see

Marlow.' After weeks of patience Coward interrupted. 'Edith,' he said, 'the line is "On a clear day you can see Marlow." On a *very* clear day you can see Marlowe *and* Beaumont *and* Fletcher.' The production was a huge success, and spawned a still-continuing vogue of Coward revivals.

Was he ever (and will he ever be) as highly regarded outside the English-speaking countries? I doubt it. He was above all a virtuoso of linguistic nuance. I cannot think that it will ever be possible to explain to a Belgian or Italian audience exactly why Budleigh Salterton is funny and Henley-in-Arden is not. One of the last and best stories I heard about Coward depends for its full effect on the choice and timing of an English proper noun. He was staying in Brighton with the Oliviers when their five-year-old daughter Tamsin saw in the street a male dog sniffing a female dog. She asked Uncle Noël what the animals were doing. 'The doggie in front', he replied, 'has suddenly gone blind, and the other one has very kindly offered to push him all the way to St Dunstan's.'

Incidentally, it is Olivier's theory that the authentic Noël Coward note in English literature was first struck by Sir John Falstaff, who says, when Mistress Quickly suggests putting an egg into his cup of sack: 'I'll no pullet sperm in my brewage.'

Not long before his death, Coward appeared in a Gillette advertisement. It required him to give a list of things that in his view had style. His reply was a brilliant, if oblique, self-portrait: 'A candy-striped Jeep; Jane Austen; Cassius Clay; *The Times* before it changed; Danny La Rue; Charleston in South Carolina; "Monsieur" de Givenchy; a zebra (but *not* a zebra crossing); evading boredom; Gertrude Lawrence; the Paris Opera House; white; a seagull; a Brixham trawler; Margot Fonteyn; any Cole Porter song; English pageantry; Marlene's voice … and … Lingfield has a tiny bit.'

About a year ago my wife and I dined at the Savoy Grill. At the next table sat Noël and his hard-core court, consisting of Graham Payn, the designer Gladys Calthrop and the actress Joyce Carey. When they had finished I felt a tap on my shoulder. It was Noël, standing beside me and explaining that he had just returned from a winter in Jamaica. The spring weather in London was warm, and my wife said he had picked a good time to come. 'Do you swear it?' said Noël gravely, unconsciously quoting from *Shadow Play*. He went on to tell us that he had recently met a very famous dwarf who had turned out to be enormously tedious. 'There's only one thing worse than being a dwarf,' he said, 'and that's being a boring dwarf.'

We were still laughing when he turned to go and we saw with a shock that he could hardly hobble. It took him more than two minutes to leave the room, with Graham Payn supporting one arm and Joyce Carey the other. His rubicund face and ebullient manner had fooled us. Noël had suffered a *coup de vieux*, and I felt sadly sure that I would not—nor did I—see him again.

Lenny Bruce

The following essay was published in 1965. In the last paragraph I wrote that: 'even if he died tomorrow, [Lenny Bruce] would deserve more than a footnote in any history of modern Western culture'. As it happened, Bruce did die a year later—on August 3rd, 1966, from an overdose of heroin, at the age of forty—thereby converting my piece into an obituary. I reprint it here as it first appeared.

Constant, abrasive irritation produces the pearl: it is a disease of the oyster. Similarly—according to Gustave Flaubert—the artist is a disease of society. By the same token, Lenny Bruce is a disease of America. The very existence of comedy like his is evidence of unease in the body politic. Class chafes against class, ignorance against intelligence, puritanism against pleasure, majority against minority, easy hypocrisy against hard sincerity, white against black, jingoism against internationalism, price against value, sale against service, suspicion against trust, death against life—and out of all these collisions and contradictions there emerges the troubled voice of Lenny Bruce, a night-club Cassandra bringing news of impending chaos, a tightrope walker between morality and nihilism, a pearl miscast before swine. The message he bears is simple and basic: whatever releases people and brings them together is good, and whatever confines and separates them is bad. The worst drag of all is war; in didactic moments Bruce likes to remind his audience that ' "Thou shalt not kill" *means just that*'. Although he occasionally invokes Christ as source material, I think he would applaud a statement recently made by Wayland Young, an English writer and agnostic, in a book called *Eros Denied*:

> Christian and post-Christian and Communist culture is a eunuch; pornography is his severed balls; thermonuclear

weapons are his staff of office. If there is anything sadder than a eunuch it is his balls; if there is anything more deadly than impotence it is murder.

If it is sick to agree with that, then God preserve us from health.

This may be the time to point out the primary fact about Bruce, which is that he is extremely funny. It is easy to leave that out when writing about him — to pass over the skill with which he plays his audiences as an angler plays a big-game fish, and the magical timing, born of burlesque origins and jazz upbringing, that triggers off the sudden, startled yell of laughter. But he is seldom funny without an ulterior motive. You squirm as you smile. With Bruce a smile is not an end in itself, it is invariably a means. What begins as pure hilarity may end in self-accusation. When, for example, he tells the story of the unhappily married couple who achieve togetherness in the evening of their lives by discovering that they both have gonorrhoea, your first reaction is laughter; but when you go on to consider your own far-from-perfect marriage, held together (it may be) by loveless habit or financial necessity or fear of social disapproval — all of which are motives less concrete and intimate than venereal disease — your laughter may cool off into a puzzled frown of self-scrutiny. You begin to reflect that there are worse fates than the clap; that a curable physical sickness may even be preferable, as a source of togetherness, to a social or spiritual sickness for which no cure is available. And thus another taboo is dented.

Bruce is the sharpest denter of taboos at present active in show business. Alone among those who work the clubs, he is a true iconoclast. Others josh, snipe and rib; only Bruce demolishes. He breaks through the barrier of laughter to the horizon beyond, where the truth has its sanctuary. People say he is shocking and they are quite correct. Part of his purpose is to force us to redefine what we mean by 'being shocked'. We all feel impersonally outraged by racialism; but when Bruce mimics a white liberal who, meeting a Negro at a party, instantly assumes that he must know a lot of people in show business, we feel a twinge of recognition and personal implication. Poverty and starvation, which afflict more than half of the human race, enrage us — if at all — only in a distant, generalized way; yet we are roused to a state of vengeful fury

3

when Bruce makes public use of harmless, fruitful syllables like 'come' (in the sense of orgasm) and 'fuck'. Where righteous indignation is concerned, we have clearly got our priorities mixed up. The point about Bruce is that he wants us to be shocked, *but by the right things*; not by four-letter words, which violate only convention, but by want and deprivation, which violate human dignity. This is not to deny that he has a disenchanted view of mankind as a whole. Even his least Swiftian bit, the monologue about a brash and incompetent American comic who tries to conquer the London Palladium, ends with the hero winning the cheers of the audience by urging them, in a burst of sadistic inspiration, to 'screw the Irish'. But the cynicism is just a façade. Bruce has the heart of an unfrocked evangelist.

I first saw him six years ago in a cellar room under the Duane Hotel in New York. Lean and pallid, with close-cropped black hair, he talked about Religions, Inc., a soft-selling ecumenical group on Madison Avenue whose main purpose was to render the image of Billy Graham indistinguishable from that of Pope John. ('Listen, Johnny, when you come out to the Coast, *wear the big ring*.') Clutching a hand mike, he slouched around a tiny dais, free-associating like mad; grinning as he improvised, caring as he grinned, seldom repeating in the second show what he said in the first, and often conducting what amounted to a rush job of psycho-analysis on the audience he was addressing. He used words as a jazz musician uses notes, going off into fantastic private cadenzas and digressions, and returning to his theme just when you thought he had lost track of it for ever. I saw him at the Duane four times, with four separate groups of friends. Some found him offensive—a reaction they smartly concealed by calling him boring. Others thought him self-indulgent, because he felt his way into the audience's confidence by means of exploratory improvisation, instead of plunging straight into rehearsed routines. Among my guests, he was not universally liked. 'Where's Lenny Bruce?' 'Down the Duane,' so ran a popular riposte. During the Duane engagement I met him for the first time—an archetypal night person, hypersensitive, laconic and withdrawn. Terry Southern once said that a hipster was someone who had deliberately decided to kill a part of himself in order to make life bearable. He knows that by doing this he is cutting himself off from many positive

emotions as well as the negative, destructive ones he seeks to
avoid; but on balance he feels that the sacrifice is worth while.
By this definition Bruce was (and is) authentically, indelibly
hip.

In the years that followed, it was not Bruce but my friends
who improved. One by one they began to discover that they
had always admired him. I recalled a saying of Gertrude
Stein's: 'A creator is not in advance of his generation but he is
the first of his contemporaries to be conscious of what is happening to his generation.' Bruce was fully, quiveringly conscious,
and audiences in Chicago and San Francisco started to respond
to his manner and his message. So did the police of these and
other great cities, rightly detecting in this uncompromising
outsider a threat to conventional mores. Arrests began, on
narcotics and obscenity charges, but Bruce pressed on, a long-
distance runner whose loneliness was now applauded by
liberals everywhere, including those tardy converts, my chums
in Manhattan. Mort Sahl, brilliant but essentially non-sub-
versive, had long been their pet satirist; but the election of
John F. Kennedy robbed Sahl of most of his animus, which had
been directed towards Eisenhower from the lame left wing of
the Democratic Party. It became clear that Bruce was tapping
a vein of satire that went much deeper than the puppet warfare
of the two-party system. Whichever group was in power, his
criticisms remained valid. Myself, I wished he had broadened
his viewpoint by a little selective reading of Marx as well as
Freud; but that, I suppose, is too much to expect of any comic
operating west of Eastport, Maine.

In the spring of 1962, he paid his first and only visit to
London, where he appeared for a few explosive weeks at The
Establishment, a Soho night club devoted to satire and run by
Peter Cook of *Beyond the Fringe*. Clad in a black tunic sans
lapels, as worn by the late Pandit Nehru, he roamed out on
stage in his usual mood of tormented derision; 90 minutes later
there was little room for doubt that he was the most original,
free-speaking, wild-thinking gymnast of language our inhibited
island had ever hired to beguile its citizens. I made notes of the
ideas he toyed with on opening night, and herewith reproduce
them:

'The smoking of marijuana should be encouraged because
it does not induce lung cancer. Children ought to watch

pornographic movies: it's healthier than learning about sex from Hollywood. Venereal disease is news only when poor people catch it. Publicity is stronger than sanity: given the right P.R., armpit hair on female singers could become a national fetish. Fascism in America is kept solvent by the left-wing hunger for persecution: "Liberals will buy anything any bigot writes." If Norman Thomas, the senior American socialist, were to be elected President, he would have to find a minority to hate. It might conceivably be midgets—in which case his campaign slogan would run: "Smack a midget for Norm".'

He went on to talk about the nuances of race relations, with special emphasis on whites who cherish the Negro cause but somehow never have Negroes to dinner; about a prison movie to end them all (starring Ann Dvorak, Charles Bickford and Nat Pendleton) in which the riot is quelled by a chaplain named Father Flotsky; about the difficulties of guiltless masturbation, and the psychological duplicity ('It's a horny hoax') involved in sleeping enjoyably with a prostitute; about pain of many kinds, and laughter, and dying. At times he drawled and mumbled too privately, lapsing into a lexicon of Yiddish phrases borrowed from the showbiz world that reared him. But by the end of the evening he had crashed through frontiers of language and feeling that I had hitherto thought impregnable. The British comedian Jonathan Miller, who watched the performance in something like awe, agreed with me afterwards that Bruce was a bloodbath where *Beyond the Fringe* had been a pinprick. We were dealing with something formerly unknown in Britain: an impromptu prose poet who trusted his audience so completely that he could talk in public no less outspokenly than he would talk in private.

His trust was misplaced. Scarcely a night passed during his brief sojourn at The Establishment without vocal protests from offended customers, sometimes backed up by clenched fists; and this, at a members-only club, is rare in London. The actress Siobhan McKenna came with a party and noisily rose to leave in the middle of Bruce's act; it seems she was outraged by his attitude towards the Roman Church. On her way out Peter Cook sought to remonstrate with her, whereupon she seized his tie while one of her escorts belted him squarely on the nose. 'These are Irish hands,' cried Miss McKenna dramatically, 'and they're clean!' 'This is an English face,' replied Mr Cook curtly, 'and it's bleeding.' A few days later a brisk, pink-faced sextet of young affluents from London's stockbroker belt booked a ringside table. They sat, half-heartedly sniggering, through jokes about money-making, sexual contact with Negroes, onanism as an alternative to V.D., and genetic hazards proceeding from fall-out. Suddenly Bruce ventured on to the subject of cigarettes and lung cancer. At once, as if in obedience to some tribal summons, the brisk, pink, stockbroker host sprang to his feet. 'All right,' he said tersely, 'Susan, Charles, Sonia! Cancer! Come on! *Cancer!* All out!' And meekly, in single file, they marched out through the door. Bruce kept tape recordings of both the McKenna and the cancer demonstrations, and made unsparing use of them on subsequent evenings.

At the end of his engagement he was rushed out of the country with the conservative press baying at his heels. The following year, Peter Cook applied for permission to bring him back to London. The Home Secretary brusquely turned down the application; Bruce, it seemed, was classified as an undesirable alien. (Off stage, he appears to have behaved quite desirably, apart from a rumoured occasion when the manager of a London hotel, awakened by complaining guests, strode into Bruce's room at 4 a.m. to find him conducting a trio of blondes whom he had taught to sing 'Please fuck me, Lenny' in three-part harmony.) In 1963 the Earl of Harewood invited him to take part in an International Drama Conference at the Edinburgh Festival. Despite the august source of the invitation, the Home Office once again said no. Lenny Bruce was too wild an import for British officialdom to stomach.

We miss him, and the nerve-fraying, jazz-digging, pain-hating, sex-loving, lie-shunning, bomb-loathing life he represents. There are times when I wish he would settle in Europe, for long enough at least to realize that capitalism—from which so many of his targets derive—is not necessarily a permanent and unchangeable fact of human existence. But even if he died tomorrow, he would deserve more than a footnote in any history of modern Western culture. I have heard him described, somewhat portentously, as 'the man on America's conscience'. Hyperbole like that would not appeal to Lenny Bruce. 'No,' I can hear him dissenting, 'let's say the man who *went down* on America's conscience … '

The Maturing
of Eric Morecambe

Early in 1973, Eric Morecambe and Ernie Wise, who are both in their mid-forties, celebrated their thirtieth anniversary as a double act. Before they were in their teens, they had appeared separately in northern working-men's clubs. They teamed up during the war and have since worked together in music-hall, radio, movies and television. They have been getting better all the time. There comes a point at which sheer professional skill, raised to the highest degree by the refining drudgery of constant practice, evolves into something different in kind, conferring on its possessors an assurance that enables them to take off, to ignite, to achieve outrageous feats of timing and audience control that would, even a few years before, have been beyond them. Morecambe and Wise have now reached that point. In their last TV series, written by the intuitive Eddie Braben, they came on as masters, fit to head any list of the most accomplished performing artists at present active in this country. What has happened to star quality in Britain? Morecambe and Wise have; or, to be invidiously precise, Eric Morecambe has, with unselfish, ebullient and indispensable help from Ernie Wise.

Every year, when their last TV show is safely in the can, they dart around the provinces carrying out what they call 'bank raids'. Twice nightly, on Fridays and Saturdays, they appear at a selected few of the biggest theatres outside London, making from these brief jaunts more money (their P.R. man half-boasts, half-complains) than thirteen B.B.C. shows would bring in. The first half of the programme is a straight variety bill; they occupy the second, which can last up to ninety minutes and consists of the legendary routines they use to warm up studio audiences and have prudently declined to squander on the tube. Last spring I saw them at the New Theatre in Oxford,

an echoing barn which they packed to the roof. 'We still get
the dry lip,' Eric had told me beforehand. 'A lot of our comedy's
based on fear.' But he was talking about television tension, the
surge of adrenalin that can lead to berserk ad libs and sudden
jumps in the script. On stage their confidence is total. But
apart from certain TV trademarks—gags about Ernie's alleged
wig and 'little short legs'; the affectionate pats, just crisp
enough to sting, that Eric bestows on Ernie's cheek; and
catch-phrases like the mysterious cry of 'Arsenal!', which was
used in one B.B.C. programme and now gets a round of
applause whenever Eric utters it—apart from these, their
style and material at Oxford reached back to their music-hall
days.

The act, so to speak, was Morecambe and Wise Mark I—
the original model, fitted with automatic gearshift and power
steering. In other words, a traditional male duo, but performed at a pace, with a delicacy, and above all *in clothes*
(matching suits from Savile Row) that would have amazed
such earlier couples as Murray and Mooney or Clapham and
Dwyer. Male double acts, once numerous, are today fairly
thin on the ground; thinner still are male-female teams,
such as Caryll and Mundy or Kenway and Young; and the
vogue for girl twosomes, like Revnell and West, Gert and
Daisy and the Houston Sisters, appears to have vanished.
Morecambe and Wise inspire reflections like these, so firmly is
their stage work rooted in pre-war vaudeville. You can also
trace the influence of Abbott and Costello and Wheeler and
Woolsey, who ranked among the top movie teams during their
adolescence. In M and W Mk. I, Ernie is the classic stooge,
dapper and aggressive, like a sawn-off Lew Hoad: Eric is the
comic off whose foolishness Ernie scores. Huge black horn-
rims are a vital part of his persona. They highlight the ocular
reactions that are among his specialities—the look of suddenly
dawning enlightenment, the blank stare aimed straight at the
camera, the smug *oeillade* that accompanies asides like: 'This
boy is a *fool*.' Behind the spectacles the face is boyish and
vulnerable, with the long upper lip that all great comics seem
to have. Wise is boyish, too. Indeed, the characters they present
in their act are both fixed at a mental and emotional age of
approximately 15. They ape the manners and vocabulary of
adults, but are always falling back on the idioms, habits and

local references of a North-country childhood. Hence they cannot deal with adult sex, except indirectly, through innuendo, as in their famous TV encounter with Frank ('Casanova') Finlay:

FINLAY (*furtively*): I have a *long felt want.*
MORECAMBE (*after subliminal pause*): There's no answer to that.

Nor would they wish to go further. As Ernie says: 'We never touch anything blue.' Such is their sexual innocence that, although they frequently share a bed in TV sketches, no whiff of queerness ever intrudes. They once did a routine in which it was hinted that Ernie might have been responsible for an illegitimate pregnancy: thirty letters of protest arrived, and they worried about it for weeks. They shun politics, too; in fact, I have no doubt that Lenny Bruce would have appalled them. Cynicism, the moral stock-in-trade of most American comics, is utterly alien to them. If, as we are always being told, comedy must have an attitude towards life, they are not comedians at all. Their laughs—and this is something very British, observable in talents as disparate as Pinter and the Goons— depend on nuance and inflexion, minute details of vocal and verbal eccentricity:

WISE: I'm going to make you the greatest singer in the world.
MORECAMBE: You're only saying that.
WISE: No, I'm not.
MORECAMBE: Somebody just did.

Morecambe's reflexes—the effortless speed and timing with which he changes expressions and tones of voice—are among the wonders of the profession. He can modulate through a series like Alarm/Aggression/Collapse/Recovery/Snide Insinuation in about four seconds, each phase being distinct in itself and leading logically to the next. My notes on the stage act include the following sequence, accomplished in roughly the same time: 'Apology/nervous cough/challenging glare/business with brown paper bag/false smile/business of adjusting glasses/ voice suddenly strident and serious.' For theatrical purposes the speed may even be excessive: after years of TV, Morecambe's style often needs the close-up camera to do justice to its intimacy and understatement.

'In the early days,' Morecambe told me, 'people kept saying to us: "You'll never be a success till you find something to hang your hat on" '—i.e. a durable routine like Sid Field's golfing sketch, or a stock trait like Jack Benny's meanness. They never found one, unless you count (as I would) the ventriloquist bit that is the high point of their variety act. Morecambe, equipped with doll, seats himself and says to the audience: 'Good evening, little man, and how are you? I'm very well, thank you. And what are you going to do for the ladies and gentlemen? I'll sing a song.' He pronounces every word at dictation speed with elaborate lip movements. The dummy's lips do not move at all. At length Wise, who has been watching incredulously, interrupts:

WISE: But I can see your lips moving!
MORECAMBE (*impatiently, as to a halfwit*): Of *course* you can see my lips moving!

Wise carefully explains that the whole point of ventriloquism is that the ventriloquist's lips should not move. This, when at last it gets through to Morecambe, strikes him as self-evidently absurd, and he confides to the audience that Wise is a crazy fantasist: 'He lives in a dream world.'

WISE (*shouting*): Don't you understand?
MORECAMBE (*shouting back*): No, but does it matter at this late stage?

Finally, under pressure from Wise, he tries to make the dummy's lips work, and in the attempt detaches the head from the body. Brandishing it by the neck, he hopefully crows: 'A throat with knuckles—they've never seen that before!' Any other comic would ventriloquize *badly*; only a Morecambe would take the wild imaginative step of not ventriloquizing *at all*. Another stage routine that might qualify, if extended, for hat-hanging status is the one in which Morecambe enters in full evening dress as a star magician. He stoops beneath the weight of an outsize tail-coat, from the bulging shoulders of which feathers are escaping.

WISE: What have you got in there?
MORECAMBE: Five chickens, three parrots, two vultures, four turkeys and a tom tit.

WISE: What does the tom tit do?
MORECAMBE: Not a lot.

They seldom address the audience directly—once at the beginning of their act, when Morecambe peers into the darkness and genially remarks: 'What a fat woman you are, madam. You. Are. Fat. Did you come on a lorry?'; and again at the end, when they invite questions from the house. They have a wide range of prepared answers and have only once been baffled. That was when a passionate voice rang out from the gallery: 'Should mopeds be allowed on the motorway?' Even Eric dried.

Their curtain calls are numerous. 'We never used to be able to do a good warm-up,' Ernie had said to me. 'Now the only thing we can't do is take a good bow.' But it really isn't true. Eric, as we know from TV, is a superb user of curtains, whether to burst through, peer round, lurk behind, or feign strangling himself with one hand in the folds of. It was he who told me the advice an old pro had given him on the art of taking bows: 'Rattle the corner of the curtain to show you're still there.' In any case, they have no need to milk applause. They are unmistakably loved—so much so that even the money they earn is not resented. 'When I'm driving through towns in the North,' Ernie says, 'people hate the Rolls until they see who's in it. Somehow they forgive us.'

Over supper after their Oxford appearance, Eric talks about comedy. Like Ernie (who had driven home to Harrow) he is a mobile repository of vaudeville lore, an encyclopedia of English-speaking gags, their genealogy, past effectiveness and current ownership. Give him a paper cup and within seconds it will have become a false nose and he'll be into a Durante impersonation. His favourite variety house is the Birmingham Hippodrome, on which I was brought up, so I quiz him about some of the lesser-known names of the '40s. Does he remember Freddie Bamberger and Pam? 'Very good act. A bit ahead of its time, maybe a bit too sophisticated. Freddie always smoked a cigar, and in the provinces a cigar means it's Christmas.' For Eric, as for most British comedians, the comics' comic is Tommy Cooper. (The American equivalent is George Burns.) 'My dressing-room', Eric says, 'is the Cooper shrine. You can tell how good he is because everyone does impressions of him.

If Tom's in the same room with a lot of other comedians, they're all waiting to see what he says next. He always surprises you.' A typical Cooper story: a man walks up to a shabby house and knocks on the door. It is opened by an anguished woman in black. 'Can I speak to Harry Jones?' asks the man. The woman bursts into tears. Another man wearing a black tie and a black arm-band appears behind the woman and asks the visitor what he wants. 'Can I speak to Harry Jones?' the first man asks. 'Harry Jones died two hours ago,' says the other man sombrely. 'I am his brother and this is his wife.' 'Oh,' says the first man, after a short pause. 'Did he say anything about a pot of paint?' If you find that unfunny, you are probably not a comedian.

Eric, who is married with two grown-up children (1 m., 1 f.), was born in Morecambe and christened Eric Bartholomew, an only child with no show-business background. His father was a corporation workman; his mother—'a very intelligent woman' —taught him music. He can still, at a pinch, play accordion, trumpet, clarinet, trombone and euphonium. Ernie Wise, a native of Leeds, was one of five children and came from a lower social level than Eric. His father worked on the railways and as a semi-pro entertainer in working-men's clubs. Ernie joined the act at the age of seven; Eric, urged on by his mother, was working the clubs at eleven; and they met in Swansea at the beginning of the war. In 1943, aged sixteen, they made their West End début in *Strike a New Note*, the hit revue that brought Sid Field to London after years in the provinces. Because Ernie was a friend of George Black, the producer, they were billed as 'Morecambe and Wise', although they didn't appear together in the show (except on a couple of occasions when somebody's illness left a hole in the programme.) Their act, Eric says, was: 'Terrible. With the full American accent. God knows why.' Towards the end of the war, Ernie went into the merchant navy and Eric was sent down the mines, an experience that left him with a weakened heart. They were reunited in 1947. In the 1950s came *Running Wild*, a disastrous TV series for the B.B.C. ('We were *pummelled*'); in the 1960s they triumphed on both channels and plunged into a frenzied period of overwork, including pantomimes, summer shows, films, and fourteen trips to the States to appear on the Ed Sullivan show. They also played the northern clubs, where they prospered in an atmosphere they did not always relish: too much drink in an audience isn't good for the finer points of comedy. Eric does a definitive impression of a club comic mumbling a hoarse stream of racist gags into a pencil mike: 'There was this Pakistani went into this synagogue ... '

In 1968 Eric had a heart attack. John Ammonds, an affable, hirsute little man who has produced all their B.B.C. shows for the past four years, believes that this setback, which seemed so shattering at the time, has had beneficial results. 'It forced the boys to give up all their outside activities and focus their attention on thirteen television shows a year. It allowed them to rehearse longer, and it made them concentrate.' Ammonds was the man who taught Eric to work to a specific camera (on asides like: 'A cunning little barb!') instead of to the studio audience. And it was from Ammonds, who copied it from Groucho Marx, that they picked up the curious skipping exit, like a sort of camp hornpipe, which they use to end their shows. (As many dance routines have disclosed, Eric is probably the most graceful bespectacled man on television.) Like Tony Hancock, and unlike almost all other British comedians, they actually improved on the way from the variety stage to the small screen. Already, in the mid-'60s, Morecambe and Wise Mark II had evolved. They were no longer comic and stooge, but two egotists in more or less equal competition. 'In old-fashioned double acts,' Eric says, 'the straight man would do something right and the comic would get it wrong. With us, Ernie would probably get it wrong as well. You get the same kind of thing with Laurel and Hardy.' Until Eric's heart attack, their scripts were written by Sid Green and Dick Hills, who also took part in the shows. Since 1969, and the advent of Eddie Braben, a Liverpudlian recluse who dispatches his scripts from Merseyside and hates coming to London, Morecambe and Wise Mark III have emerged, and Eric in particular has burgeoned into one of the most richly quirkish and hypnotic performers in the history of the box.

It is doubtful whether much that is memorable will be left in print about him. He may well be a literary casualty, because he lacks the easily identifiable characteristics by which other comics impress themselves on the memory. He is not a tramp, like Chaplin. He is not a lecher, like Groucho. He is not a boozy misanthrope, like W. C. Fields. Nor does he fall down or get kicked in the pants, like Norman Wisdom And Cast Of Thousands. Some of the time he is simply a pro comic making pro-comic jokes, e.g.:

QUEEN VICTORIA (*Glenda Jackson*): This audience is finished.
DISRAELI (*Eric*): Rubbish. They're good for another ten minutes yet.

But if you study the team's recent work closely, you will find that the primitive, Mark I relationship has been radically changed. Nowadays Ernie is usually the idiot—writing his terrible plays, composing his vacuous doggerel, giving his atrocious impersonations of James Cagney, etc. If someone must appear in drag, it is Ernie, not Eric. The new Ernie is like a rubber beach toy, slapped, shoved and prodded by his partner. Eric, meanwhile, has moved into the power vacuum. 'Eddie Braben', he says, 'has made me tougher, less gormless, *harder* towards Ern.' He is brisk, verbose, officious; always the imposer, always (however inefficiently) in command, whether quietly dropping *verb. -sap.* hints (as when, seeing his little pal with Frank Finlay, he intrudes with elaborate unconcern to mutter into Ernie's ear: 'A drunk from the audience. On your left. *A drunk.*') or suddenly hectoring Ernie in measured cadences of fruity, high-pitched intensity. There is a remarkable passage in the Finlay show where Eric has a long speech explaining to Ern, who has dressed up as a woman to save his sister's honour from Casanova, that if he goes thus clad to the great lover's bedroom, 'it could be a touch of the Hello-folks-and-how-about-the-workers.' Faced with incomprehension from Ernie, Eric repeats the entire speech three times, syllable for syllable. Another comedian would have made it louder every time, with diminishing comic returns; Eric uses the same even, rational tones throughout, and brings down the house.

The new Eric is a quasi-managerial type, jumped-up perhaps, but inspiring confidence with his balding dome and look of beady-eyed myopia; radiating a sense of leave-it-to-me and watch-it-buster; never quite humiliated, always quick to strike back, capable of accelerating from discomfiture to triumph in 0·7 seconds; and betraying vestigial signs of insecurity only by fleeting adjustments of the spectacles or momentary saggings of the jaw. He can even bully André Previn and the London Philharmonic. What other soloist, rebuked from the podium for not playing the right notes in the Grieg Piano Concerto, would seize the conductor by the lapels, lifting him well off the ground, and snarl into his face: 'Listen, sunshine— I'm playing all the right notes, but not necessarily in the right order.' Not long ago the boys tried out a sketch in which Eric was maltreated by Ernie, who played a temperamental movie director. It didn't work: because the new Eric would have rebelled and slapped Ernie down. What has happened is more complex than a simple reversal of roles. Ernie today is the comic *who is not funny*. And Eric—the dominating character who patronizes the comic—is the straight man *who is funny*. The combination is brilliant, wholly original, and irresistible. How much of it is due to Braben, and how much to the performers, is hard to determine; but we know that the scripts are heavily modified in rehearsal, and that most of the changes come from Eric.

I am not sure what will become of him. Towards the end of the last B.B.C. series Braben was making the team stretch itself by writing longer and longer sketches: there was one about the British Empire and the North-West Frontier that went on for over thirty minutes and never flagged for a second. The three films they've made so far have been as leadenly infantile as films starring British comedians traditionally are: Eric thinks they need a script plotted by somebody else, with Braben to write in additional gags. He is utterly uninterested in what, for every British comic before him, would represent the summit of ambition: starring in his own West End show. 'It would have no appeal for me,' he says politely. Why, after all, try something that might hurt the act, could not possibly help it, and might tie them down for a long time in a town that, being 'Northern comics' (a phrase dinned into their ears from childhood), they cannot think of as home? They have decided to avoid TV next winter, for fear of being over-exposed; but they must clearly do something. Eric views the future with pragmatic apprehension. When I asked him why so many comedians voted Tory, he replied, 'Because of tax.' Money is important to him. The history of comedy, especially in the TV era, is a graveyard of suddenly eclipsed reputations. (Rowan and Martin, where are you now?) 'For Ernie and I to play one minute without a laugh is murder,' Eric told me. '*It is fear.*'

Whatever happens, there will be no more where he came from. Because they started so young, he and Ernie form a unique link between pre-war vaudeville and contemporary television. The halls are closing; the clubs cannot develop comics with Eric's range and finesse; the British cinema has never created a great comedian (except possibly Peter Sellers); and you cannot learn from films or TV the ability to control a thousand people by your physical presence. I asked Eric what he thought of American comedy today. 'There's one thing I miss,' he said. '*There are no funny men*. There are funny lines, but no funny men.' The night before I met him, I dreamed about a surrealist show in which Eric kept stalking on stage in a burnous, bellowing: 'Where are my shock troops? I knew I should never have sold that wicker table.' Even with lines like that, I would trust Eric Morecambe to convince any English-speaking audience on earth that he was an incomparably funny man.

Q. Is there not, faintly detectable beneath the mask of the clown, an undertow of pathos, a strain of that inconsolable melancholy that haunts all sublunary things?

A. No. There is not.

Merman in London

(1)
February 19th, 1964

> I'm chipper all the day,
> Happy with my lot ...

—So runs the verse of a song that Ethel Merman didn't sing last Wednesday during her triumphant London début at the Talk of the Town. It comes from Gershwin's 'I Got Rhythm', one of the many numbers she can surely be said to have created, if created means made flesh.

Style is the effortless projection of content, the hammer that releases the chime, the seamless blending of instrument with purpose; and Merman, with her background of classic shows written for her by Gershwin, Cole Porter and Irving Berlin, is the strutting incarnation of style in American musicals. She almost invented the mode, with her carelessly accurate voice, brandished like a banner and glowing like sunrise over Brooklyn Heights; and so majestic is her timing that she can stroll around the stage in a tempo different from that of the song she is singing.

This is Annie who got her gun, for whom there's no business like show business; the hostess with the mostest on the ball; supremely the savage show-business momma for whom (in *Gypsy*) everything's coming up roses—the tops, the Palladium, the John F. Kennedy stadium.

Above all, she is a lesson in economy. From Merman one learns that there is no need to strain, wink, scream or wail. All that is necessary is a clean, clear voice, monumental breath-control, built-in timing and sincerity. She can mould a ballad ('They say that falling in love is wonderful ... ') as movingly as the brashest marching song—this stocky, middle-aged girl who might have gone westward with the wagons, this matchless technician who can make her notes blossom into a flamboyant *vibrato* or hold them down to a Sistine purity, this embodiment of the life-loving exuberance we have long associated with Broadway musicals and now see for the first time in the flesh.

Merman celebrates herself and us, sans pathos or rabble-rousing. The big room rocks to her; we rise to her indomitable simplicity, and wonder, as our palms steam with applause, what there ever was about Callas that we deemed worthier of our tears.

(2)
   September 10th, 1974
Last night Merman played the Palladium for the first time. An electric occasion, with standing ovations and the star at her militant best—she in whose hands musical comedy became a martial art. I love her defiance, the sense she communicates that she could swagger her way through Armageddon and survive: as with Seneca's heroine, you are sure that, even if Gibraltar tumbles, '*Medea superest*'. And the Rolls-Royce ease of her style: young audiences today expect the visible (and often risible) strain and sweat that pop stars provide. Merman's golden flow dumbfounds them. America is a democracy and Merman is American to the core; yet she sums up one of the contradictions of American democracy when she buoyantly sings:

> Some people
> May be content,
> Playing bingo
> And paying rent ...
> *But some people*
> *Ain't me!*

Another deeply American fact about her career is that Cole Porter (of all contrasting people) wrote many of his best songs for her—the dapper upper-class wit, dazzled and inspired by the brassy broad from Queens. This kind of thing would have been inconceivable in England: we can't imagine Ivor Novello or Noël Coward writing for Gracie Fields. (Incidentally, Merman could do worse than add a few Coward tunes to her repertoire—'Twentieth Century Blues', for example, or 'Sail

Away', not to mention the wonderful, underrated 'Sigh No More'. She epitomizes that gallant, rise-above-it quality that so many Coward songs celebrate.)

There won't be another Merman, because there is no need today for a voice like hers. Last night, in her mid-sixties, she used a radio mike, but on Broadway she never needed anything but the minimikes in the footlights, and often not even them. Barbra Streisand might have become her successor, but Streisand starred in only one Broadway show (*Funny Girl*) before plunging into movies. Streisand will never be able to give a solo performance like Merman's because nobody has ever written a show for her. Almost everything Merman sings was custom-made for the special strengths of her voice: and it shows. The colours suit her, the clothes fit like second skins. Let her juniors make do with reach-me-downs; Merman carries her own wardrobe with her, and it is full of original models.

Always she keeps her distance. What she sells is the song, not herself; every syllable comes over with stereo crispness. (Never in her Broadway career did she have to address her audience directly, as now: she always played character parts in book shows.) There are stars you admire and stars with whom you identify. Merman is one of the former, who are rapidly becoming extinct. The Palladium audience called her back for ten minutes, begging for encores. She thanked them but, although her accompanist was still present, she declined to sing any more. 'I haven't any more music rehearsed,' she said. Professional to the gilded hilt, she would not insult her admirers by giving them anything less than perfection.

Two or Three Things
I Know of Marlene

These are aspects of Dietrich as they surface in my memory, coloured no doubt by fifteen years of knowing her and some thirty years of quietly lustful admiration.

First, there is my friend the nurse—the sender of appropriate pills, the source of uncanny medical tips, the magic panacea. For this Marlene, healer of the world's wounded, I have often been thankful. Her songs are healing, too. Her voice tells you that whatever hell you inhabit, she has been there before, and survived. Some trace of ancient Teutonic folk-wisdom— many would call it witchcraft—still adheres to her. For example, she can predict a child's sex before its birth. This must, of course, be inspired guesswork or shrewdly applied psychology. She calls it science, as any witch would.

Then there is the self-punishing worker, daughter of an exacting German father, brought up to take pleasure as a prize and a privilege, not as a birthright. This is the Marlene who worships excellence—a high-definition performer who daily polishes her unrusting skills. A small eater, sticking to steaks and greenery, but a great devourer of applause. For some people (said Jean Cocteau), style is a very complicated way of saying very simple things; for others, it is a very simple way of saying very complicated things. Marlene is one of the others. Her style looks absurdly simple—an effortless act of projection, a serpentine lasso whereby her voice casually winds itself around our most vulnerable fantasies. But it is not easy. It is what remains when ingratiation, sentimentality and the manifold devices of heart-warming crap have been ruthlessly pared away. Steel and silk are left, shining and durable.

And a tireless self-chronicler. For the first half-hour of every meeting with this Marlene, you will be told how she wowed them in Warsaw, mowed them down in Moscow, savaged them in Sydney, was pelted with poppies in Ispahan. It is all true and, if anything, understated. She is merely keeping you up to date. Then she moves in—critical, probing and self-abnegating —on your own life and its problems. For the time being, you transfer your burdens to the willing shoulders of this gallant Kraut.

From the flat screen she stormed the senses, looking always tangible but at the same time untouchable. Her eyes were a pair of mournful rebukes, twin appeals to us not to lose our heads by becoming 'emotionally involved': but the milk-soft skin (which still shows no signs of curdling) gave the lie to them. And how cynically witty were her lips! This was not the fatal woman panting for fulfilment, like Theda Bara and the rest: it was the fatal woman fulfilled, gorged and sleek with triumph. The aftermath (*vide* Ovid) is sadness, and it was sadness that Dietrich communicated, even in her first youth. 'There is a gloom in deep love,' said Landor, 'as in deep waters.' But Dietrich had not alone the earth-melancholy of Lilith: she could awake and sing, brandishing her hips like Eve defying the Fall. 'Beware the *amazing* blonde women!' she cried in one of her early songs: and there was in her voice that note of quasi-military harshness you find in so many Germanic heroines. The order rings out riotously, and men come cringing to heel: the rule is instant obedience, the sheep must beg to be slaughtered. That, anyway, was the Dietrich myth, and it has its echoes in fictional women as disparate as Wedekind's Lulu and La Mort in Cocteau's *Orphée*. Many women, according to an old joke, have gender but no sex. With Dietrich the opposite is true. She has sex, but no particular gender. Her ways are mannish: the characters she played loved power and wore slacks, and they never had headaches or hysterics. They were also quite undomesticated. Dietrich's masculinity appeals to women, and her sexuality to men. They say (or, at least, *I* say) that she was the only woman who was allowed to attend the annual ball for male transvestites in pre-Hitler Berlin. She habitually turned up in top hat, white tie and tails. Seeing two exquisite creatures descending the grand staircases, clad in form-hugging sequins and cascading blond wigs, she wondered wide-eyed: 'Are you two in love?' '*Fräulein*,' said one of them frostily, 'we are not Lesbians.' This Marlene lives in a sexual no man's land—and no woman's, either. She dedicates herself to looking, rather than to being, sexy. The art is in the seeming. The semblance is the image, and the image is the message. She is every man's mistress and mother, every woman's lover and aunt, and nobody's husband except Rudi's—and he *is* her husband, far off on his ranch in California.

She believes in the stars but makes her own luck. Impresarios unnerve her. She has no agent or business manager except herself. Where once, in the high noon of the thirties, she depended on Joseph von Sternberg, she now looks to Burt Bacharach, her arranger and conductor. In his absence, she frets; at his excuses, she expressively shrugs. Burt is her generalissimo, the musical overlord on whom, quite asexually, she dotes.

She laughs a lot, making a honking sound that is not without melancholy. A special note of mournful bitchery invades her voice when the conversation turns to jumped-up starlets who need to be put down. ('What *about* that picture? She has to be out of her mind. Honey, it's to *die*!') This professional Marlene is not what anyone would call a woman's woman. I was not surprised to learn that she had never met Greta Garbo, her major rival in the World Eroticism Stakes of the pre-war era. She venerates many kinds of men—great strenuous helpers of our species like Sir Alexander Fleming; great life-enhancing performers like Jean Gabin and Orson Welles; great self-revealing writers like Ernest Hemingway and Konstantin Paustovsky; great masters of timing and nuance like Noël Coward; and men of great power like General Patton, John Fitzgerald Kennedy and—the latest recruit to the clan— Moshe Dayan. Marlene relishes the breath of power. She is rabidly anti-war, but just as rabidly pro-Israeli. This paradox in her nature sometimes worries me.

Aloof, imperious, unfeeling, icy and calculating: these are some of the things she is not. Proud, involved, challenging, ironic and outgoing: these are apter epithets. On stage, in the solo act to which she has devoted the last decade or so, she stands as if astonished to be there, like a statue unveiled every night to its own inexhaustible amazement. She shows herself to the audience like the Host to the congregation. And delivers the sacred goods. She *knows* where all the flowers went—buried in the mud of Passchendaele, blasted to ash at Hiroshima, napalmed to a crisp in Vietnam — and she carries the knowledge in her voice. She once assured me that she could play Bertolt Brecht's *Mother Courage*, and I expect she was right. I can picture her pulling a wagon across the battlefields, chanting those dark and stoical Brechtian songs, and setting up shop wherever the action erupts, as she did in France during the Ardennes offensive — this queen of camp followers, the Empress Lili Marlene.

What we have here, by way of summary, is a defiant and regal lady with no hobbies except perfectionism, no vices except self-exploitation, and no dangerous habits except an infallible gift for eliciting prose as monumentally lush as this from otherwise rational men. Marlene makes blurb-writers of us all. She is advice to the love-lorn, influence in high places, a word to the wise, and the territorial imperative. She is also Whispering Jack Schmidt, Wilhelmina the Moocher, the deep purple falling, the smoke in your eyes, how to live alone and like it, the survival of the fittest, the age of anxiety, the liberal imagination, nobody's fool and every dead soldier's widow. On top of which, she has limitations and knows them.

She is now on public show in person for the first time in New York. Roll up in reverence.

Magnetic Pole: a portrait of Polanski

In January, 1971, halfway through the shooting of *Macbeth*, they tried to fire Roman Polanski. This was quite audacious of them, since he was not only directing the picture, he was also the producer. He had decided in the spring of 1970 that he wanted to make a movie of Shakespeare's play. Together with a friend named Andrew Braunsberg, he formed a company to produce it; he asked me to write the screenplay with him, which took us six weeks; Hugh Hefner read it and agreed to finance the production. Shooting began in November, 1970, on location in North Wales. Now, barely two months later, came the explosion.

Let me explain that it wasn't Hefner or his advisers at *Playboy* who plotted the *coup d'état*. The sequence of events was as follows: having agreed on a budget ($2,400,000) with *Playboy*, Polanski and Braunsberg sought out what's known as a completion guarantor, whose business it is—in return for a substantial fee—to guarantee delivery of the finished picture to the distributors, and to pay any costs over and above the budgeted figure. These costs would be repaid only after *Playboy* had recouped its investment. By mid-January, Polanski was already way behind schedule; and the guarantors determined, one cold Wednesday morning, to show their teeth. They exercised their contractual right to replace Polanski and Braunsberg as producers; and their substitute, a professional troubleshooter, duly arrived at Shepperton Studios near London with chauffeur-driven car and stilt-heeled secretary. Moreover, they announced that unless Polanski caught up with the schedule by the end of the week—an impossible task—they would take him off the picture altogether.

Morale in the *Macbeth* unit slumped, even in the upper echelons. The word on the set was that a director of blood-stained quickies, recently seen lurking in the commissary, had already been signed to finish the movie. Telephone wires between Shepperton and Chicago pulsated with pleas and threats, imprecations and exculpations. Everyone lost his last shred of cool. Everyone except Polanski.

On the last working day of what was to have been his last week on the picture, he walked jauntily off the floor for lunch with three desperate colleagues in pursuit, begging him to cut a couple of the remaining crowd scenes, to eliminate the expensive fantasy sequence, to cancel his plan to spend an additional week on location. They halted to let a girl in a blue Mini Cooper go by, and suddenly Polanski was gone, skipping sideways at amazing speed, squinting in at the driver's seat, grinning and waving and shouting, 'Listen, what's your name? You're *beaudiful* ... ' On the way back to London that evening, he told Andrew Braunsberg, who knew him well enough to need no telling, that not only was he not going to cut a single shot out of the script, he was not going to cut an adjective or even a semicolon. He intended to shoot the picture at his own speed, because he didn't know any other. Very late that night he talked to Hefner in Chicago, marshalling his arguments with Napoleonic skill. Within twenty minutes he had obtained a budget increase large enough to pay for the extended schedule and to buy out the completion guarantors. Everyone breathed again, except Polanski, who had not stopped breathing for an instant. Next day I asked him how he had managed to be so spookily unconcerned. 'I tell you,' he said. 'The same thing happened to me in 1968, when I was in Hollywood making *Rosemary's Baby*. Paramount wanted to fire me because I was going over budget. I was walking across the lot feeling pretty drastic. Then Otto Preminger came up to me and asked what was the matter. I told him, and he put his arm around my shoulder and said, "Look—directors get fired when their dailies are lousy. They get fired when some big star doesn't like them. But nobody ever got fired for going over budget. So go eat your borscht in peace." And I checked up, and you know, he was right!'

Nobody is harder to faze than this cocksure Polish gnome. He armours himself against showing anything that might be construed as weakness. He probably feels—to rephrase Lord Acton—that all weakness corrupts, and absolute weakness corrupts absolutely. And what else would you expect? When he was a child in Poland (he is now thirty-eight) both his parents were taken to concentration camps: his mother died in Auschwitz. From then until the grotesque and ferocious night that robbed him of his wife in the summer of 1969, life has schooled him and steeled him to be a one-man survival kit. His aim is quite simply to be invulnerable, physically as well as psychologically—not the easiest of tasks, if you are only a few inches over five feet tall, and not an ambition calculated to inspire universal affection. (He has been described by an ill-wisher as 'the original five-foot Pole you wouldn't touch anyone with'.) He has the necessary fitness of a hunted man, and he holds himself with the compact, aggressive tension of a crossbow. With either leg extended in front of him, he can do fifty full knee-bends on the other, and his stomach is like an iron shield. Tests of strength have an unfailing appeal for him. As he arrived at Shepperton one morning, a member of the crew pointed silently at a little construction that he and his colleagues had set up. It consisted of a piece of wood—two inches thick and six inches square—resting like a lintel on two up-ended bricks. Polanski surveyed it for a moment and then, standing astride it, clenched his fist and punched sharply downward. The wood split down the middle. He shrugged mock-boastfully and passed on.

He both skis and drives like a maniac, and takes pride in the friendship of people (like the racing driver Jackie Stewart) who risk their lives professionally and get away with it. That his physical powers might one day decay is a possibility he refuses to entertain; whatever age may do to others, it is never going to wither *him*. I once heard him talking to a friend—a man in his mid-forties—who had been suffering from troublesome migraines.

'You were always a healthy bugger,' said Polanski. 'You're just going through the male menopause.'

'I suppose so.'

'Will that happen to me?'

'Yes.'

'Up your arse.' Polanski held up the middle finger of his right hand. 'It's all psychological.'

He has the assurance of all the great imposers. Let me clarify the concept of 'imposing'. Derived from the French verb *s'imposer*, it is a quality of temperament or personality. It denotes the ability not only to impose one's will on others (although that is a part of it) but to dictate the conditions — social, moral, sexual, political — within which one can operate with maximum freedom. In other words, assuming one has talent, the gift of imposing is what enables one to exercise it to the full. It does not merely stake one's claim, it asserts one's authority over a given field of work. 'Inside this field,' it says, 'you will defer to me.' Laurence Olivier, Orson Welles, Harold Pinter and Marlon Brando are among the show-business people in whom I have recognized this quality. An imposer is one about whom you worry whether his response to your next remark will be a smile or a snarl. You shrink from his scorn and cherish his praise. Unfortunately, many un-talented people have the knack of imposing; the arts are full of them, and very nasty they are. On the other hand, many talented people are quite unable to impose, being too gentle and reticent; and these are the saddest cases of all. Success or failure, fulfilment or frustration in almost every sphere of human activity is dependent on whether or not one has the trick of imposing. Polanski has it in spades — sometimes to an extreme degree. He tends to make a request for the first time with the exasperation of a non-imposer making it for the tenth; and he never apologizes, no matter whom he has offended, or how. With people like this, there is always a sense of danger, as anyone can testify who ever had a drink with Ernest Hemingway.

Like many imposers, he divides the world into Lenin's categories of 'Who' and 'Whom' — those who do, and those to whom it is done. Some of his opinions verge on the reactionary. He mistrusts trade unions, especially in the British film industry, where he regards the closed shop as a conspiracy to suppress talent; and he is in favour of strict legislation to forbid un-official strikes. (His failure to identify with the proletariat is partly a rebellion against the dogmatic communism that was poured down his throat during his adolescence in postwar Poland. Similarly, his distaste for religion has its roots in the years he spent living with a Catholic family between the ages of eight and twelve. But although he claims to have rejected the Party and the Church, they have both left their mark on the cast of his mind. Reading that capitalism is headed for yet another crisis, he is likely to murmur: 'Maybe Marx was right'; and he would often puzzle the *Macbeth* unit with obscure jokes about the Pope's ring and the sex lives of cardinals. 'Those Catholics,' he once said to me, 'they really left me *bent*.') Towards girls his attitude is not so much feudal as tribal. He beguiles them into submission with his urchin charm; but if they presume to engage him in argument, he soon grows bored and petulant. Women's lib arouses him to a high pitch of bewildered fury. While we were writing the *Macbeth* script in his study, there would often be a brace of girls draped around in the living-room, reading magazines and playing records. One evening, when we had finished work, a recumbent darling rose to her feet and said she was going into the kitchen to make some coffee. Polanski rounded on her as if stung. 'What are you — some kind of militant?' he said. 'If you want coffee, ask my housekeeper.' I realized that for him there were only two acceptable female postures: sitting down and lying down. To get up unasked — even if only to enter the kitchen, symbolic dungeon of oppressed womanhood — was tantamount to an act of insurrection. This message is implicit in the first object you see on crossing his threshold. It is a piece of sculptured furniture designed by the English artist Allen Jones — a coffee table consisting of a sheet of plate glass supported by a life-size girl on all fours, modelled in fibre glass and wearing nothing but long gloves, laced leather boots, tightly fitting knickers and a corset. Her back is arched, and her expressionlessly pretty face contemplates itself in a mirror thoughtfully placed on the floor.

The master–servant relationship has always fascinated Polanski. *Le Gros et le Maigre*, a short he made in Paris in 1960, deals with a fat, overbearing tyrant and his cringing slave (played by Polanski himself), who ends up by embracing his own self-abasement. Here, as in much of his early work, Samuel Beckett is a potent influence. Two years later in Poland, Polanski wrote and directed *Mammals*, a brief fable about two men who alternate the parts of master and servant, taking turns to drag each other across a snowbound landscape on a sled. They are constantly squabbling, and during one of their fights a third man steals their property. (This was Voyteck Frykowski, who thereafter vanishes from public view until 1969, when he reappears as one of the victims in the massacre that killed Sharon Tate. Polanski is not superstitious; but he seems to be something of a lightning conductor, and he is not altogether kidding when he jokes about the way in which people close to him tend to get hit. David Stone, an English writer who translated his script for *Repulsion* from French into English, died recently of appendicitis, of which *nobody* dies; Krzysztof Komeda, who wrote the music for all Polanski's films except *Repulsion*, collapsed in a Hollywood street two years ago and died of a brain haemorrhage. Zbigniew Cybulski, the unforgotten dark-spectacled star of *Ashes and Diamonds* and an intimate chum of Polanski's, contrived to get himself killed jumping on a train; the Polish director Andrzej Munk, who gave Polanski his first job on a feature film, was eliminated in a car crash; and soon after starring in *Cul de Sac* the same fate befell Françoise Dorléac. The other day Polanski told me a long and hilarious story about an eccentric Polish schoolfriend. 'What happened to him?' I asked. 'Oh,' said Polanski, 'I heard he jumped off a roof about two months ago.') In *Cul de Sac*, Lionel Stander plays a gangster on the run who takes over an isolated castle and turns its master into his servant. The gangster himself is awaiting instructions from *his* boss, the omnipotent Katelbach, which happens to be the surname of the actor who played the tyrant in *Le Gros et le Maigre*. The question so icily answered in *Rosemary's Baby* is: what happens to a man's life and that of his wife when he consciously enslaves himself to Satan? And the whole plot of *Knife in the Water* — Polanski's first full-length film — revolves around the attempts of two men to impose on one another: a journalist approaching forty and a young hitchhiker compete for mastery of the journalist's wife.

To Polanski, most people are either arse-lickers or licked arses. I discovered during *Macbeth* that he has a respectful admiration for his own buttocks. He had just shot Lady Macbeth's sleepwalking scene, in which Francesca Annis appears naked. She played it beautifully and was utterly unfussed by the nudity, so much so that the wardrobe lady, who crouched like a sprinter throughout each take, ready to dash in with the dressing-gown the moment Polanski said 'Cut,' seemed rather superfluous. Over lunch Polanski began to talk about the female body. Breasts, he said, were secondary to him; bottoms were what counted. We debated the relative merits of some archetypal movie bottoms. I proposed Natalie Wood's; he shook his head and said: 'Jane Fonda.' 'A bit boyish?' I suggested. 'So what?' he said, and, leaping to his feet in the middle of the studio restaurant, invited me to inspect his own bejeaned rump. 'As a matter of fact,' he said proudly, '*I* have the greatest arse in the entire film industry.' I said I still preferred Marilyn Monroe's. 'Oh well,' he said, resuming his seat, 'if you're going to talk about dead people, Sharon had a pretty good bottom.' If this sounds callous, I will swear that was not how Polanski meant it. It was a facing of facts and a candid tribute. Polanski has a terrible past with which to live, and it would be out of character for him (as well as bad therapy) to wrap it up in sentimental ribbons. In order to survive and function, he has had to immunize himself against nostalgia; and from time to time he deliberately administers to himself little jabs—booster shots, you might call them—like the remark I have quoted. An apt motto for Polanski would be the enigmatic catchphrase used by the indomitable old Captain in Strindberg's play *The Dance of Death*: 'Cancel—and pass on!'

Polanski's code of honour is simple and inflexible. It prescribes absolute loyalty to people who show fealty to him, and absolute contempt for people who betray him. But while he expects fealty, flattery bores him; and he is deeply suspicious of behaviour that smacks in any way of ingratiation. One day, after seeing the rushes of a sequence in which Jon Finch, the young actor who plays Macbeth, rides home in triumph after a battle, I innocently asked: 'Don't you think he might smile a little? After all, he's a victorious general.' Polanski was baffled by the question. 'Why should he smile?' he said. 'Only cunts smile.' He pointed a finger at my face. '*You* smile,' he said, grinning broadly. And he was right, a faint apologetic grimace *had* congealed on my lips.

Imposers are often lonely and Polanski is no exception. The measure of his loneliness is that he is never alone. Most days after shooting he would fling himself exhausted into the back seat of the big Rolls with the smoked-glass windows, and, murmuring 'Who shall I gratify tonight?', thumb through a constantly amended list of candidates. Then he would grab the car telephone and the hunt would be up. If any special buddies were in town, such as Warren Beatty or Mike Nichols, they too would be roped in, and the party would probably end up after midnight at Tramp in Jermyn Street, the currently fashionable Mayfair discothèque. Next morning, promptly at 7.45, the host would pick me up at my home. Although he was never in the strict sense hung over (he drinks hardly at all), there were days when, hiding behind dark glasses, too weary to talk, he would sleep like a child all the way to the studio. But mostly he would be uncannily restored, bright-eyed and bushy-tailed, vivacious and observant as ever, chattering away like a magpie, missing nothing from the moment I climbed into the car:

'You had garlic for dinner last night, my friend. Open the window ... How you like this new tape? Elton John. Fantastic, huh? ... Listen, I screwed a Chinese lawyer last night. She's a barrister from Hong Kong. Beaudiful! ... You see the guy driving that Jensen? He's wearing a wig ... Peter Sellers and I and some chicks had dinner at Parkes' with this Persian guy who writes poetry, the one I told you about who's always stoned out of his mind. When we sat down he said, "I am estoned" — Persians are like Spanish, they put an "e" before "s" at the beginning of words. We all ordered blanquette de veau and the Persian just sat there, not moving, with his head bowed down like he was praying ... That's a 747 over there, going into that cloud ... After we waited for some time the Persian suddenly said, quite loudly, 'I want to change my wheel.' So naturally we thought he must be hallucinating, and we laughed, and Peter said maybe he would like his oil changed as well, and how about a phone in the back seat? But he kept saying, "I want to change my wheel," over and over. Then I finally remembered what we had ordered. *All he wanted was to eat something else instead of veal!* ... Listen, I'm going to Gstaad this weekend with those two chicks I pulled at the party that Victor gave for Warren ... You remember, there was the one with the drastic hot pants? Sure you know the type, sort of between a starlet and a secretary ... Or is it the party *which* Victor gave? What's the *exact difference* between "that " and "which"? ... ' We stop at a red light and there is a pretty girl standing on the corner. Without hesitation Polanski rolls down the window and leans out. 'Hey, miss, excuse me, you have a beaudiful arse, where are you going?' The chances are good that the girl will end up in the car. During his marriage to

Sharon, Polanski once shouted a similar compliment at a girl in Beverly Hills whose rear view attracted him. When she turned round he saw that it was his wife.

He puts into his films the solitude he compulsively shuns in life. As Ivan Butler says in *The Cinema of Roman Polanski*, 'All his characters convey a powerful impression of "aloneness".' There is Carol, the psychotic heroine of *Repulsion*, left on her own for a weekend in that sombre South Kensington apartment which becomes the setting for a carnival of bloodshed; Rosemary, of course, cut off from all help in *Rosemary's Baby*; the husband and wife in *Cul de Sac*, fugitives from reality on their lonely peninsula; the three trapped people on the boat in *Knife in the Water*. And now, to add to the list, there is Macbeth, alone at the end in his besieged castle, deserted by his supporters, his wife dead, his best friend murdered by his own command. What Polanski once told an interviewer sounds perfectly credible: that he would like to make a film that had only one character. Typically, he counts among his favourite movies a macabre curiosity called *Peeping Tom*, made in 1957 by the baroque English director Michael Powell. Its central character is a hermit photographer living in a state of complete psychological isolation. A voyeur imprisoned in his own fantasies, he revenges himself for a horrendous childhood by murdering women and taking pictures of them as they die. He calls himself a student of fear.

Polanski subscribes to the view (which he calls 'realistic' and I call conservative) that life is a jungle in which, despite occasional truces with other men for mutual advantage, we are all on our own. He is a fierce competitor who loves winning; and so long as society makes sure that none of its members is actually starving, he sees no reason why the lion's share of the spoils should not go to the most talented. Predictably, he is a great believer in Robert Ardrey's 'territorial imperative' — the theory that man's basic instinct is the desire, bequeathed by his animal ancestry, to conquer and defend territory, to proclaim that what he has he holds. I would sometimes give Polanski an argument on this, pointing out that in the course of the long journey up from all fours we had succeeded in tempering and civilizing many such atavistic impulses. At this the Pole would explode:

'Listen — if you come into your house and a strange guy is

sitting there, the blood goes to your head, right? You resent him, right?'

'First I'd have to know why he was there. He might have come to mend the icebox—'

'*I'm not talking about motives!* Jesus Christ, you try to rationalize everything! What I'm talking about comes *before* reason. It's a *primitive impulse*. You see that guy in your house and *you hate him*!'

This attitude towards intruders—and I can imagine Polanski's rage on hearing an explanation so rational—is not surprising in a man whose homes have always been temporary and imperilled. Even among film buffs, you can win money by betting people that they can't name his birthplace. The usual answer is Warsaw, and it is wrong. The 'in' group smiles and says Cracow: wrong again. Polanski was born on August 18th, 1933, in Paris, where his father, a Polish Jew, was working for a record company; his mother, also a Polish citizen, came of Russian stock. When he was three, the family moved to Cracow, and it was here, in 1940, that he remembers seeing German troops building a wall across the end of the street where he lived. Though he did not understand at the time what was happening, they were sealing off the ghetto. In the following year both his parents disappeared into concentration camps. Polanski (then aged eight) escaped from the ghetto to the countryside, where he lived on a farm with a Catholic family, 'friends of friends of my father'. One hot summer afternoon he climbed a hill to pick blackberries. Far in the distance he saw a group of three or four German soldiers, reclining in a field. He did not give them a second thought until, several minutes later, he heard a high-pitched whirring noise, close to his head, followed by a bang. One of them had taken a shot at him as if he were a rabbit. He threw himself to the ground and stayed there for a long while. That was the first time anybody tried to kill him. Back in liberated Cracow a day or two before the final German surrender, he remembers going to the lavatory late one evening and breaking the blackout regulations by turning on the light. He was instantly blown through the door, badly injuring his left arm. The only bomb dropped in almost the last German air raid of the war had fallen on his house. That was his second experience of dicing with death.

The war ended and Stalinism replaced Nazism in Poland.

Polanski's mother had perished in the camp; and he chose not to live with his father, who survived and remarried. Instead, he moved into lodgings (with financial aid from his father) and went to art school in Cracow. When he was sixteen the third attempt on his life took place. He was obsessed with bicycle racing, and one day he met in a café a young man who offered to sell him a racing machine at an absurdly low price. They arranged a rendezvous next day, to which Polanski brought along a friend. The young man told the friend to wait and escorted Polanski into a nearby park where there was an underground concrete bunker, built by the Germans. It was pitch-dark inside except for a faint glow from a tiny skylight. As they entered the man motioned Polanski to lead the way and, striking a match, lit a rolled-up newspaper he was carrying.

'After a few steps I asked him where is the bicycle? "At the end," he said. "But I can see the end, sir," I said. For some reason I found myself calling him sir. "It's around a corner," he said. And he was whispering. For years after I was scared of anyone who whispered. Then I thought I felt an electric shock. I thought maybe I'd touched some exposed cable down there. I didn't allow myself to think he had hit me on the head.'

But he had, five times, with a rock concealed in the newspaper, after which he stole Polanski's wristwatch and money and fled.

'I don't know how long I was knocked out. When I woke up blood was pouring down into my eyes like water. I didn't take a shower for a long time after that. Even now, when I step into a shower and feel the water dripping down my face, I can taste blood. I staggered out of the bunker and nearly bumped into a woman in the street. "What's the matter, young man?" she said. "Nothing," I said, and I remember pushing her away and leaving a bloody hand print on her raincoat. Then a garbage truck pulled up at the kerb and sitting in the front seat was the guy who hit me. What had happened was that my friend saw him come running out of the bunker. He chased him, and two garbage collectors who were passing in a truck got out to help. Together they caught him.'

They hauled Polanski aboard and took their prisoner to a police station. It did not take long to identify him because, as it turned out, he was already wanted for three murders. To commemorate the incident, Polanski still bears five livid scars on his skull.

From art school he went on to spend five years at the famous State Film School at Lódź. (Polanski is a living vindication of the principle of state-aided cinema.) There in 1958 he wrote and directed for his senior thesis the haunting surrealist short, *Two Men and a Wardrobe*. Other shorts followed; then came a prolonged trip to Paris, after which he returned to Poland in 1962 to make *Knife in the Water*. Back in France, he wrote the scenario for a bizarre comedy called *Aimez-Vous Les Femmes?*, about a chic set of contemporary urban cannibals whose *spécialité* is garnished girl. The international success of *Knife in the Water* brought him to England, where he arrived in 1965 — speaking more or less five languages (Polish, Russian and French more, Italian and English less) — to direct *Repulsion*, the film that launched him with a resonant splash in the English-speaking cinema. In 1966, *Cul de Sac* won him the Golden Bear at the Berlin Film Festival; and although his highly personal Gothic fairy tale, *The Fearless Vampire Killers*, disappointed many who approached it merely as a burlesque horror movie, his next picture, *Rosemary's Baby*, caught the full tide of popular and critical approval. That was in 1968. The bad times, it seemed, were over for good; in Sharon, he had found the only girl who ever moved into his life on equal terms; and professionally he was in a position to write his own contract anywhere in the world. Then came the incredible summer morning in 1969 when one picked up the paper and read the shattering news from California.

In a way it is no wonder that Polanski chose *Macbeth* for his next film — when at last, the following spring, the notion of work began once more to make sense. The world of the play is one to which, from childhood, he has been no stranger — a place of considered cruelty, of ambush and unforeseen loss, of tyranny founded on bloodshed, of bright omens leading to pits of howling despair, of revenge brutally visited not only upon enemies but upon their kin. (In passing, one of the remarkable things about Polanski is not, as people often allege, that his films reveal 'a taste for violence', but that so much of his most characteristic work — *Knife in the Water* and *Rosemary's Baby*, for example — contains no violence at all.)

Good things of day begin to droop and drowse,
Whiles night's black agents to their preys do rouse ...

Polanski needed no maps to find his way about in *Macbeth*
country: it was like a homecoming.

In the spring of 1970 he asked me to collaborate with him
on the script and to act as artistic adviser during the shooting.
As I write, the shooting has only just ended, and it's much too
early for me to venture any comment on what the finished
movie will be like; but it may help to complete my account
of this volatile, extravagantly gifted Pole if I set down some of
the notes I made during the long months of our work together.

May/June, 1970. First script discussion. Roman and I agree
that the Macbeths should be young. Nothing in the play
contradicts this; and it seems far more likely that a deadly
swordsman (which we know him to be) would be youthful
rather than middle-aged. If the Macbeths are young, they have
everything to win or lose and are risking their whole future
— far more thrilling than a sudden and inexplicable access of
homicidal mania on the part of a postmenopausal Darby and
Joan. The parts are conventionally played middle-aged because
the old Shakespearean actor-managers usually *were* middle-aged
by the time they had their own companies. Query: is this why
the play has nearly always failed in the theatre? Of the many
Macbeths I've seen, Laurence Olivier's at Stratford-on-Avon
in 1955 was the only one that worked. Roman luckily comes to
the play unintimidated by its bad record: he has never seen it
on stage ...

Cast almost any actor as Macbeth, and he will come on
looking doom-laden, already aware that he is in a Great
Tragedy. But the point about the Macbeths is that *they do not
know they are in a tragedy*. They think they are in a story that is
going to have a triumphantly happy ending. When the witches
prophesy that Macbeth will be king, he is filled with exhilaration, like a man who has come into an unexpected fortune.
That is the dream. Rushing to fulfil it, the Macbeths encounter
the reality of their own natures, which hitherto neither of them
knew; and that is the tragedy ...

Essential not to tiptoe up to the text with excessive awe. If
asked whether it is a great tragedy written by a great

philosopher, or a great melodrama written by a great poet, we would favour the latter. This doesn't, of course, mean that it's no more than a Highland story of partners in crime, subtitled 'My Bonnie Lies Over The Clyde' ...

Roman and I have been seeing some Shakespearean films. Of the Orson Welles *Macbeth* he says, 'It's a tragedy of bad plumbing—a universal sewer filled with incestuous warlocks.' But we both admire the Russian *Hamlet*, with Smoktunovsky as the prince ...

Except for odd lines like Banquo's 'In the great hand of God I stand,' we decide to eliminate overt religion from the script. Not on doctrinaire grounds but because, if we let it in, we have to show what *kind* of religion—Christian or pagan? Priests or high priests? Incense or entrails? Once embarked on that course you are apt to end up inventing symbolic figures like the ghastly Old Man with the cross in Orson's picture. There is plenty of *evil* in the play; and, though he denies it, I suspect that Roman believes in the existence of evil as an active force in the world. Certainly he takes a fairly low view of human motives. So does the script: the only sympathetic characters of any note are Banquo and the Macduffs, and of them only Macduff survives to the end ...

I'd expected that I would be mainly concerned with the verbal aspect of the script and Roman with the visuals. But not at all: he knows the text inside out, and many of the staging ideas are coming from me. Etymology fascinates him. He racks my brains to find out the distinction, in Shakespearean English, between 'shall' and 'will' ,'thou' and 'you'. He has a polymath's appetite for knowledge. When the phone in his car breaks down, he gives me a two-minute lecture on the principles of electronic dialling; he is corresponding with a professor on the science of optics; and he often starts conversations with brusque, Olympian remarks like: 'I just solved the problem of the tides ...' But it must always be practical knowledge. Abstract argument bores him ...

Roman is a rigid purist where screen writing is concerned. He absolutely forbids the kind of vague, emotive stage directions (e.g. 'the atmosphere is threatening', 'he seems uneasily pre-occupied') with which many scripts are padded. He insists that we confine ourselves strictly to what can be seen and heard: 'Anything else is cheating.' Example of his passion for concrete detail: we discuss a shot of the advancing English army and he asks, 'Should they move right to left across the frame, or left to right?' I rashly say, 'Does it matter?' 'Of course it matters,' he says. 'To the Western eye easy or successful movement is left to right, difficult or failed movement is right to left.' He sends out for a children's comic to prove his point. On the first page a canoe is shooting the rapids left to right, and a man is climbing a mountain right to left. The English army advances left to right ...

Roman rejects the idea of 'metaphysical' witches, abstract spirits of evil. Instead they will be real old women who live in a real place and mix real potions. Their first scene—only eight lines long—has already gone through a dozen revisions. Sometimes I get impatient with the way he frets over minute details of description—even of layout on the page. He grins and says, '*Je suis un enculeur de mouches*' ('I'm a buggerer of flies') ...

Today Roman writes a letter to his old friend and adversary John Trevelyan, the British film censor, who is a declared opponent of screen violence. Gravely he warns Trevelyan that he is working on a subject which involves the cold-blooded murder of a reigning monarch by a member of the aristocracy, and the decapitation of his successor. He adds that the plot also includes infanticide and a detailed recipe for calling up the devil ...

Shakespeare left the murder of King Duncan offstage not out of aesthetic decorum (he showed kings being killed in other plays) but because *Macbeth* was written to be performed in the presence of a Scottish king, James I. There is thus no reason for us to keep the murder offscreen. Roman insists that we act out various ways of slaughtering Duncan. It's a hot day, and we are working stripped to the waist in his little mews house near Eaton Square. He makes me lie down in the spare bedroom with my eyes shut, and announces the unattractive news that he is going to come at me with a paper knife. He does so. I manage to disarm him; he unfairly produces a second weapon; and we roll over and over on the floor. We repeat this with many variations, alternating the roles. Suddenly I notice that, on the balcony of the house overlooking Roman's garden, a group of middle-aged people are watching us, holding sherry glasses. Their eyebrows are politely raised, their heads bent forward in mild curiosity, their faces impassive. Roman darts to the window and beckons them to join us, but they turn fastidiously away—none too keen, I imagine, on the idea of participating in the arcane rituals of a pair of sadomasochistic queers ...

Lady Macbeth must be nude in the sleepwalking scene. It's true that in the text she is said to put on a 'nightgown' (Elizabethan for 'dressing-gown') after getting out of bed; but then Shakespeare had no alternative but to clothe her in something, since the part was played by a boy. This convention created necessities that are not binding on us. And the historical evidence is unequivocal: in the Middle Ages everyone slept naked. Moreover, in an ironclad embattled castle, she will look effectively vulnerable. And apart from anything else, as Roman says, it is pleasant to look at a naked girl ...

Assassins break into Macduff's castle during his absence and murder his wife and children. I have not looked forward to working on this scene, which we finished today. There was one difficult moment when I queried Roman's estimate of the amount of blood that would be shed by a small boy stabbed in the back. 'You didn't see my house in California last summer,' he said bleakly. 'I know about bleeding.' This is the only reference he has made to his private tragedy since we started work ...

September, 1970. Flying back last week from Paris to London, Roman saw on the plane a face that rang a distinct bell. He fraternized and found that it was Jon Finch, an actor he first noticed in a casting directory a few days ago, now finishing a TV series in France. Last night Finch flew to London again and I met him and Roman for supper: he is in his late twenties and looks very possible, cool, composed and dominant. Roman took him back to the house and for several hours we put him through the scene with Banquo's two murderers. I faded at 2 a.m., leaving Roman still busily recording his performance on a video-tape machine ...

The advantage of a youthful Lady M. is that she can bring sexual pressure to bear on her husband: the killing of Duncan becomes a test of his affection and virility. Today Roman tested six young actresses for the part. He patiently explained that there was no need to *thunder* at Macbeth like the conventional stage gorgon. They all nodded, and proceeded to thunder *quietly*. Only Francesca Annis (Nicol Williamson's Ophelia in his New York production of *Hamlet*) got the point and worked on Macbeth like a tearful, disappointed little girl ...

November, 1970–April, 1971. Shooting starts on location in Wales: gale-force winds and freezing horizontal rain. The rushes are not the only things that grow green hereabouts: grass does as well. On windless days—which are few—a thin haze of pot smoke hangs over the hotel where the company is billeted ...

Roman's attitude towards the actors is one of jocular contempt. 'Send for the comics!' he cries when a take is imminent. Today he noted with glee that bananas had been served for their breakfast: 'Quite right—they are monkeys!' He seriously warns me against discussing with them anything of real consequence in the script: 'It might look as if there are things open to negotiation, and there aren't.'

His knowledge of all branches of film-making is daunting and encyclopedic. In addition to dictating the choice of lens and camera angle, he supervises props, make-up, costumes and lighting. Many directors cover themselves by shooting sequences from several different angles, sometimes using three or more cameras. Characteristically, Roman prefers to go for broke, like a high-wire artist without a net. He hardly ever uses more than one camera, and he favours long takes on which he must stake everything, since this method makes it impossible for him to delete anything without causing an unacceptable jump-cut. Having committed himself to a single camera setup, he lets the takes multiply. The crew already echoes his refrain: 'That's mudge bedder, beaudiful—*once again!* ...'

Roman's English is much more polished than when I first knew him five years ago. Douglas Slocombe, his cameraman on *The Fearless Vampire Killers*, recalls a moment when Roman was failing to explain himself clearly and someone gently pointed out that he was a foreigner. 'As far as I'm concerned,' Roman yelled, 'you're *all* foreigners!' He resents inaccurate journalistic attempts to reproduce his accent. Clement Freud, grandson of Sigmund, has recently written an article that falls into this phonetic trap. Roman has sent the following letter to Freud's editor: 'Zis piece about me feelming *Macbet* vas vonderful, very funny. But being a Pole I deedn't know zet I speak viz accent of an Austrian psychiatrist ... Looook, vhen Hefner reads zis article he vill say, how can zis alien parrot direct our moooovie! Zo I'm in beeeeg trouble …'

Undying image of Roman on Christmas Eve, wearing a preposterous paper hat left over from Christmas lunch in the commissary, capering around a muddy studio courtyard directing horses, goats, donkeys, geese, chickens, pigs, falcons and extras. 'Make the fucking geese hit their marks, goddamn it!' 'They're only *birds*, Roman,' says his assistant plaintively. 'I don't care! Point the pigs at them. Geese hate pigs. *Then* the geese will hit their marks …'

After several rather drab takes, Francesca plays a key scene in a state of high emotional turmoil. It works splendidly. Later Roman tells me that just before the crucial take he gave her a popper—i.e. crushed an amyl-nitrate capsule under her nose …

Macbeth tells one of Banquo's murderers, 'There's blood upon thy face.' Directing the actor, Roman says, 'Put your hand up quickly to rub it off—you know, the way you react when people say "There's shit upon thy face." ' *What kind of a life is Roman leading in which that is an everyday remark?*

Inescapably, *Macbeth* is a gory play. A gallon jug of blood is always on hand, and I have many memories of Roman spraying the claret all over the set and complaining, 'This blood looks only good when it's fresh.' This morning he shot the murder of Lady Macduff's children. With enormous tact and grace, he explained to a shy little four-year-old girl that she must lie down and pretend to be dead while he put 'red paint' on her face. 'What's your name?' he asked, daubing away. 'Sharon,' she unbelievably said …

We finish the scene at the witches' cauldron, featuring twenty-two naked old ladies and four goats: a sinister spectacle. Roman is in boisterous form: 'No, Elsie, there's no more toil and trouble until I give you the cue … Listen, I think Maisie is on fire … Throw some herbs on her, for Christ's sake … *All right, hags, let's shoot!*' He is about to dismiss the cast when someone reminds him that tomorrow is Hugh Hefner's birthday. In honour of this event he shoots an extra sequence. It will be sent to Hefner unannounced in the next batch of rushes—two dozen naked crones singing. 'Happy birthday, dear Hughie, happy birthday to you' …

During the sword fight with Young Siward, Jon Finch received a wound in the hand that needed twelve stitches and put him out of action for several days. Today, in the middle of a take, he launched a full-blooded swing at Macduff and gashed him right through to the cheekbone. The cast is beginning to believe the ancient rumour that there is a curse on *Macbeth*. My own explanation for the bad luck that traditionally dogs the play is that a great deal of the action takes place on battlements in pitch-darkness, causing people to plunge off sixteen-foot rostrums and break their legs. Which is why we have set as much of the film as possible in broad daylight ...

April 23. End of the twenty-fifth and last week of shooting. The original schedule was sixteen weeks. Symbolically, it is Shakespeare's birthday. Someone asks Roman, 'Are you going to give Shakespeare equal billing?' 'Why should I?' he buoyantly replies. 'For one thing, it's already fairly well known that he is the author. For another thing, he hasn't got an agent.' Roman now retires to the cutting room, where the final choices must be made. Thousands of flies are still waiting to be buggered.

The Testing of Antonio Ordoñez

The announcement was made early in August, 1972. It said that on September 7th three old matadors were to fight six bulls for charity in a second-category bullring in southern Spain. At once the *aficionados* rejoiced and it was agreed that the *corrida* in question would be the most important event of the taurine year. The toreros were the three senior men on Spain's active list of some one hundred and thirty full matadors. Their average age (roughly forty-six) would be the highest ever recorded in a professional bullfight; and the bulls would probably be well below the legal minimum weight, since on charitable occasions the authorities tend to relax their customary vigilance. Yet an hour after the box-office opened, every one of the five thousand seats had been sold.

To explain the excitement, I need only tell lovers of the bulls that the three matadors were Antonio Bienvenida, Luis Miguel Dominguín and Antonio Ordoñez, and that the occasion was the traditional Goyesca bullfight in Ronda, for which the toreros dress up in costumes based on Goya's etchings. Other readers may require some background briefing.

Antonio Bienvenida ('Tony Welcome' to loutish English tourists), now aged fifty-one, is the oldest man still practising the curious art of killing bulls gracefully. It was he who, in 1953, uttered a famous and outspoken attack on the scandalous habit of horn-shaving. He thereby risked ostracism by the fashionable star matadors who regularly fought bulls with horns that had been clipped and filed down to near-inoffensiveness. But the risk paid off; bullfighting was cleaned up, and though some of the dirt returned in the heyday of El Cordobés, the integral bull is still seen in Spanish rings far more often than it was before Bienvenida's outburst. Since then the *aficionados* have forgiven him many bad afternoons in recognition of his services as crusader. And that, for the moment, is all we will say of this modest and stout-hearted man, whose knowledge of bulls is immense, whose art (despite his stocky build) can be exquisite, but whose best days are long past.

What caused the uproar of anticipation was the conjunction of Dominguín, Ordoñez, and Ronda. Ronda is a little Andalusian town perched astride a gorge in the sierra, high above the tourist ghettos of Marbella and Torremolinos. It is accessible by five scenic and serpentine mountain roads, all of them in appalling condition for long stretches. It calls itself, with much justification, the cradle of bullfighting. Here Pedro Romero was born, the first great matador, who flourished in the eighteenth century. His statue stands in a park beside the ravishingly pretty stone bullring, which is the oldest in Spain. Ronda was the birthplace, too, of Niño de la Palma, a celebrated torero of the 1920s, who appears—renamed 'Pedro Romero'—as the bullfighter in Hemingway's *The Sun Also Rises*. Antonio Ordoñez, likewise born in Ronda, is Niño de la Palma's third son. (By coincidence, Dominguín and Bienvenida are also the third sons of toreros.) It was Ordoñez, in the 1950s, who rekindled Hemingway's *afición*, Ordoñez, whose rivalry with Dominguín overshadowed everything else in the memorable season of 1959, about which Hemingway wrote a pious but oddly unsatisfactory reportage, marred by hero-worship and entitled 'The Dangerous Summer'.

In the last twenty years the main reason for going to bullfights has been to observe the maturing art of Antonio Ordoñez. Not, of course, the only reason. Dominguín had his thousands of partisans; just over a decade ago an amazingly knowing boy from Sevilla named Paco Camino took the first steps of a career that has mingled artistry with apathy in proportions of approximately one to five; and another *Sevillano*, Curro Romero (whose moon face turns livid green when suffused with panic, as it frequently is), has built a strange reputation for extreme and unbridled fear which can modulate, perhaps one afternoon in twenty, into pure, imperturbable genius. But for consistency over the long haul, for broadening mastery and deepening emotion, Ordoñez (born in 1932) has been the great figure— many *aficionados* would say the greatest of all time. In the seasons of 1958 and 1959 he reached the apogee of his youthful period.

He had lately married the attractive younger sister of Luis Miguel Dominguín; there was a quarrel between the two families; and to patch it up, a series of *corridas* was arranged for 1959 in which the brothers-in-law would fight *mano a mano* — taking on six bulls between them, without the participation of a third matador.

There were sound commercial, as well as domestic, reasons for this. Luis Miguel, a tall and insolently handsome Castilian, was not only the most glamorous bullfighter of the age (friend of Ava Gardner's and Picasso's, hobnobber with jet-setters), he was also the supreme technician of the art, with bull-knowledge so encyclopedic that he could, if he wished, dominate anything the breeders could throw at him. He had been the young challenger to Manolete's throne in the middle 1940s; was on the same programme when the maestro was killed in the ring at Linares in 1947; and he had shortly afterwards affronted the critical Madrid public by raising his right index finger skyward in their presence and proclaiming himself 'el Número Uno'. And so, for a while, he was; until Ordóñez, six years his junior, came along and began to show the difference between science and art.

In 1959 they were beautifully matched. No one could approach them in prestige and skill. The posters simply announced LOS DOS; there was no need to print their names. Their greatest afternoon came on an August Sunday in Malaga, when, from six Juan Pedro Domecq bulls of (it must be admitted) less than stupefying size, they cut between them eleven ears, four tails and three hooves. I sat a few seats away from Hemingway, and tears were trickling down into his beard. A couple of weeks later Luis Miguel was nastily gored in Bilbao, where the bulls tend to be giants, and before long he retired from the Spanish rings, confining himself to rare, highly paid appearances in Central America.

Fans of the art will have noticed a glaring omission from my survey of bullfighting in the past twenty years. Wasn't there someone called El Cordobés? Well, yes, there was a performer of that name. His fame was vast in the 1960s, the tourists loved him, and he was paid more than any torero had ever been paid before. But although he was brave and tireless and possessed remarkable reflexes, he was essentially a clown, a circus act, a picturesque mountebank. Less forgivably, the

Cordobés era undermined the standards of bullfighting more thoroughly even than the Manolete epoch, when the mass production of undersized bulls with truncated horns first disfigured tauromachy. With Cordobés, such abuses returned; and he lacked Manolete's redeeming virtues — the power of conveying deep emotion, and the ability to kill honourably. Perhaps worst of all, a whole generation of toreros fell to imitating his tricks. There is a professional code that forbids one matador to attack another in public. Bearing that in mind, consider the following conversation I had with Ordoñez not long ago:

TYNAN: Has El Cordobés had a good influence on bullfighting?

ORDOÑEZ: You must ask El Cordobés.

TYNAN: Why has no first-rate classical torero emerged in the last decade?

ORDOÑEZ (*deadpan*): Same answer.

Sometimes in big *ferias* — devastatingly at Madrid in 1965 — Ordoñez would appear the day after Cordobés, with the evident intention of showing him up; but the two never fought together. This was partly due to Ordoñez's pride. He had said he would not appear with anyone who was being paid more than he was, and although Ordoñez earned some enormous sums ($50,000 for one afternoon in Tijuana), there is no doubt that El Cordobés got more. But another, more potent reason was that artistic competition between the two was inconceivable. They were not really in the same business, except in the nominal sense that Laurence Olivier is in the same business as Milton Berle.

In 1971 three vital taurine decisions were taken. Luis Miguel, with time and money both running out on him, came back to the ring. In August, after a bad afternoon in San Sebastian, Ordoñez suddenly announced his immediate retirement, and cancelled all his contracts for the rest of the season. Whether the still flourishing Cordobés cult had anything to do with his withdrawal, he did not reveal. The third decision came later in the year. El Cordobés declared that he, too, was giving up the bulls.

The scene was now set for the Ronda fight. 1972 would be the first taurine season without El Cordobés in more than a decade. And an idea took shape in Ordoñez's mind. He would return to the ring, but just for one *corrida*, staking all his prestige

on a single gesture. He would put together for the event a
cartel that would reassert the lost values of classical bullfighting.
With conscious irony, he invited two other veterans to join him
— the ironic point being that only ancients could remember or
recreate what bullfighting had been in the years B.C. — Before
Cordobés. And what lent the project its special, crowd-pulling
piquancy was the fact that 'Los Dos' would be appearing
together for the first time in thirteen years.

Hence the sellout. Then disaster struck. Four days before his
appointment in Ronda, Luis Miguel fought in the French
plaza of Bayonne and was tossed, receiving on the way up
several horn wounds in and near the scrotum (twenty-five
stitches) and a badly dislocated shoulder when he hit the
ground: no joke for a man in his forty-seventh year. That
ruled him out of Ronda, and there was no one of anything like
comparable experience who could replace him. In this crisis
some felt that Ordoñez should have invited a young torero with
classical ambitions to fill the gap, thus emphasizing that there
was still continuity between the past and the future of bullfighting. Stubbornly, he chose another course. He determined
to fight three bulls himself, and made the *corrida* a *mano a mano*,
Ordoñez-Bienvenida.

The bumpy roads to Ronda were jammed that Thursday
morning. All the major Spanish critics had made the trip, and
the key members of the Spanish *afición*, who are predominantly
Ordoñistas. The Conde de la Union, with whom Ordoñismo is
an obsession, would be attending his first bullfight of the
season; for nearly twenty years he has seen every *corrida*
Ordoñez has fought, and no others. The international bull-
followers were also well represented. I noticed Matt Carney,
the tall, ageless American who, as even the Spanish concede,
runs more bravely and spectacularly with the bulls at Pamplona
than anyone else. The legendary Alice Hall of Georgia was
there, doyenne of the bull fancy, friend of many matadors, a
spinster schoolteacher of bandbox aspect who has managed, by
discreet economies, to dedicate the long summers of her retirement to the bullfight. From London, among many others, had
come Michael Wigram, a young banker whose zeal for the
bulls is so intense that the logbook in which he scribbles
throughout every *corrida* contains (it is said) even such details

as the colour of the paper frills on the banderillas. This time, to make sure of missing nothing, he had brought with him a private film unit.

The ambiente was supercharged with expertise—I saw very few tourists—but in the excitement there was much nervous apprehension. After all, Antonio (which in the taurine world always implies 'Ordoñez') had had a dismal year in 1971 and had not fought a *corrida* for over twelve months. Certainly, he had trained for the event by caping and killing a dozen bulls in private; but whether, at forty, after a long layoff, he could stand up to the pressure of such an occasion was a question that nagged at many minds as we pushed our way through the thronged and flag-bedecked streets to the bullring.

Here are the notes I kept, sardine-packed in my *barrera* seat:

'4.30: the band blares out the *pasodoble* and the two matadors in their Goya suits lead the procession across the ring. Ordoñez in white silk jacket and blue silk pants (both embroidered in black), carrying the black sickle-shaped hat of the period. Great ovation. He looks astonishingly youthful, much slimmer than for many years: obviously he's tuned his body to concert pitch. Man from the Ministry of Labour steps out and pins to his chest the Gran Cruz de la Beneficencia. (He's renowned for his benefactions: in the little Moorish town of Tarifa, a whole workers' housing estate has been built on the proceeds of 14 *corridas* in which he fought there unpaid.) More applause.

'First bull for Bienvenida as senior matador, and the first surprise: it isn't a midget of the kind you expect at charity affairs, but a *toro* of respectable size and armament. Ordoñez picked the animals himself from the ranch of Carlos Nuñez, one of his favourite breeders, and if No. 1 is anything to judge by, he did not choose them for ease and comfort. [*Next day the critics agreed that the bulls had presence and bravura, were neither small nor easy, and would not have disgraced the biggest plazas in Spain.*] Bienvenida dedicates his *faena* to Ordoñez, gets through some fluent and delicate work with the muleta, and kills quickly. Perhaps overgenerously, the president awards him two ears.

'Hiss of expectation as the crowd shushes itself to silence, all eyes on Ordoñez. His face is not particularly interesting, if by interesting we mean beautiful (like Luis Miguel) or dramatic (like Manolete, the so-called "Knight of the Sorrowful Countenance"). It is simply a full, dark-brown oval, slightly weathered, with thinning black hair slicked straight back, shrewd brown eyes, and a lazily charming smile. His concentration is casual but total, and can ripen into rapturous serenity when things are going well. But if I pointed him out to you in a bar as a lawyer from Sevilla, you wouldn't suspect a hoax. He does not seek to impress out of the ring. I never knew a man more secure in his identity, more tranquil in his awareness of himself as an absolute maestro.

'He moves out to the bull (larger than No. 1) in light, cat-footed steps, plants himself before it, shakes out the cape and ushers the horns through six of his famous slow-motion *verónicas*. Olés and ovation. Buoyant, he signals to his picador to treat the bull gently and requests the president to allow only one pair of banderillas to be placed. Taking the muleta, he starts to show us what we go to bullfights to see: the difficult made easy.

'The fundamental rules of the art, though simply stated, are easily forgotten. You stand still; you extend the cloth to provoke the charge; you slow it down to a tempo and a rhythm of your choosing; and you take the bull off his natural course so that you are using his aggressiveness to make a pattern of your designing. The classic way of doing this is to move the leg further from the bull forward as soon as the charge begins, so that it is placed directly in his path, and then to take him around and beyond it with a single sweep of the muleta. This is what Antonio does in groups of linked passes — three series with the right hand followed by three with the left. After the last pass in each right-handed group, he twirls slowly on his toes, transferring the cloth behind his back to the left hand, floats it across the bull's dazzled eyes, and, completing his turn with uptilted head, walks softly away into a roar of applause. He goes in to kill well, leaning over the right horn, but unluckily hits bone twice before getting the sword in. He still receives two ears but is visibly irked by his failure to kill cleanly. ['*For Antonio*', *a critic wrote afterwards*, '*those two unsuccessful stabs were like two discordant notes in a magnificent concerto.*']

'The third bull goes to Bienvenida, who dispatches it discreetly but drably, cutting no trophies. [*He did the same with the fifth.*] It's clear that the afternoon is going to stand or fall by Ordoñez's ability to rise to the occasion: he must take on himself the heavy responsibility of demonstrating single-handed that pure *toreo* isn't dead. Again one curses that Luis Miguel isn't here to give him the spur of competition.

'Bull No. 4, and it's difficult; tends to stop in mid-charge; won't lower its head to follow the lure but plunges through with horns perilously high. Such a bull needs patient and powerful teaching. To make the struggle beautiful — to combine the instruction the bull needs with the artistry the crowd wants — this is the sort of challenge we expect great matadors to accept. It would be easy to avoid it, to settle for a few punishing passes and a swift kill. The crowd, though disappointed, would be tolerant.

'Antonio, as he must, accepts it. [*'In the great classroom of the plaza of Ronda,'* said a critic, *'the professor gave his lecture.'*] First he tests the bull with both hands, gauges its flaws and merits, noting the angles and distances that dispose it to charge, and then sets about the arduous business of involving it in art. Halfway through a right-hand pass it stops. The horns swing up, a foot or so from Antonio's body. Unmoved, he insists with the muleta. The bull looks from him to the cloth and back again; then, some crucial interior decision having been forced upon him, lowers his head and follows the cloth. This moment is the key that opens the floodgate. Passes of all kinds now flow without impediment, guided by Antonio's marvellous wrists. The bull is literally his creature. 'Every bull is a world,' he once said, and how completely he has explored this one! All is done with such courtesy: man and animal are collaborators, not adversaries. I recall a characteristic statement of Antonio's: "It is not a question of dominating the bull, but of *coinciding* with him." Over in the sunny seats, the crowd explodes into that syncopated flamenco applause — clap, clap, clap, clapper-clapper-clapper clap — which you hear only in Andalusia, and there only when something superlative is happening. This time Antonio makes no mistake with the sword. One thrust, two ears and tail, delirium ...

'Nothing can stop the triumph now. The sixth bull, though no pushover, presents fewer problems, and Antonio shows us all the treasures of his repertoire. This would not be a good bullfight to see if it were your first. In these sure hands everything looks too safe and simple. To appreciate Antonio in this vein it is necessary to know how monstrously hard the job is, to have seen what a botched, disorganized mess can be made of it, even by the best. Passes with both hands, high and low; whirling *molinetes*; *naturales* citing from the front, facing the horns head on so that an error with the cloth means a certain goring; circular passes, taking the bull right round the body — and all performed in the same small area of sand. Elegance is matched by economy. Have I ever seen Antonio better than this? In individual bulls, yes. For a whole afternoon, no. [ANTONIO ORDOÑEZ IN HIS PLENITUDE *was the headline in* El Ruedo, *the leading bullfight magazine. Its review began: 'The maestro of Ronda, whose* toreo *is at this moment a perfect synthesis of the styles of the two colossi called Joselito and Belmonte, gave today a matchless recital of all that classical bullfighting should be.' Joselito, who could do everything well, and Belmonte, who could do a few things unforgettably, were the twin heroes of bullfighting's Golden Age, more than half a century ago. I have sometimes — though rarely — heard a modern matador likened to one or the other; never before to both. Even allowing for the extravagance and sycophancy of much bullfight criticism, this is a unique tribute.*] Another fine kill, two more ears, another tail, and the crowd on its feet shouting *"To-re-ro!"* as Antonio circles the ring. The hometown audience rises to its hero: for whatever the national repercussions may be, this is above all a local occasion, its aim the raising of money for Ronda's hospitals.

'Imperceptibly the chant changes to *"So-bre-ro!"* The *sobrero* is the substitute bull that must always be available in the corrals in case one of the others is underweight or in any way lamed or incapacitated before the fight. The public is asking Antonio to buy it for them. The taurine regulations nowadays forbid this once common practice on the grounds that it gives rich matadors an unfair advantage over poor ones. But this is a special day; the crowd's clamour is shaking the ancient bullring; and when Antonio crosses to the presidential box and begs, hat in hand, for permission, the president wisely grants it.

'The *toril* gate is only half open when the bull charges in and splits it in two with his horn. This is easily the biggest of the afternoon. And a beauty: noble as well as powerful.

'Pointless to list the passes. The fight unfolds in an atmosphere of intoxication, with Antonio the cool centre of the tumult. As with all great displays in the ring, it's as if bull and man were both drawing on the same profound source of energy — animal impulse compressed and canalized into deliberate

THE TESTING OF ANTONIO ORDOÑEZ 115

beauty. The cape slowly billowing, the bull surging with it, never less and seldom more than a foot from its folds; the whole making an image like a great ship under sail. At this level bullfighting temporarily heals the rift, dissolves the tension, between reason and instinct, intellect and passion. The animal, by the end, is part of us. We no longer regard it as an alien force, outrageous in its violence, at all costs to be vanquished. Beneath an apparent contradiction—the bull's power versus the man's intelligence—we perceive a deeper harmony. Failure to achieve this perception was the fatal error of King Pentheus in Euripides' masterpiece, *The Bacchae*, who tried to suppress the animal in man instead of accepting it, and died horribly in consequence.

'Appropriately, Antonio kills (at the second attempt) in the rare and dangerous fashion called *recibiendo*—not running at the bull with the sword, but awaiting the charge, accepting it.

'The crowd is a snowstorm of waving handkerchiefs. Two ears; the tail; still the storm persists. A hoof is cut; then another. Awarding hooves is also against the modern rules; but since it was illegal to fight the bull anyway, who cares? Admirers swarm into the ring—old men as well as boys—and Antonio is lifted on to their shoulders, and borne out with the news into the rejoicing streets of Ronda.

'Scanning my notes, I make a discovery of purely statistical significance. In this *corrida* Antonio has cut 8 ears, 3 tails and 2 hooves. Unless I'm mistaken, this adds up to more trophies than any matador in the whole history of bullfighting has ever won in a single afternoon. [*I was not mistaken.*]'

I walked back in silence to the hotel, grabbed a table at the bar, and ordered twenty-four dry sherries for myself, my friends, and anyone else who might need them. Conversation—apart from exchanges of understanding nods and smiles—was out of the question for a long time. One merely wanted to savour the experience while it was fresh in memory. (Apart from anything else, one was crying.) If anyone at that instant had denied that the man we had just been watching was one of the greatest artists in the world, I would probably have hit him. A minor torero I know slightly came up and whispered in my ear, 'Today we have drunk from the fountain of bullfighting.' (They really talk like that.) I offered him a sherry to top it off. No doubt about it, Antonio had made his point. The throne was not empty, the king not deposed. All was as it had been before the clowns arrived.

There was a party until dawn at the matador's house in Ronda. Next day the critics all raved in their different manners, but one word appeared in every review: 'Apotheosis'. Typical of many was the man who said: 'Don Antonio returned with the same majesty and mastery as before—if not more. His four *faenas* have already passed into the history of bullfighting.' Another writer recalled what Ordoñez had said when asked how he felt after a successful *corrida*: 'I do not know how to say it. All I know is that when you have fought as you wish to fight, your bones ache, right to the marrow.' 'On this great day,' the writer continued, 'the pain of art came upon Antonio Ordoñez and penetrated more deeply than his bones. It must have reached the marrow of his soul.'

Last spring Ordoñez said to a friend, 'Sometimes when I cape bulls in the country and I am feeling well and strong, I begin to think that perhaps ... But as soon as I take a shower, the water washes away those wicked thoughts of returning to bullfighting.' I saw him a week after the Ronda fight and asked if he had had any wicked thoughts lately. He grinned and shook his head. 'The shower washed them away again,' he said. 'Next year will be the same as this year. I shall fight only one *corrida*. The Goyesca at Ronda.'

The date is the first week of September. The nearest airport is Málaga. The best hotel in Ronda is the Reina Victoria. Already, I am told, the demand for rooms is heavy.

Section Two

Section Two

A Rehearsal Logbook

The National Theatre's triumphantly successful production of George Farquhar's *The Recruiting Officer* opened at the Old Vic on December 10th, 1963. It was the fourth production in the company's short history, which had begun on October 22nd with *Hamlet* (directed by Laurence Olivier; Peter O'Toole as the prince), followed by Shaw's *Saint Joan* and Chekhov's *Uncle Vanya*. *Hamlet* was a *mise en scène d'occasion* and a play in which both director and star had appeared before. The Shaw and the Chekhov were transfers from the Chichester Festival. All three were acclaimed, especially *Vanya*; but *The Recruiting Officer* was the first National Theatre production to which everyone involved came absolutely fresh.

It was rehearsed for five weeks and some odd days. Its director, William Gaskill, came to the National Theatre on the strength of a high reputation gained at the Royal Court Theatre and at Stratford-upon-Avon. John Osborne's *Epitaph for George Dillon* (which he also staged on Broadway), and two plays by N. F. Simpson—*A Resounding Tinkle* and *One-Way Pendulum*—were among his Royal Court productions. For the Royal Shakespeare Company he directed *Richard III*, *Cymbeline*, Brecht's *Caucasian Chalk Circle*, and *Infanticide in the House of Fred Ginger*, a stark and disturbing first play by Fred Watson. His last West End production before joining the N.T. as one of Olivier's two Associate Directors (the other being John Dexter) was Brecht's picaresque early work *Baal*, with Peter O'Toole in the leading role. Gaskill was born in Yorkshire, and when *The Recruiting Officer* opened he was thirty-three years old.

The notes that follow were jotted down during rehearsals. The N.T.'s temporary offices consist of a row of flimsy huts on a bomb-site near Waterloo Bridge, of which the Rehearsal Room is the largest. The spartan surroundings, the frequent emergencies, the regular briefing sessions are all redolent of Biggin Hill. One has a distinct sense of participating in the theatrical equivalent of the Battle of Britain.

Week One. A striking beginning: Gaskill dispenses with the traditional read-through, explaining to the cast that the lines are the last stage of a process that must begin with a thorough investigation of character and situation. The first morning is devoted to improvisations unconnected with the text. Seated in a circle, the cast are told to pass an imaginary object from one to another; as each person receives the 'object' he must transform it by means of mime into something else. Next, Gaskill places a chair in the middle of the circle and challenges the actors to use it as something other than a chair. One rides it like a horse; another makes love to it; a third combs his hair with it. Then comes an exercise in association: Gaskill walks round the group carrying a brief-case, asking each actor to state spontaneously what it reminds him of. Finally, we have improvisation in pairs. Two people carry out an unrehearsed mime of their own choice (e.g. painting a wall). After watching them for a few moments, a third intervenes and changes the action into something else (e.g. a game of tennis). These exercises are a kind of limbering-up, psychological as well as physical. The aim, in Gaskill's words, is 'to help you relate to each other's imaginations'. He announces that every day before rehearsals he will hold an optional movement class, lasting half an hour.

Using a model of the set, Gaskill tells the cast where the scenery will be, but makes no attempt to dictate to them where they should move. He approaches each scene in four stages. (1) Seated, the actors read the text. (2) On their feet, but without scripts, they improvise on the basis of what they know of the scene: e.g., in i.i., Sergeant Kite's basic 'action' is to persuade the local lads to enlist, and theirs is to resist his efforts. (Gaskill makes great use of the terms 'action' and 'resistance'.) This scriptless exercise is repeated several times, with widely differing results. (3) Gaskill quizzes the actors about the social background and motivation of the characters they are playing: 'What do you do for a living? How much do you earn? Less or more than you would in the army? Would your wife mind if you enlisted?' etc. (4) They perform the

scene again, this time with scripts. In all this, there is no direc-
torial coercion: characterization emerges by question and
answer, trial and error. Among the more extrovert actors I
note a tendency—probably unavoidable—to go for glib laughs
during the improvisations by merely replacing period idiom
with modern slang.

Gaskill to cast: 'I know you're all skilled comic performers—
otherwise you wouldn't be here. I take that skill for granted.
But what audiences live on is the *relationships* between characters. And that means going to the sub-text—the real action
that underlies the words spoken.' He cares little at this stage
for externals, and never suggests business.

Max Adrian's baptism of improvisation: not, I should say,
this veteran actor's natural mode, though he tackles it bravely.
Someone asks Gaskill the point of improvisation. He replies,
'To establish a sequence of emotions in the actor's mind.'
Directing Adrian, he bids him remember that Justice Balance's
surface *bonhomie* is not fundamental to his character; his class
interests as a J.P. and a landowner are what really govern his
behaviour. These must be revealed if the part is to be honestly
played. Similarly, Gaskill says of i.i., 'Recruiting isn't *fun* to
Kite and Captain Plume, although the scene itself is comic. It's
their living and they're ruthless about it. You've got to show
that. Otherwise the laughs are superficial.'

Olivier, absent for the first few days of rehearsal because of
administrative duties, joins the group. He and Gaskill have not
worked together before: one wonders whether they will see eye
to eye (which in the theatre means ego to ego). Once having
seized on the emotional core of a part, Olivier usually pays
fanatically fastidious attention to details of movement, business,
costume, make-up, vocal inflexion, etc.; Gaskill, by contrast,
stresses motives, 'drives', 'pressures', etc., seldom mentioning
externals. I expect tension when Olivier is asked to improvise.
Forebodings unjustified: he plunges in with zest and great in-
ventiveness. He improvises in character, but sometimes goes far
beyond what actually takes place in the scene—i.e. he invents
things for Brazen to do and say which are perfectly consistent
with the character but which, when followed through, bring the
scene to a different conclusion from Farquhar's. Thus by improvisation one can discover aspects of character overlooked or
(for dramatic reasons) suppressed by the author.

At first Olivier's conception of Captain Brazen is too foppish and perky—a sort of Mr Puff in uniform. Guiding him towards the right tone of boorishness and sleazy vulgarity, Gaskill points out that the world of *The Recruiting Officer* (first performed in 1706) is quite different from Congreve's: small-town realism is the keynote, with no urban airs and graces. Olivier responds and his lines begin to take on the elephantine loquacity of the pub bore.

General note from Gaskill on pronunciation: avoid coy archaisms such as 'obleege' for 'oblige' and 'avarsion' for 'aversion'.

Week Two. Maggie Smith hasn't yet found the right note of candour and directness for Silvia; she is tending to make her too sly. In the male impersonation scenes Robert Stephens (Plume) is having trouble addressing her as if he really accepts her as a man: he can't help being ever so slightly deferential and gallant. This is no fault of Maggie S.'s: the problem arises wherever breeches parts are concerned.

Dealing with the court scene (v.v.), Gaskill asks the cast to bear in mind the 'social subtext': Farquhar is demonstrating how Justice worked in cahoots with the Army to get recruits, in spite of the Act of Parliament forbidding such collusion. For example, Balance invites Plume to sit beside him on the Bench, and Kite is allowed to describe himself as 'Counsel for the Queen'. Of the three J.P.s, Scruple alone takes any trouble to give the defendants a fair hearing. 'Balance', says Gaskill, 'is really an old fascist.' The stage direction 'Plume reads the Articles of War' is to be literally interpreted: Gaskill has prepared a potted version of the Articles of War for 1706, to illustrate the immense variety of offences for which the penalty was death.

His insistence on realism is already paying off. The actors are not falling back on the fussy extravagances that commonly pass for 'Restoration style'. He repeatedly warns the cast to cut gestures down to a minimum: the prose rhythms encourage manual flourishes, which must be resisted. The countrymen especially are to remember that after a day's work in the fields one's arms are tired and hang heavily.

II.iii. (which ends with Plume's successful bid to trick the rustics Pearmain and Appletree into the army) is clearly going to be outstanding. It's very funny, yet the underlying ruthlessness comes powerfully across, and there's a bitter inevitability about Pearmain's final capitulation. Gaskill to Kite and the two victims: 'At the beginning of the scene, don't just play drunkenness—it's too easy. Don't obscure the social points the lines are making, like Appletree's remark that a J.P. is more powerful than any emperor.'

The longest scene in the play, iv.iii., in which Kite dresses up as a German clairvoyant to ensnare recruits, hasn't yet got off the ground. It was obviously written as a set-piece for a virtuoso clown. Gaskill has added some effective bits of business (e.g. Kite spearing cards on his sword while telling Pluck's fortune) but now seems determined to cut them. His unwillingness to 'improve on' the text here works against him; I suspect that the scene was composed with just such 'improvements' in mind. (As finally acted, it was much reduced in length.)

By the end of the week, technical considerations—moves, sight-lines, etc.—are starting to intrude: 'If I cross here, he can get round behind me without masking her … ' But still no run-through.

Week Three. Maggie S. is settling into the breeches scenes with a deeper voice and a more convinced swagger; she now has the right air of dapper caddishness.

Improvisations are held on what has been happening immediately before the play begins. Gaskill asks questions about the life of agricultural labourers in the early seventeenth century. How many hours a day did they work? Have they just come in from the fields when Kite arrives? Have they ever seen a recruiting officer before? (Answer: yes, it was probably an annual visitation; Plume's illegitimate child was sired during his last trip.) How much did they know about the laws relating to impressment? Do they approve of recruiting drives? (One member of the crowd says yes: it's better to send unemployed men overseas than keep them idle at the expense of the parish.) Were army conditions so much worse than their everyday lives? Gaskill adds: 'If you haven't any lines in this scene with Kite, you must find reasons for saying nothing.' From the improvisations the final form of the scene emerges. The towns-folk listen to Kite's sales-talk with no reaction at all; their 'resistance' expresses itself in sullen immobility, and Kite has to force them to pay attention.

The fortune-telling scene: Colin Blakely (Kite) is now giving a wonderfully subtle comic display, but on a scale rather too intimate for the Old Vic. Gaskill tells him, 'As an actor you tend to lose yourself in other people.'

Maggie S. discovers a very moving moment in her enlistment scene with Plume (iv.i.). Her voice quavers just perceptibly when she says that no matter what perils life in the army may hold, 'they would be less terrible to me than to stay behind you' — and a twinge of genuine feeling disturbs the façade of badinage and imposture.

Week Four. The first full run-through: mood of general exhilaration. The recruiting scenes have been firmly earthed and the production will stand or fall by them. The Melinda–Worthy sub-plot is flimsier stuff, hard though the actors try to give it substance; and there isn't the right temperamental contrast (sincerity versus affectation) between Maggie S.'s Silvia and Mary Miller's Melinda. Some of the early expository passages with Balance, Plume and Silvia look static and too baldly 'plotty'. But no one's in any doubt that the basic structure is sound. Incidental music is to be confined to 'The British Grenadiers' and 'Over the Hills and Far Away', played on flute and fiddle; and it will be enough. Gaskill detests music when used as an adventitious, 'atmospheric' device.

The director's comments on the run-through: (1) some of the scenes that have been intensively rehearsed have become too casual and intimate — 'the plot and action are getting lost between your noses'; (2) too many of the actors have acquired a habit of *launching* themselves into big speeches with a grunt, an exclamation or a slight stamp of the foot — 'if you're properly prepared for the speech it should fly like an arrow from a bow. The flow should be as effortless as Mozart'; (3) there's still a tendency, at times, not to trust the text — to overstress, underline and wink at the audience: 'Only when it's been *proved* that a line doesn't work can you afford to regard it as less than pure gold.'

As an experiment, Gaskill makes Silvia and Melinda exchange roles in some of their scenes together — so that each can judge the other's character from the outside: the acting equivalent of seeing ourselves as others see us.

Throughout the week the final scene of discovery and re-

conciliation remains somewhat lifeless. My deadpan suggestion that the recruits should march in at the end with banners
reading 'Marlborough Needs You' and 'Malplaquet By
Christmas' is thanklessly spurned. The assistant director un-
earths a few curious phrases of military exhortation from an old
army handbook: given to Brazen and delivered to the troops,
they help to lift the closing moments.

First run-through on the Old Vic stage. Decision is taken to
cut the Plume–Brazen exchange in v.iv. where Brazen asks
Plume's advice as to whether he should invest in a privateer or
a playhouse. Olivier feels that, since he is investing his career in
a national playhouse, it might sound too much like a private
joke; and the lines aren't funny enough to justify the risk.

Week Five. Trouble with the court scene, which doesn't quite
live up to the expectations aroused by its position in the play.
The blame here is Farquhar's, for failing to clarify his heroine's
motives. When the constable arrests the disguised Silvia on a
charge of having raped the hoyden Rose, why is she so anxious
to appear in court before Balance, her father? Answer, supplied
by Gaskill: in Act II Balance has made Silvia promise never to
marry without his consent. Hence her decision to dress as a
man and enlist with her beloved Plume. But her sense of
honour demands that her father should publicly and legally
order her to go off with him. Hence her eagerness to be haled
into court. But little of this is explicit in Farquhar's text; and
short of rewriting, there is no way to make it so.

Gaskill enumerates the three principal 'actions' (or objectives) of the play, to which all else is ancillary:
(1) Silvia's determination to get Plume.
(2) Plume's and Kite's determination to get recruits.
(3) Worthy's determination to get Melinda.
Silvia's male impersonation brings (1) and (2) together;
while Brazen's designs on Melinda link the recruiting theme
with (3). Gaskill warns the cast that it is easy to lose sight of
these vital objectives in the diffuse second half of the play —
with resultant confusion in the audience's mind. From Silvia's
point of view, he adds, the climax comes when she learns (in
v.vii.) that Plume has agreed to discharge her from the army:
this means that she has failed in her attempt to use the recruiting drive for her own romantic ends.

Gaskill decides to transpose v.v. and v.vi.: thus the Brazen–Worthy–Melinda sub-plot is settled before the court scene, which leads naturally into the Plume–Silvia dénouement.

Week Six. Dress rehearsals on Sunday and Monday. Gaskill watches each act from a different part of the house, checking sight-lines and audibility. Olivier broods over whether to use, as Brazen, the business of clicking his heels and getting the spurs entangled which he invented as Saranoff in *Arms and the Man*, nearly twenty years ago: he finally decides against it. The whirligig set works smoothly, and the cast is confident. Am I right in suspecting that, here and there, the text is not quite strong enough to stand up to the realistic scrutiny to which Gaskill has subjected it? Possibly. But this is a quibble, effectively silenced by the production as a whole. The play's muscles and bones have been trusted, tested and found to work. A Restoration masterpiece has been reclaimed, stripped of the veneer of camp that custom prescribes for plays of its period, and saved for the second half of the twentieth century.

Tuesday at 7: curtain up.

Olivier: the Actor and the Moor

My theme is the growth of a performance, first mooted early in 1963 and brought to birth at the Old Vic Theatre on April 23rd, 1964, in honour of William Shakespeare's four hundredth birthday. Let me begin by discussing the performer.

Laurence Olivier at his best is what everyone has always meant by the phrase 'a great actor'. He holds all the cards; and in acting the court cards consist of (a) complete physical relaxation, (b) powerful physical magnetism, (c) commanding eyes that are visible at the back of the gallery, (d) a commanding voice that is audible *without effort* at the back of the gallery, (e) superb timing, which includes the capacity to make verse swing, (f) *chutzpah* — the untranslatable Jewish word that means cool nerve and outrageous effrontery combined, and (g) the ability to communicate a sense of danger.

These are all vital attributes, though you can list them in many orders of importance (Olivier himself regards his eyes as the ace of trumps); but the last is surely the rarest. Watching Olivier, you feel that at any moment he may do something utterly unpredictable; something explosive, possibly apocalyptic, anyway unnerving in its emotional nakedness; the lion's paw may lash out. There is nothing bland in this man. He is complex, moody and turbulent; deep in his temperament there runs a vein of rage that his affable public mask cannot wholly conceal. I once asked Ralph Richardson how he differed, as an actor, from Olivier. He replied: 'I haven't got Laurence's splendid fury.'

Fame, which isolates men from all but their closest colleagues and servitors, has enabled Olivier to preserve in his late fifties the hair-triggered emotional reactions of adolescence. He has never developed the thick social skin of conformity beneath which most of us hide our more violent or embarrassing impulses. With him they are still close to the surface, un-ashamed and readily accessible. The volcano remains active, the eruption for ever imminent. This is an actor ruled by instinct, not a rational being or a patient arguer or a paragon of consecutive thought; and when you ally this intuitive fire with exceptional technical equipment and a long knowledge of audience responses, you have something like the theatrical equivalent of the internal combustion engine.

Out of a sense of duty, he has occasionally tried to play what is insultingly known as 'the common man'—the seedy school-master, for instance, in the film *Term of Trial*. He seldom suc-ceeds. That outsize emotional candour cannot help breaking through, the actor impatiently bursts the seams of the role, and the common man becomes extraordinary. That is why he has spent the greater part of his professional life with his trousers off—playing bare-legged or in tights the great excep-tional characters around whom the playwrights of the past built their tallest tragedies and highest comedies. He has acted in many good movies, but seldom at the height of his talent: partly because the reticence of movie acting is awkward for him, but mostly because his performances need to be seen as flowing, consecutive wholes, not chopped up into long-shots and close-ups and spread over months of shooting.* You cannot make love by instalments, and Olivier's relationship with his audience is that of a skilled but dominating lover. He is one of that select group of performers (great athletes, bullfighters, singers, politicians, ballet dancers and vaudeville comedians are some of the others) whose special gift is to be able to exer-cise fingertip control over the emotions of a large number of people gathered in one place to witness a single unique event. He can do other things, of course; but that is what he does peerlessly and irreplaceably. His absorption in the hows and ifs and whys of his craft is total. How does he vote? What is his religion? What is his philosophy of life? The questions simply do not arise. Although I have worked quite closely with him in the last few years, I have no idea what his convictions are on any other subject than acting. This separation of work from private beliefs is not necessarily a virtue in him; but I suspect that it contributes to his acting its curious amoral

* 'In films', he once said to me, 'there is no performance! You just shoot a lot of rehearsals and pick the best.'

strength. He approaches each new character quite unencumbered by preconceived value judgments.

The best British actors often come in pairs. A century and a half ago we had John Philip Kemble, all dignity and word-music, and the galvanic rule-breaker Edmund Kean, all earth and fire. People accused Kean of mangling blank verse, but Coleridge said that when he acted it was like reading Shakespeare by flashes of lightning; and Hazlitt's comment on his death-scene in *Richard III* is a set-piece of unforgettably dramatic criticism:

> He fought like one drunk with wounds: and the attitude in which he stands with his hands stretched out, after his sword is taken from him, had a preternatural and terrific grandeur, as if his will could not be disarmed, and the very phantoms of his despair had a withering power.

In modern terms John Gielgud is Kemble to Olivier's Kean — the aesthete, as opposed to the animal. 'John is claret,' as Alan Dent once put it, 'and Larry is burgundy.' The difference between them reminds me more of Edmund Burke's famous essay on the Sublime and the Beautiful. According to Burke's definition, the Beautiful (i.e. Gielgud) comprises that which is shapely, harmonious and pleasing; while the Sublime (i.e. Olivier) is irregular, jagged and awe-inspiring, like thunder over the Matterhorn. A dozen or so years ago it looked as if a similar conflict might be stirring between Paul Scofield the poet and Richard Burton the peasant; but Burton went filmwards, and battle was never joined. Incidentally, one of Olivier's most cherished possessions is the sword that Kean used in *Richard III*. It was a gift from Gielgud, inscribed with a characteristically generous tribute to his performance.

Young actors trust and venerate Gielgud, but the man they tend to copy is Olivier. What, after all, could be more seductive than performances like his Richard, his Macbeth, his Henry V, his Oedipus, his Coriolanus — acting explosions that opened up new horizons for each of these parts, so that we felt we had never truly seen them before? His mimics are countless, but they always miss his essence. One half of Olivier loves ceremony, hierarchy and ritual — the full panoply of the *status quo* — and I even suspect that he would not mind being the first theatrical peer.* The other half loves eccentricity: he relishes the abnormal, the antisocial, the offbeat, the bizarre. You could see this split in his direction of *Hamlet*, the inaugural production of the National Theatre at the Old Vic in October, 1963. It combined, not always too happily, an atmosphere of fanfare and glamour with sharp, gleeful insights into unglamorous quirks of character. Ophelia, for example, behaved in the mad scenes like a suicidal nymphomaniac. In 1944, the two sides of Olivier's nature met and married in one supreme coalition: he played a raging psychotic who adored pomp and circumstance—Richard of Gloucester, multiple murderer and anointed king.

It was not easy to persuade him to play Othello. At least, he made it seem difficult; perhaps, deep in his personal labyrinth, where the minotaur of his talent lurks, he had already decided, and merely wanted to be coaxed. Elia Kazan once told me that the adjective he would choose to sum up Olivier was 'girlish'. When I looked baffled, he elaborated: 'I don't mean that he's effeminate—just that he's coy, he's vain, he has tantrums, he needs to be wooed.' It took careful wooing to talk him into Othello, the only major role in Shakespearean tragedy that he had not played. He pointed out that no English actor in this century had succeeded in the part. The play, he said, belonged to Iago, who could always make the Moor look a credulous idiot—and he spoke with authority, since he had played Iago to Ralph Richardson's Othello in 1938. 'If I take it on,' he said, 'I don't want a witty, Machiavellian Iago. I want a solid, honest-to-God N.C.O.' The director, John Dexter, fully agreed with this approach. He and Olivier went through the play in depth and detail, at the end of which process the National Theatre had cast its Othello.

Soon afterwards I passed the news on to Orson Welles, himself a former Othello. He voiced an instant doubt. 'Larry's a natural tenor,' he rumbled, 'and Othello's a natural baritone.' When I mentioned this to Olivier, he gave me what Peter O'Toole has expressively called 'that grey-eyed myopic stare that can turn you to stone'. There followed weeks of daily voice lessons that throbbed through the plywood walls of the National

* A stroke of prophetic intuition: in 1970, six years after this essay was written, he accepted a peerage and became Lord Olivier.

Theatre's temporary offices near Waterloo Bridge. When the cast assembled to read the play (on February 3rd, 1964), Olivier's voice was an octave lower than any of us had ever heard it.

Dexter, dapper and downright, made a bold preliminary speech. After two or three days of 'blocking' (i.e. working out the moves), there would be a first run-through with books. Of the text as a whole, he said that 'this is the most headlong of the plays'; for the purposes of this production, it would be assumed that the action took place within roughly forty-eight hours – a night in Venice, a night in Cyprus, and a final night during which Desdemona is killed. The settings (by Jocelyn Herbert) would be sparse and simple, with no elaborate scene-changes and almost nothing in the way of furniture except the indispensable nuptial couch. Pride, he said, was the key to all the characters, especially to that of Othello; already he was touching on the theme that was to be the concealed mainspring of the production – the idea of Othello as a man essentially narcissistic and self-dramatizing. The germ of this came from a famous essay by Dr F. R. Leavis, which Dexter and I had already studied with Olivier. 'Othello', Dexter told the cast, 'is a pompous, word-spinning, arrogant black general. At any rate, that's how you ought to see him. The important thing is not to accept him at his own valuation. Try to look at him objectively. He isn't just a righteous man who's been wronged. He's a man too proud to think he could ever be capable of anything as base as jealousy. When he learns that he *can* be jealous, his character changes. The knowledge destroys him, and he goes berserk. Now let's have a good loud reading this afternoon.'

That first read-through was a shattering experience. Normally on these occasions the actors do not exert themselves. They sit in a circle and mumble, more concerned with getting to know one another than with giving a performance. Into this polite gathering Olivier tossed a hand-grenade. He delivered the works – a fantastic, full-volume display that scorched one's ears, serving final notice on everyone present that the hero, storm-centre and focal point of the tragedy was the man named in the title. Seated, bespectacled and lounge-suited, he fell on the text like a tiger. This was not a noble, 'civilized' Othello but a triumphant black despot, aflame with unadmitted self-regard.

So far from letting Iago manipulate him, he seemed to manipulate Iago, treating him as a kind of court jester. Such
contumely cried out for deflation. There are moral flaws in
every other Shakespearean hero, but Othello is traditionally
held to be exempt. Olivier's reading made us realize that
tradition might be wrong; that Othello was flawed indeed with
the sin of pride. At the power of his voice, the windows shook
and my scalp tingled. A natural force had entered the room,
stark and harsh, with vowel-sounds as subtly alien as Kwame
Nkrumah's; and the cast listened pole-axed. I wondered at the
risks he was taking. Mightn't the knockdown arrogance of this
interpretation verge too closely for comfort on comedy? Wasn't
he doing to Othello precisely what he deplored in the Peter
Brook–Paul Scofield *King Lear* (or '*Mr Lear*', as he called it) —
i.e. cutting the hero down to size and slicing away his majesty?
Then he came to 'Farewell the plumed troop,' and again the
hair rose on my neck. It was like the dying moan of a fighting
bull.

Like the cast, I was awed. We were learning what it meant to
be faced with a great classical actor in full spate — one whose
vocal range was so immense that by a single new inflexion he
could point the way to a whole new interpretation. Every
speech, for Olivier, is like a mass of marble at which the sculptor
chips away until its essential form and meaning are revealed.
No matter how ignoble the character he plays, the result is
always noble as a work of art. I realized how vital, for an actor,
is the use to which he puts the time available to him before his
bodily resources begin to flag. In the last fifteen years Olivier
has played more than twenty stage parts, ancient and modern.
During the same period Marlon Brando — once, potentially, an
American Olivier — has not appeared on stage at all. He had the
quality; but quantity is the practice that makes quality perfect.

Othello was rehearsed for nine weeks before it opened on tour
at the Alexandra Theatre, Birmingham, on April 6th. For
three of the nine weeks Olivier was absent, suffering from a
virus infection which (as he put it) 'shook me like a dog shakes
a rat'. Rather than follow his performance as it evolved day by
day, I propose to deal with it scene by scene, using the notes I
kept during rehearsals of what was intended and what was
achieved.

Act I Scene ii. His first entrance: an easy, rolling gait, enor-mous sly eyes, and a tender-tigerish smile. It is clear from the start that whatever else this performance may be, it is going to be a closely studied piece of physical impersonation. (Odd how rare this element is in contemporary theatre: modern actors in general — as Max Beerbohm said of Duse — 'never stoop to impersonation', wrongly holding it to be a facile and suspect skill.) In the opening exchanges with Iago, Olivier displays the public mask of Othello: a Negro sophisticated enough to conform to the white myth about Negroes, pretending to be simple and not above rolling his eyes, but in fact concealing (like any other aristocrat) a highly developed sense of racial superiority. This will not be a sentimental reading of the part, nor one that white liberals will necessarily applaud.

Note on props: during the early part of the scene he sniffs at and toys with a long-stemmed pink rose. Is this a foreshadowing of the lines in v. ii.

> ' ... When I have pluckt the rose,
> I cannot give it vital growth again,
> It needs must wither ... '?

'Keep up your bright swords, for the dew will rust them' is delivered almost affably, with a trace of sarcastic condescension in the second half of the line. Othello's mere presence is enough to silence a brawl. This is a man who does not need to raise his voice to be obeyed.

Act I Scene iii. The Senate scene: a midnight meeting, convened in panic at the impending Turkish threat. Dexter tells the senators to chatter among themselves about what really concerns them — namely, the effect on their own pockets if the Turks seize a trading centre as important as Cyprus: 'Look at the economics of the scene. It's not about religion, it's not about politics, it's about money.'

Othello, a fully 'assimilated' Moor, wears a crucifix round his neck and crosses himself when Brabantio accuses him of having won Desdemona's love with witchcraft. For the great account of the wooing, he is still and central. 'Her father — loved me' is directed straight at Brabantio, in tones of wonder-ing rebuke. There is lofty pride in the re-telling of his magical adventures; and when he reaches the line about 'the Cannibals, that each other eat,/The Anthropophagi,' he utters the Greek word by way of kindly parenthetical explanation, as if to say, 'That, in case you didn't know, is the scholarly term for these creatures.' He also manages to convey his sardonic awareness that this is just the kind of story that Europeans would expect Africans to tell. (All this in a single phrase? Yes, such is the power of inflexion when practised by a master.) 'She wisht she had not heard it: yet she wisht/That heaven had made her such a man' modulates from gentle, amused reminiscence to proud, erotic self-congratulation. 'Upon this hint I spake' is preceded by a smiling shrug, the actor dwelling on 'hint' as a jocular understatement, and forcing the senators to share his pleasure. On 'This only is the witchcraft I have used,' Olivier isolates the word 'witchcraft' so that you can almost hear the inverted commas, deliberately making the second vowel harsh and African, and pointedly eyeing Brabantio as he delivers it. Throughout the speech, he is at once the Duke's servant and the white man's master. Every time we rehearse it, the room is pin-still. For some of us, this is the high point of the performance.

Act II Scene i. The arrival at Cyprus, after a hot, wild hurricane that signals our entry into a world quite different from that of super-civilized Venice. Embracing Desdemona, Othello is beside himself with deep, internal joy, wreathed in smiles and barely able to speak. He greets the Cypriots as old friends; they are closer to him in blood than the Venetians.

Act II Scene iii. Contrary to custom, Iago's first song ('And let me the canakin clink') is a homesick soldier's lament instead of the usual rousing chorus: a perceptive idea of John Dexter's. The Cassio–Montano squabble develops (as Stanislavsky suggested in his notes on the play) into a popular riot, with the mutinous Cypriots rising against their Venetian overlords; thus Othello has something more to quell than a private quarrel. He enters nursing a scimitar; Iago lines the Venetian soldiers up before him, as if on parade.

Act III Scene iii. The great jealousy scene, the fulcrum that thrusts the energy of the play towards tragedy. To Desdemona's pleas for the reinstatement of Cassio, Othello reacts with paternal chuckles, a man besotted by the toy white trophy he has conquered. For the duologue with Iago, Dexter deliberately makes things technically hard for both actors. Othello usually sits at a desk, riffling through military documents while Iago begins his needling; Dexter forbids the desk, thereby compelling the actors to make the scene work without recourse to props. He is swiftly proved right. With no official tasks to perform, Othello ceases to be a sitting target, and Iago must struggle to hold his attention: both actors must find reasons deeper than accidents of duty to keep them together long enough for the deadly duologue to be irrevocably launched. Stroke of genius by Olivier: no sooner has Iago mentioned Cassio than *he* takes the initiative. Iago seems to be hiding something, so Othello determines to quiz *him*, in order to get a full report on Cassio's character; after all, Desdemona wants the lieutenant reinstated, and the general owes it to his wife to find out all the facts. 'What dost thou *think*?' he asks with avuncular persistence, like a headmaster ordering one prefect to tell tales on another. On 'By heaven, he echoes me,' he is mock-severe, rebuking Iago for talking in riddles. His whole attitude is one of supreme self-confidence. (Query: will the public and critics realize that this is an egocentric Othello, not an egocentric performance?) What he expects is that Iago will disclose a story about a mess bill that Cassio left unpaid, or some similar peccadillo. At this point Othello is cat to Iago's mouse.

As Othello's interrogation progresses, Iago retreats and hedges, refusing to reveal his thoughts. A showdown is the last thing he wants to precipitate; he is unprepared for anything so drastic. Driven into a corner, he suddenly says, 'O, beware, my lord, of *jealousy*.' This is pure improvisation, a shot in the dark. The notion has never before crossed Othello's mind: he thought they were discussing matters of military discipline, and his immediate response is angry incomprehension. When Iago continues, 'But, O, what damned minutes tells he o'er/Who dotes, yet doubts, suspects, yet strongly loves!'—he replies 'O misery!' with a bewildered emphasis that implies: 'Yes, it must be miserable to feel like that, but what has it to do with me?'

Next development: Othello explodes in outrage, and Iago is almost frightened by the ferocity he has inadvertently un-leashed. But having gone so far, he must now go further, stressing that a girl unnatural enough to deceive her father and marry a black is capable of anything. Such is Olivier's shame that he cannot face Iago while delivering the treacherous order: 'Set on thy wife to observe.' Once Iago has departed, his ego reasserts itself: 'Why did I marry?' is uttered with the first person singular heavily italicized, as if to say: 'I—of all people.'

The entry of Desdemona: when Othello complains of 'a pain upon my forehead,' he presses two fingers above his eyebrows, indicating to us (though not to her) the cuckold's horns. At 'Come, I'll go in with you,' he leads her off in a close, enfolding embrace that will end in bed. During his absence, we have Iago's seizure of the handkerchief dropped by Desdemona. Note: in Frank Finlay's interpretation, endorsed by Dexter, Iago has been impotent for years—hence his loathing of Othello's sexuality and his alienation from Emilia.

When Othello returns ('Ha! ha! false to *me*?'), he has been unable to make love to Desdemona; he sniffs his fingers as if they were tainted by contact with her body. He ranges back and forth across the stage for 'Farewell the tranquil mind!'; the speech becomes an animal moan of desolation, the long vowels throbbing and extended, and the 'ear-piercing fife' rising to an ecstasy of agonized onomatopoeia.

On 'Villain, be sure thou prove my love a whore,' Olivier locks Finlay by the throat and hurls him to the ground, threatening him with a trick knife-blade concealed in a bracelet. (He will later—in v. ii—use the same weapon to cut his own jugular vein.) This assault leaves Iago hoarse and breathless. From now on Othello is a boundlessly destructive force, needing only to be steered to its target.

Dexter risks a textual emendation to hammer home the hero's egoism. Instead of: ' ... her name, that was as fresh/As Dian's visage, is now begrimed and black/As mine own face.'— he reads: ' ... *my* name, that was as fresh' etc.

The danger with all Iagos is that they make Othello seem too credulous. Unless we find their lies plausible, the play becomes a tale of an oaf gulled by a con man. Dexter asks Finlay to play the whole scene as if he really believed that Cassio was sleeping with Desdemona. Only thus can he create provocation enough to trigger off Olivier's gigantic passion. Approaching the scene in this way (as of course he should; Iago's hypocrisy must be perfect and impenetrable), Finlay almost bursts into ears while recounting Cassio's dream — 'In sleep I heard him say, "Sweet Desdemona,/Let us be wary, let us hide our loves" ' — as if he could not bear to think of the general being so vilely deceived. This is a long step towards the true Iago, the one who could fool *us*. As I had expected, Olivier gets through 'Like to the Pontic sea … ' — eight lines of blank verse — with only one pause for breath. His cadenzas hereabouts are hypnotic. After 'Now, by yon ma-a-a-arble heaven' — a surging atavistic roar — he tears the crucifix from his neck and flings it into the air. Othello's a Moor again.

Act III Scene iv. The handkerchief scene. As Othello tells the story of this talismanic heirloom ('there's magic in the web of it'), we get a glimpse of the narrative spell-binder who conquered Desdemona with his tales. She sits at his feet to listen, drawn back once again into the exotic world of the Anthropophagi. These will be their last peaceful moments together. Her rueful comment on the missing handkerchief ('Then would to God that I had never seen't!') produces a sudden, terrific spasm of fury: *'Ha! wherefore?'* — the words detonate like thunder-claps. Before his exit, Othello repeats 'The handkerchief!' three times. Olivier reaches a climax of pointblank intimidation in the first two, but for the third and last he finds a moving new inflexion, uttering the line like a desperate suppliant, whimpering for reassurance, his hands clasped before him in prayer.

Act IV Scene i. Othello is now Iago's creature. The new lieutenant is merely a passenger aboard the great plunging ship of Othello's wrath. 'All you have to do,' says Olivier to Finlay, 'is toss him a bit of meat from time to time, and he gobbles it whole.' Dexter to Finlay: 'At this point you're like Lady Macbeth after Macbeth's killed Duncan — there's really nothing left to do except go mad.' Iago and the Moor enter together and drift slowly downstage; the sinister responses and repetitions are murmurously chanted, like a satanic litany spoken in a trance:

> 'Or to be naked with her friend in bed
> An hour or more, not meaning any harm?'
> 'Naked in bed, Iago, and not mean harm … '

The two men even begin to sway gently from side to side, locked together in the rhythm of Othello's pain. In the epileptic fit Olivier pulls out all the stops; but, as always, there is science in his bravura. The symptoms of epilepsy (the long, shuddering breaths; the head flung back; the jaw thrust out) are painstakingly reproduced; and when he falls thrashing to the ground like a landed barracuda, Iago shoves the haft of a dagger between his teeth to keep him from biting off his tongue.

Othello's re-entry after eavesdropping on the Cassio–Iago scene and Bianca's intervention with the handkerchief: he circles the stage, a caged jungle king *in extremis*, with Iago immobile at the centre. Dexter to Finlay: 'Think of yourself as a ring-master. Just give him an occasional flick of the whip — like "Nay, that's not your way" — to keep him in order.'

The arrival of Lodovico from Venice: as Dexter points out, this changes the whole situation. Iago's moment of triumph is over, his peak is passed. From 'O, beware, my lord, of jealousy' right up to this instant, he is in complete control; from now on he is at the mercy of events. The news of Othello's recall to Venice and of Cassio's appointment as governor of Cyprus throws all his plans into confusion; he is forced to improvise, this time with disastrous results — viz. the bungled attempt on Cassio's life.

Othello strikes Desdemona across the face with the rolled-up proclamation he has received from Lodovico. Her reaction (as played by Maggie Smith) is not the usual collapse into sobs; it is one of deep shame and embarrassment, for Othello's sake as well as her own. She is outraged, but tries out of loyalty not to show it. After the blow, she holds herself rigidly upright and expressionless, fighting back her tears. 'I have not deserved this' is not an appeal for sympathy, but a protest quietly and firmly lodged by an extremely spunky girl.

'Cassio shall have my place': Olivier turns this line into an ironic *double entente* — hasn't Cassio already usurped his place in bed?

Act IV Scene ii. The interrogation of Emilia (Joyce Redman) and the confrontation with Desdemona, whom Othello now openly treats as a prostitute. The scene is a nightmare of cruelty, and Olivier plays it to the hilt: the superman runs amok, the bull wrecks the china-shop. On lines like:

' ... turn thy complexion there,
Patience, thou young and rose-lipt cherubin, –
I there look grim as hell ... '

Olivier resorts to shrill and wailing headnotes that savour slightly of self-indulgence. Answer: it is Othello, not Olivier, who is indulging himself emotionally. Question: yes, but will the audience know the difference?

At 'O thou weed,/Who art so lovely fair, and smell'st so sweet,' he crawls across the stage and lies on top of Desdemona: for a moment, desire almost overcomes disgust: or rather, both emotions co-exist. Othello comes close to committing the crime of which Brabantio accused his daughter: he very nearly 'falls in love with what he fears to look on'.

Act V Scene i. The street scene, including the abortive stabbing of Cassio by Roderigo, and the latter's murder by Iago. Othello's brief and dramatically pointless appearance is cut, in accordance with sound theatrical custom.

Act V Scene ii. The killing of Desdemona in the bedroom. Entrance of Othello: white-robed and dark-limbed, picked out by a shaft of moonlight through a grille over the chamber door. On 'Who's there?', Desdemona wakes up in a convulsion of fear, as if from a nightmare; then says with a sigh of relief, 'Othello!' The 'murder, which I thought a sacrifice' is accomplished with relentless, implacable precision; honour having been offended, the prescribed penalty must be enforced.

Turning-point of the case against Iago: Emilia can prove that her husband is a dirty-minded gossipmonger, but not until Othello reveals that he has seen Cassio with the handkerchief ('I saw it in his hand') can she prove that Iago is guilty of conspiracy to murder. It takes her a second or two to react to the implication of what Othello has said; but then she bursts out with 'O God! O heavenly God!' – and after this clinching double-take it is all up with Iago, since she now reveals that she gave him the handkerchief. The end of Iago: he offers himself masochistically to Othello's sword. 'I bleed, sir; but not kill'd' is spoken with quiet satisfaction. The end of Othello: kneeling on the bed, hugging the limp corpse of Desdemona, he slashes his throat with the hidden stiletto we saw in III. iii. And slumps like a falling tower.

About six months after the production opened, the Italian director Franco Zeffirelli saw it for the first time. Of Olivier's performance he said: 'I was told that this was the last flourish of the romantic tradition of acting. It's nothing of the sort. It's an anthology of everything that has been discovered about acting in the last three centuries. It's grand and majestic, but it's also modern and realistic. I would call it a lesson for us all.'

Section Three

An Unpublished Interview: 1970

PLAYBOY: Whatever else *Oh! Calcutta!* may have proved, at least it's shown that the New York critics can't always kill the things they hate. But although the show's a box-office success, did the reviews upset you?

TYNAN: Not really. We did, of course, get worse reviews than any other major show in my lifetime; I can think of only three other productions that have survived such terrible daily notices: *Abie's Irish Rose*, *Tobacco Road* and *Hellzapoppin*. They all got stinkers from the daily critics, and survived. It's a bizarre group, isn't it? Impossible to say whether we're in good or bad company. But the thing about *Oh! Calcutta!* is that it didn't invite the usual sort of critical reaction: the critics all went along with their wives, and as soon as one saw these very nice men—my former colleagues, in fact—sitting with their wives, one thought of their children at home, and said to oneself: My God, I'm inviting them to say publicly, in their columns, that the sight of the girls' breasts and bottoms gave them an erection. Because, after all, that is one of the criteria by which the show is to be assessed. And it was unthinkable that they should respond like that, it's still impossible in our society for that kind of enjoyment to be publicly admitted. So I wouldn't blame them. I wasn't upset, or angered, by the reviews, I just wished that the real reasons for disliking the show could have been stated: what use are comments like 'badly written'? They're irrelevant to a show that's trying to be erotic, unless you say 'badly written, because written in a non-stimulating way' or 'irrelevant to sex'—that sort of thing might be worth saying. To say merely that it's badly written isn't enough, when the response we're inviting is not the response to normal drama. What we are asking for is a

143

response to private acts performed in public. And I don't think there's a vocabulary for that yet, certainly not a critical one.

PLAYBOY: But even when it's found, the language employed to criticize the public performance of the act is going to be fairly simple, isn't it?

TYNAN: No. An erotic show—the ideal erotic show—will be, must be, so much more than the mere act, so much more complex. I don't think I'd find the act itself, on the stage, stimulating. I mean, I don't find the male genitalia particularly exciting, and I don't find watching them in conjunction with the female genitalia particularly exciting. What is arousing is the foreplay, the dance of sex, the ritual element, the lead-up, the approach-withdrawal-approach rhythm. These excite me far more than watching the act itself, so whether or not the act takes place is, to me, not important at all.

PLAYBOY: Is there no theatrical moment at which it might be essential?

TYNAN: The sort of plays in which fucking was essential might well be plays that I shouldn't like. For instance, if a Moral Rearmament supporter wanted to put on a play demonstrating that sex between old men and young girls was vile and evil, he might very well want to show an old man fucking a young girl on stage to prove his point, to show how disgusting and horrifying it is. Now that wouldn't much move me one way or the other. However, the act might be used constructively in a play in a way which would interest and involve me, and still not excite me sexually. Suppose you had a play about two couples, two pairs of young lovers: one pair enjoy each other's jokes, each other's intelligence, and, socially, have a marvellous, unbroken façade of witty unanimity—but they can't make it in bed. The other two are always throwing glasses at one another, insulting one another, kicking one another: but *they* have a marvellous time in bed. Now in order to make that point, you'd have to show both couples in bed; and so, in that sort of play, fucking would be dramatically relevant. But it wouldn't be, to me, very exciting. It would be there to reveal character in action. To be exciting, the approach would have to be oblique, not head-on.

PLAYBOY: Then surely, the playwright, or director, or movie-maker needn't push limits any further than where they're set at present: sex totally implicit, 99 per cent explicit, and all the erotic foreplay you could wish for?

TYNAN: I think the audience has to have the *possibility* of total revelation in order that what leads up to it may be exciting and erotic. It must know that there is nothing to prevent the two partners from fucking, should the action lead them to it. If the audience knows that no matter how subtle and delicate the approach, the final revelation can't be made, they're not going to be held.

PLAYBOY: Are you saying, then, that you've never been sexually stimulated by any public performance? After all, nothing that's been presented openly so far has fulfilled the demands you're making.

TYNAN: In all honesty I suppose I'd have to say that some — very rare — things have operated on my imagination to the point where the possibility of total revelation didn't matter. But they *are* rare: I once tried to gather clips from existing films to put in a TV programme, *Eros In The Arts*, and I sat through hours and hours of film, and there was very little at the end of it — there's a scene between Tony Curtis and Marilyn Monroe in *Some Like It Hot*, in which he's playing a Cary Grant character unable to get an erection, and she's wearing an extraordinary see-through dress and is doing her best to excite him, in all innocence and in order to cure this bogus impotence of his, and I found that a very erotic sequence. But playfully erotic: funny and sexy at the same time. What will always leave me literally cold are films of which the soundtrack is composed largely of heavy breathing interlarded with aaaahs and oooohs, with Vivaldi playing in the background. They turn me off completely and instantly. I didn't find, for example, *Les Amants*, the Louis Malle film, at all sexy. I found it to be merely a passable performance of — what was it? — Brahms or Vivaldi? The images accompanying the music were of a portentousness that cancelled desire.

PLAYBOY: That sort of studied seriousness is probably bound to end as sexual melodrama, isn't it, and therefore to be unerotic?

TYNAN: Yes. If a sequence designed to arouse is either very serious or very funny, then it doesn't stand a chance of being erotic. Of course, the possibility of playfulness ought to be there. For me, too, a great many of the most erotic things in films have been accidentally so — a certain look in the eyes of a teenage actress, a certain way a woman crosses her legs. There were wildly erotic moments in a hell of a lot of 1930s films, which certainly weren't intended to be anything of the sort. Eroticism is, I suppose, almost as individual a taste as beauty; at one time Harold Pinter was going to direct *Oh! Calcutta!* and he and I had long talks about it, during which he demonstrated symbolically what he thought an erotic show should be like. He put a table napkin over a glass and slowly drew it off, very, very slowly, and he said that even if there was just a tiny whisper of scotch in the glass, the slow revelation of that scotch could be enormously exciting to him.

PLAYBOY: But unlikely, I'd have thought, to fill a theatre?

TYNAN: Well, certainly, Jacques Levy, who did direct *Oh! Calcutta!* — Harold went off to do a filmscript, and we decided to go to Broadway, anyhow — Jacques would consider that much too devious and tentative. If Harold had directed it, the show would have contained almost no movement, just the occasional crossing of a leg, the sound of a silk stocking sliding against another silk stocking, perhaps an occasional flash of knickers or bra, the effect would have been in the nuances, the hints, the psychological raping. Jacques is at the opposite pole, a Billy Graham of the flesh, if you like, an evangelist for group living, for feel and exposure; he would consider Pinter's approach anti-human. Somewhere between these two attitudes lies the ideal.

PLAYBOY: I'm fascinated by the thought that, somewhere, there is an Ideal Erotic Experience. Is it possible for you to visualize, or at any rate describe, it?

TYNAN: In one of Dali's autobiographies, I think it may be *The Secret Life of Salvador Dali*, he described — and it's always stayed with me — his ideal erotic experience. Which involves two people who would train one another's responses to such a hair-trigger pitch that, although they would start out naked in bed, making love, they would then refine that experience to the point where, finally, they would be able to appear at opposite corners of a huge baronial hall, fully clothed except for slits for the eyes, and by looking at one another in a certain way, they would be able to achieve orgasm. That would be, I suppose, the ideal erotic show: if one could get an actress to look at an audience like that, that would be it.

PLAYBOY: It'd take a hell of a time to train the audience.

TYNAN: That's the point. You see, *Oh! Calcutta!* is little more than a first sketch, or, let's say, a series of trailers for a possible erotic show that someone might be able to do in ten years' time. Once that crippling audience embarrassment has been eliminated. It's going to be a long process, and a great effort will have to be made, probably not— I hope not—by me.

PLAYBOY: But even that achievement—the full all-see all-experience erotic heterosexual show, and the audience with you all the way—will only be a stage in the triumph, won't it? If all the restrictions currently operating, legal, public, private, or whatever else, if all these are lifted, a lot of shows that are far more bizarre, deviant, more curiously erotic than yours are going to demand, and get, a staging. Are you happy that areas of experience, or, at least, imaginative experience, are going to be open to large audiences upon whom the private and social effects might be deleterious? And almost certainly unforeseeable?

TYNAN: I think that's a chance worth taking. It's probably a very good thing to awaken people to areas of sexual response they weren't previously aware of in themselves, because it increases the possibility of self-knowledge and pleasure, and anything that does that can't be bad. I don't believe, any more than I do in the case of pornographic literature, that you can create a taste which is not already there. I believe that all you can be awakened to by a book, or a play, or a film, is what is already in you, either acknowledged or unacknowledged. And the act of acknowledging something within you can be beneficial. Even if it disturbs and upsets you very much at the time. Some of the most exciting theatrical experiences in my life have also been some of the most disturbing and worrying, and, in some cases, guilt-producing: one doesn't judge a theatrical experience by the degree to which it fails to change one. Every powerful experience *modifies* your sensibility, and ought to: it will not, though, create something out of nothing. Just as a hypnotist may hypnotize you, and tell you that there is somebody sitting in that chair whom you ought to kill, and actually make you stab that chair with a carving-knife—you will not do it, you will not kill, unless the predisposition is there. This is true whether the hypnotist is an actor or actress, or an author.

PLAYBOY: But, surely, if he is the one to elicit that predisposition—an antisocial or dangerous predisposition which controls or circumstances have so far prevented you from acting upon—then he is responsible, isn't he? If it turns out that deep within me I have the urge to kill someone, and he actually makes me kill, isn't it his fault, rather than mine? And can't this argument be transferred to the theatre as justifiably as yours?

TYNAN: Obviously it can. But how can one ever know what possible damage may be done? We should end up by writing and performing nothing at all. The most dangerous book I have ever read was shown to me at the end of the war: it was a military Small-Arms Manual, which had a detailed description of how to bayonet people—how to put in the knife, how to twist it, how to inflict the maximum agony, all that—and as I read it, I felt sick. I thought: This ought to be banned, it's evil, it's militarist, it's sadistic, it's antisocial to the highest degree. But, on reflection, I knew I couldn't ever be the one to say: Ban this book. I suppose it may have corrupted a lot of young men, but that supposition is not strong enough to make me advocate suppression and censorship. Similarly, if I were a drama critic and watching a play extolling anti-semitism, I should attack it, and I should hope that everyone I could get to attack it would do so, in every magazine and newspaper and on every TV and radio channel. But I shouldn't suggest closing it.

PLAYBOY: I don't think we ought to lose, since it's more important than sexual incitement, that example you just gave: incitement to race-hatred. Goebbels is probably just as responsible as Hitler for seducing the German people, and he did it through art. Propaganda, but art—books, magazines, broadcasts, films, party rallies. Would you not have banned *Der Stürmer*?

TYNAN: The concentration camps would have happened with

or without *Der Stürmer*. The camps were policy, *Der Stürmer* was simply there to prepare public opinion for that policy, and it was an irrelevance. Extermination would have been carried out, as in fact it was, with maximum secrecy, irrespective of where public opinion lay.

PLAYBOY: I don't agree at all. Insofar as the mounting of any political campaign to persuade people to follow a leader is a work of art, that is, an idea which uses dramatic methods, creativity and media to put itself across, Nazism could be said to be a great work of art, magnificently staged, superbly dressed, perfectly timed, and flawlessly geared to its audience. Who, because of the words and the music and the spectacle and the actors, were completely taken in by it, and loved it.

TYNAN: All right, if that's so, then it's up to you to bring the people out of their theatre and into yours, not to burn theirs down, or close it. The only answer to a rotten book is not a bonfire, but a better book.

PLAYBOY: I agree, were the world an ideal world, and were evil not usually more attractive than good. If you can't seduce the people away from evil towards good, shouldn't you choose the most expedient way of eliminating the evil?

TYNAN: I don't accept that good can't be made more attractive than evil — look at C. S. Lewis's novels. People don't automatically side with the villain in a Western; they don't automatically get bored when Everest is climbed; they aren't automatically horrified when a heart transplant succeeds, or a mass murderer is caught. More people went on the freedom march to Washington than ever went to a Nuremberg rally. It's surely not that hard to make good seductive?

PLAYBOY: I think you would have been hard put to do it in Germany in 1938. But let's take America in 1970, and let's taken an institution somewhat more concrete than demo-cracy: marriage. Now, it's clearly not too difficult to seduce people away from the idea of marriage with the offer of excitements and infinite possibilities that lie outside the marital stockade. Things which in our present society could conveniently be described as wicked, if not actually evil; certainly, things which would play hell with traditional ideas of family loyalty, security, the stability of children, and so on. And it seems to me that the current mood may be working rather irresponsibly towards that breakdown. May we not be left, after the cult of permissiveness has passed, with nothing but wreckage?

TYNAN: One of the things that plays and books are for is to test institutions, to submit them to certain stresses and strains to see if they will stand up to criticism and pressure. If they will, then fine; if they take umbrage, or crack, it may be because of some real weakness in them. Take wife-swapping: as I understand it, it's generally intended to strengthen rather than undermine the institution of marriage. It is intended to perpetuate matrimony by giving people a sexual outlet that is not possible within the rigid forms of monogamy and therefore it's a sort of safety-valve; it's designed to keep marriage going. It may, of course, not work like this in practice because of an inequality between the two partners' desires to swap, or an inability to cope with the further implications of swapping. If one really wanted to perpetuate monogamy, one probably ought to build into the marriage contract a clause specifying that both partners must be unfaithful at least three times a year, otherwise the marriage becomes invalid.

But in the United States today there is certainly a movement towards group-living, towards situations where seven or eight young people will be living in the same apartment, some of them in monogamy, others in a more free-ranging way, but all regarding themselves as a social unit: one for all and all for one. Jacques Levy is a great supporter of that, and some of the group-touching scenes in *Oh! Calcutta!* were intended to lead to that sort of idea in the audience's mind. Personally, I feel monogamy to be irrelevant. There is nothing in the institution that indicates that it's likely to be eternal in duration or universal in scope: it seems to me to be simply something that works at the present time in certain parts of Western society, that's all. It happens to work for me, but I know people for whom it's sheer torture. Therefore, I think it legitimate to suggest that the overthrow of monogamy might be a good thing for the human race, and here I'm thinking of the earlier writing of Wilhelm Reich: particularly *The Sexual Revolution*, in which he draws a very powerful analogy between the patriarchal family and the patriarchal state, suggesting that any society which idealizes the patriarchal family unit, with the father at the top of the hierarchy as wage-earner and law-giver, is likely to be a society which will tolerate dictatorship. Germany comes to mind. Whereas an open society, where group-living is tolerated and there is not one patriarch running the family unit, may be less tolerant of dictatorship. So one could say that by working towards that system of group-living, which I might well be doing if I were twenty years younger, one is in fact striking a liberating and humanizing blow.

PLAYBOY: The problem, surely, is that matrimony could only be overthrown effectively by the sort of revolution which overthrows capitalism, an extremely rapid professional revolution which would change the system within a month and impose a dictatorship of a different sort. You can do that with a political system, but not with a sexual one. Wouldn't your idea of gradually liberating people produce extreme uneasiness within the society, for a long period?

TYNAN: It depends what you call long. It would take less than a generation. Even in our own lifetime, we've seen things that would have outraged our fathers and mothers to the point of horror gradually coming to be understood; not necessarily welcomed, but understood, tolerated, dealt with as a simple phenomenon of life rather than something terrifying from the mouth of hell. But, all right, it's a slowish process: when the Russians tried in the early days of the revolution to promulgate free love, communal child-raising, and so on, it was too quick, and they went back to the patriarchal family unit, with the astute connivance of Stalin. Who must, I think, have seen — perhaps only subconsciously — that with that family unit, the father figure could quite happily rule the country, whereas the movement towards free love had been favourable to a kind of anti-hierarchical society that would not be so easily ruled by one man.

PLAYBOY: And you're confident that the current movement towards sexual freedom in the West is an unqualified good?

TYNAN: Not confident, but reasonably hopeful. And not, of course, unqualified: we're wandering into a land without maps, after all. For example: I had a long talk the other night to an American girl who's one of the most swinging, liberal-minded girls in London. And she said to me, late one night, 'I'm twenty years younger than you, and I've had literally hundreds of men in the last five years. But I've only had three orgasms!' So I said, naturally, 'You poor thing, that's terrible. Why?' Whereupon she went into what amounted to a diatribe *against* the permissive society as it affected women. 'When you were my age,' she said, 'twenty years ago, if you wanted to go to bed with a girl, first of all you had to like her a lot and make her aware that you did, and then you had to spend time and care in exciting her physically, didn't you, to bring her to the point where she was unable to resist taking what was then a major step? Nowadays, if I'm not instantly excited as soon as he touches me, the boy immediately goes on to someone else. I either say yes immediately, and he fucks me, or I've lost him. But if I do say yes, *he* comes like a flash and *I'm* left high and dry — I've masturbated a damned sight more times than I've come!' And she was getting quietly hysterical about this. 'How can I live this way?' she said. And it suddenly occurred to me that there was an advantage, both a human and a sexual one, built into the system that I grew up with: which demanded that you had to learn a girl's body as if it were a foreign language, because unless you got her really excited, she wouldn't let you make love to her; I was left wondering just how common her experience was.

PLAYBOY: I'd have thought she was pretty unlucky with lovers. With three orgasms in a hundred times as many attempts, one could be forgiven for thinking the fault wasn't entirely on the other side. I'd not have thought that 99 per cent of men would be contented with a sexual game in which their mate was left unsatisfied, would you?

TYNAN: Well, I must say she moves with a pretty far-out group, full of men who are, to say the very least, somewhat incompetent at personal relationships. But nevertheless, the developing atmosphere of sexual licence must be partly responsible for her neurosis, and that risk is something that society will have to be prepared to take, perhaps not permanently, but certainly for some time to come. Certainly, today, virtually all writing about sex, fictional writing, is about sexual neurosis or mismanagement or maladjustment.

Couples, *Portnoy's Complaint*, best-sellers and nothing but sexual hang-ups.

PLAYBOY: What's the difficulty in writing about sexual happiness and fulfilment?

TYNAN: The worst thing is that no one seems able to write about it without becoming sacramental and mystical. The tyranny of the Holy Union. In order to write about ful-filled sex, we still seem to be forced to employ semi-religious language. And too many of us still accept the absurd notion that it's wrong to fuck people you don't love, which is like saying that it's wrong to travel except by Rolls-Royce.

PLAYBOY: There nevertheless appears to be a fair amount of high-toned prose devoted to extolling the virtues of off-beat sex, doesn't there?

TYNAN: Well, I don't think there's one ideal sexual experience towards which we should all aspire, and with which writers should exclusively concern themselves. I mean, well-judged masturbation may be the ideal sexual experience for some people, while for others coitus in the missionary posture may be. For a few — who knows, perhaps for many — kissing a high-heeled shoe may be the ideal, completely fulfilled sexual experience. It's the *tone* of pornographic writing, not the subject-matter, that sometimes bothers me. Take Pauline Réage's *Histoire d'O*: there, the whole sexual initiation of a girl is made analogous to the initiation of a nun. It's a fascinating use of religious symbolism: she enters a strict order, endures its weird and degrading disciplines, and in the final sentence of the book she asks to be martyred. Achieving, presumably, some sort of union with the infinite. And even in hard-core pornography writers often insist on using religious parallels.

PLAYBOY: How far would you guess people will translate what they pick up from pornography or erotic art into their personal sexual habits? How far might sexual experiment, for better or worse, be stimulated, or even invented, by literature?

TYNAN: All the experiments have already been made. There are no new sexual experiences. Even if the whole American nation were temporarily turned on by a multi-channel mass-orgy, a coast-to-coast TV fucking spectacular in which the whole country was put into an erotic trance, you'd find that, afterwards, the viewers would all go back to their own predilections — some would want to lick high heels, some would want to be beaten with golf umbrellas, some would want half a dozen partners, some would retire alone to a quiet closet, and the majority would take to their heterosexual beds. One thing I should just like to say here, while we're talking about the response to pornography, is that four-letter words, those great taboos, are not in themselves at all erotic. I first got this idea from my tutor at Oxford, C. S. Lewis, a great and formidable man; I was talking to him about D. H. Lawrence and Lewis said, 'In the great periods of literature, when great erotic works were being written, four-letter words were never used. And the reason they weren't used was precisely because they were anti-aphrodisiac. If you want to excite me, you must go around the subject; you must use analogy, metaphor, simile, periphrasis; but as soon as you deal with it explicitly, you are forced to choose between the language of the nursery, the gutter and the anatomy class; and I cease to be aroused. Traditionally, literature has used four-letter words only for the purpose of satire, scurrility and comedy.' I think he was dead right.

PLAYBOY: Do you think there's anything that particularly characterizes the landscape or furniture of American sexual fantasy, that doesn't appear in anyone else's?

TYNAN: In the fetish field, a leather-booted woman armed with a whip seems to dominate the American male sexual imagination far more than she figures in European fantasy. Of course, she's an international image, a much-loved member of the Sacher-Masoch Touring Company, but she enjoys her greatest triumph on Sixth Avenue, where about 30 per cent, I should say, of hard-core pornography relies on her participation. I honestly don't know why. The shiny casing may have something to do with it, and I'm not joking; it's a long time since I had an affair with an American girl, so I'm a little out of touch, but when I was having affairs with American girls, they often seemed to come in a capsule, as highly polished as vinyl — they had a marvellous, hard-plastic surface, weatherproof, bombproof, waterproof, sexproof, but if you pierced that, then underneath there was a warm wet marshmallow that would cling with an unbelievable tenacity: you'd never brush it off. Once you got them into bed, their collapse was so complete, their surrender so total, that your immediate thought was, My God, how can I possibly end this affair? I also found, for reasons I can't explain, that American women were fonder of *fellatio* — the sin that dares not speak its name, because its mouth is full. Of course, I'm talking mainly about New York professional girls, actresses, advertising women, journalists, that kind of thing, who are rather a special breed. I don't know what it's like in Akron, Ohio.

PLAYBOY: Moving from the effect of pornography or staged eroticism on an audience, and how far their lives or personalities are likely to be influenced by it, could we perhaps talk about the general effect of drama upon the spectator? Are great theatrical performances likely to be as telling on an audience today as they were before there were so many alternative dramatic media?

TYNAN: To me, the average play is infinitely more boring than the average film; the most deeply inscribed performing moments I can remember have come from the live theatre. Like Olivier's Oedipus, in 1944, with that unforgettable, ineradicable moment when he discovered that he actually was the murderer of his father and the fucker of his mother — he let out those two famous cries that all but shattered the balcony of the New Theatre in London. After a quarter of a century, there is still a sort of kinship between those who were there and heard him, as if they'd been on the Somme together. I found out later, in conversation with him, that he'd been on an ermine ranch in Canada, years before, and he'd heard the sound that an ermine made in a trap — a terrible, high-pitched wailing — and he consciously reproduced that noise. It's reverberated in my mind ever since as the sound that people make in life's extremities. That is exactly how he operates as an actor: he's an observer of all detail, and he uses it quite ruthlessly; rather than let the noise come from inside him, he observes it outside himself, and then absorbs and hoards it. But, you see, that noise, the extravagance of it, is something that would seem absurd on film. It's only possible in a large room where one man can face his audience; and that is theatre.

And something more than theatre: it's no accident, no coincidence, that history has often been made in closed or private assemblies, or in front of limited or carefully selected numbers of listeners—Pericles addressing the people of Athens, Churchill talking to the House of Commons—and, as you've said, on the bad side, at the Nuremberg rallies. There is a particular excitement when one man talks to a limited group of people and deliberately plays upon their imaginations. Perhaps this is why so many of the people I've truly admired and liked have been those whose great gift has been to control a thousand people in a mostly darkened room. I suppose that those who want to do it are in some ways dangerous: the direct manipulation of other people's feelings, the ordering of them to laugh, or cry, or feel pain or hate; and the temperament that wants to do it and can do it, must be fairly sadistic. Even frightening: it would be awful to live in a world inhabited solely by great actors. But when a great actor occurs, I want to be there. Sadly, it's going to occur less and less often. Today, in the performing arts, one finds a lack of great actors, particularly great comedians, audience-manipulators on the grand scale. There are so very few places now where a great soloist, actor or comic, can learn the art of getting a thousand people into the palm of his hand and playing with them. There are always nightclubs, I suppose; but who can be expected to compete with drunks and birthday parties and waiters and God knows what other distractions? I think what I regret most in the world of entertainment is this loss of giants. Can you imagine W. C. Fields domesticated down to the level of 'situation comedy'? There'd be no room for him, he'd be too offensive for a TV audience. And where would a new Fields train?

PLAYBOY: In subsidized theatres, perhaps? Or even subsidized vaudeville? Is that inconceivable in the States?

TYNAN: It would certainly be more difficult to mount in America than in England, and God knows it's been tough enough here. In the States, there is a great fear of subsidy, because it carries with it connotations of dictatorship, either by the State authorities, or by Federal authorities 'trespassing on States' rights'. Americans have always resisted this; one has to keep pointing to the B.B.C., or the

National Theatre, or similar British institutions to prove to them that state ownership doesn't imply dictatorship, but they just don't believe it. Perhaps if they had a better civic theatre tradition ... In England, there's a tremendously rich provincial theatre, which America lacks. Whether I should be in favour of artificially creating a theatrical tradition where there wasn't one, I'm not sure. It may be that in a soil so responsive to TV and movies it would be wanton and perverse to try to plant theatre. It's always been very much a minority art, a hothouse plant, and unless it's thriving in its own climatic conditions, as it does in England and in most of Europe, it might wilt and die very quickly indeed.

PLAYBOY: Listening to you now, and remembering that not so long ago you were the golden boy of theatre, who knew and felt more about it than anyone on this side of the footlights, a great and influential critic on both sides of the Atlantic, remembering this, one wonders why you gave up reviewing.

TYNAN: I think it's the sort of job you shouldn't do for more than about ten years. I'd been doing it since 1951 when I gave it up in 1963. The psyche gets trampled on; you find yourself no longer capable of responding to anything. That's when you know it's time to pack it in. And, for me, a natural continuity presented itself; I think I managed to create a certain amount of intelligent interest in the theatre, to lead audiences where I wanted them to go, I'd told them the sort of thing I wanted to see and wanted them to want to see; and suddenly I was offered the opportunity to help put the first fully-subsidized English state theatre on to its feet, and I thought, fine, splendid, this is the way I should now like to go. As Literary Manager, I became involved in trying to steer the National Theatre in certain directions, sometimes succeeding, sometimes failing, mainly trying to make sure that the wrong courses weren't taken—it meant becoming a sort of tugboat, trying to guide this enormous ship into the right harbour. I enjoy it tremendously, but it's very much undercover work, and it isn't work which leads one into positions of great power or authority or fame. But one sees to it that plays are written, that actors are hired, that the directors one wants are commissioned, that a certain series of plays is planned, one is creating a whole theatrical environment; and we can plan ahead, we can foster, and even dictate, new developments. And we can prophesy, which is only possible in a subsidized theatre; in the commercial theatre, you can't prophesy beyond the next opening night. We're in the crow's nest of the theatre, we can see what's happening on the horizon. The critic tends to look at the minute-hand of the theatre; we can look at the hour-hand as well. That's what the state can do when it's benevolent. As for me, it was like coming out of the restaurant as a customer and going back into the kitchen. Like writing the menus, instead of reviewing the meals. And I honestly enjoy it more, even though I don't get the satisfaction of seeing my by-line in print.

PLAYBOY: You've acted, produced, managed, reviewed. Have you never wanted to *write* a play?

TYNAN: Ha! I should *like* to be a sculptor, I should *like* to be a painter, I should *like* to rebuild St Paul's — there are very few limits to what I should like to do. But I know that I'm really a piece of blotting-paper, a reactor rather than a creator; I have been since the age of twelve. My first urge was to review the theatre, to commemorate its transience; my first review was the result of anger at reading other critics' reactions, which I disagreed with. I have always been someone who's reacted to existing phenomena, not a maker of new ones. I'm a reporter of events, whether they're plays, or bullfights, or coronations. Very few professional reporters become playwrights. I am a watcher, an observer, a reflector; not an instigator. Art is — to quote from Thomas de Quincey, who was probably quoting from someone else — art is *idem in alio*: the same thing in another form. It's a transposition, it's the author taking a little from this man he knows, and a little from that man he knows, and various bits from various people, and rolling them all together and turning them into a different character. But I am different from the author: I'm interested in you as you, not you as a future component of somebody else, not you translated or transposed, not you as a symbol. That's what makes me a journalist instead of a novelist or playwright. I would guess that about 70 per cent of novelists are just journalists evading the libel laws by changing their black-haired Irish chums into blond Swedish ch aracters in their books; I think that only about 30 per cent, if that, of our present novelists should be writing novels. The rest would do better writing about reality.

PLAYBOY: You mean turn to the sort of work that Norman Mailer's now doing?

TYNAN: Exactly that. Norman is a giant reporter, and as soon as he got on to reality and was tied down by the rigidity and inflexibility of reality, he became a great writer, instead of a sort of lost Herman Melville chasing the Moby Dick of creativity. As soon as he was shackled to the concrete, it inspired him. And I think that a great many others were like that, or would have been, but felt that it was somehow a mark of superiority to change their black-haired Irish friends into blond Swedes, that it was more 'creative', whereas to write about their black-haired Irish friends was somehow pedestrian. And it isn't. Not if you get to the essence of that black-haired Irishman. Most fiction is a hybrid: there is the part that the writer observes, and the part that is his fantasy. I should like to see more separation of these elements; if you can get hold of a fabulist, and ensure that his fables remain unencumbered with reality, you may end with something fine and fascinating and hypnotic. Likewise with what one might call a factualist. For myself, the one book I should like to write would be the first totally honest autobiography. I have not yet seen an autobiography which is that, and I should like to read it almost as much as I should like to write it.

PLAYBOY: Do you feel that there is a particular need now, late in the twentieth century, for interpreters of fact and information? A particular need, more than ever before, for honest reporters?

TYNAN: A need for witnesses, certainly, and articulate witnesses of the highest order: for Norman Mailer at the Democratic Convention in Chicago, for Susan Sontag in Hanoi. For people who will bring forward private evidence, and present it with absolute candour and accuracy. Apart from any other, wider considerations, the need for this evidence and these witnesses is something that I feel personally.

PLAYBOY: Personally?

TYNAN: Look, I think I know what sort of society I should

like to live in, what sort of administration I should like to live under. But, quite frankly, since the invasion of Czechoslovakia, which was on the way to becoming that sort of society, but was destroyed, I have become more interested in private life than in public politics. I respond to the sort of things that Norman writes about, that Mary McCarthy and Susan Sontag—at their best—write about. That kind of writing, personal testaments, concrete reports, interests me more than writing concerned with abstractions and generalities, aesthetic, political, sociological, what you will. I may not be able to explain this reaction adequately, but let me try; from about 1950 onwards, it was clear to me that the possibility of changing, *fundamentally* changing, a large-scale industrial society like the United States or Russia was non-existent. They were immutable and impregnable. But I retained the hope that small countries *could* change, be changed, and move more towards the sort of society one wanted. Cuba survived—perhaps not quite as the place one hoped it would be; North Vietnam, unhappily, got involved in a siege economy that prevented the development of what one hoped one would see there after Ho Chi Minh got the French out; but then one saw, suddenly, in Czechoslovakia, something which one thought actually worked. In my own generation, in Europe, I saw that radical change *was* possible, and that socialism and freedom were compatible. And for the first time, the arts behaved as one had dreamed they would behave—they weren't just developing, but leaping ahead. Prague, in 1965, 1966 and 1967, had the best theatre in Europe, the best younger cinema, it had marvellous poets, marvellous novelists. Out of socialism had come what one had always hoped would come, an incredible, enthusiastic, almost frenzied creativity. And then, when one saw *that* crushed by the Russians in 1968, it meant finally that the possibility of radical and total change, even in a very small country, was no longer to be considered. Because one or other of the great powers would step in and kill it. And at that point, I felt a sad, overriding need for a period of withdrawal, a period of concentration on the private life. And that's an involved way of telling you why it is that I'm now more interested in private evidence than in public theory.

PLAYBOY: And what about the presentation of that evidence? Apart from documentary writing, do you see it shaped into other forms for public delivery?

TYNAN: To take one example, I should like to see a theatre devoted to the restaging of great trials. Trials to me are basic theatre. Of course, it's extremely difficult to condense all the evidence of a major trial into two-and-a-half hours, it would necessitate agonizing selection, but suppose you did that, and suppose you got a jury out of the audience, every night, and asked them to decide, on the evidence they'd heard on stage, whether they would have found the defendant guilty or not guilty — wouldn't that be tremendous theatre? And I don't mean just murder trials, but political trials, the Soviet purge trials, for example, the Eichmann trial, trials from all countries and periods. I think it would be fascinating, because again, it's testimony — my witnessed experience against yours, judged by the world. That seems to me a very valid form of theatrical activity.

PLAYBOY: More matter with less art?

TYNAN: The word 'art' is now really no use to me at all. I mean, are Mailer's books art, or what? Is it even an interesting question to ask? When I hear the word 'art' now, I begin to yawn; to me, it's somehow a cop-out word, a word to dodge and hedge with, a word that means something different in everyone's mouth. The senses in which it's used are so various, so mutable, so contradictory, that I should think it's almost a test of good writing nowadays to see whether you can get by without using the words 'art' or 'artistic'. I've lately been rereading some of the Renaissance treatises on art, written by people who tried to confine writing to a strait-jacket, to categorize it into comedy, tragedy, and so forth — but they always took as their definition of art 'that which instructs through delight'. I'd like to go back to the definition, and forget what it defines: I would simply ask myself the question, 'Does this instruct me? Does it delight me? Does it do both?' If it does, then I think it is good. But let's not use the word 'art', it's a befouled word, it means too much, it means anything and so it means nothing. I've tried, in everything I've written over the last five years or so, to avoid using the word, and it's surprisingly easy to do. And apart from the irrelevance

6

of the question 'what is art?', one must also ask oneself constantly about the relevance to life of many things which we formally describe as art. Let me put it this way: people who are able to share one another's minds and bodies, people who are able to fulfil themselves adequately by their relationships with others, these healthy people spend much of their thinking- or reading- or watching-time in venerating the visions and moral insights of neurotic people who are frequently unable to live a shared and fulfilled life themselves, and these latter are known as artists and politicians. And I feel that an unhealthy amount of attention is paid, an undesirable intensity of reverence is shown, to what are often visions and precepts and ideologies that arise out of a failure to live a fulfilled private life. Much of art consists merely of messages transmitted from the lonely to the lonely. There is too much veneration accorded to the imaginative visions of failed human beings. Total happiness, as Cyril Connolly said, is the enemy of art. Forced to choose between the two, I would recommend happiness.

PLAYBOY: Yes, but he also complained that 'the pram in the hallway is the enemy of promise.' He would not seem to be as clear about his priorities as you. Aren't you really saying that it's better to bring happy babies into the world than good books?'

TYNAN: Not quite that. But when one listens to extremely nice, happy, fulfilled, rational, humane people desperately trying to accommodate themselves to admiring some perfectly hysterical and ludicrous daub passing as a work of art, one wants to shout *Stop!* One sees more and more of this, of happy people growing miserable through trying to enrich their already satisfactory lives by struggling to appreciate some vapid trash which they've been persuaded they must understand in order to improve themselves.

PLAYBOY: Surely, though, even the most fulfilled private life can be enriched in texture by an exposure to what is genuinely good?

TYNAN: Oh, even the happiest people will need — and want — to shift themselves into new emotional environments, yes. The main reason anyone reads anything is to borrow another pair of eyes with which to see the world, to immerse himself in someone else's sensibilities, and thereby escape from the prison of himself, escape into someone else's perception. The desire to see with another man's eyes is the most humanizing and worthwhile thing about what is called 'art'. But there's no need to sanctify that experience by dubbing it Great Art. I remember a book of Aldous Huxley's in which he quoted, as one of the most moving bits of writing he had ever read, a suicide note left by a man in a London suburb whose wife had walked out on him. Just four sentences, but absolutely heartrending. Huxley felt that, in those few sentence, he was seeing the whole of a man's life through the man's own eyes.

PLAYBOY: How far would you say that 'seeing through other men's eyes' influences the moral and social climate? Does art change things, or is it itself changed by them?

TYNAN: Writing, plays, films, can act as signposts; they can't build the road. The writer is a back-seat driver, but not the man at the wheel. He'll say 'Let's go that way!' but he cannot do more than point.

PLAYBOY: So that we can't be led into decadence, as is so often claimed, by writers and communicators, or reformed into something better than we are by them, as much as by legislators and politicians?

TYNAN: Well, writers have, of course, often worked directly with politicians, on Parliamentary committees, on Senate committees; they've given their *advice* on such things as censorship, or law reforms, or whatever. But that wasn't in a creative role, but rather as expert commentators in a given field. I'd say, though, that some progressive politicians may have been made more progressive, or felt supported in their progressiveness, by exposure to books and plays and films by artists who spoke on behalf of inarticulate people suffering from the effects of ancient oppressions. Men like H. G. Wells or Bertrand Russell certainly influenced what politicians thought and did, not only by their books, but also by the examples they set. Men like that, or like Maxim Gorky—who was ostracized in the States for travelling with a woman not his wife—not only advocated sexual reform as desirable, but *behaved* as if it were. And they were noticed, and, with luck, respected. It's the effect of that which finally ends in legislation. But when one says that sexual permissiveness or other forms of private liberty advocated or demonstrated by artists are leading the nation like the Gadarene swine to perdition—that's nonsense. Marx and Lenin would have laughed that off as a lovely bit of obfuscation: when you're being forced at bayonet-point into an inferno, it isn't the fact that you're nude at the time that's to blame for your doom! In other words, when a whole society, economically and militarily and politically, is being led to hell, when its members are being killed in war abroad or polluted physically and intellectually at home, how on earth can a little sexual licence be made to carry the can for what is called decadence? The basic movement of society is not affected *at all* by the fact that queers are living together, or that couples are interswapping—they are merely a convenient means of distracting attention from the really destructive impulses at work.

PLAYBOY: Do you think this deeper decadence, this motion towards destruction, is particularly defined in contemporary America?

TYNAN: You have to bear in mind my belief that all centralized societies of more than about fifty million people are evil. They command such power, such authority, such tyrannous means of enforcing the ruling will, as to be unchangeable. And that is evil. I remember talking to Conor Cruise O'Brien, who was teaching a year or so ago at N.Y.U. He is a convinced socialist, but he said that it worried him when the youth of America got too rebellious, because he didn't want to see them cut down in the streets by tanks, and if there were a full-scale youth revolt, that, he said, is exactly what would happen. It is, in fact, rather like what is happening to the Black Panthers.

PLAYBOY: You believe that American troops and police would fire as readily on students, white and black, as they would on Panthers?

TYNAN: If a country that large, in possession of so much power, with the knowledge of how to wield it, with the skill in its application that the police and the military have, finds its fundamental beliefs and attitudes and institutions challenged, it will not tolerate it. There may be mounting and terrible frustration in the United States over the next few years, and if it expresses itself in organized revolt, there will be no radical concessions from the rulers but, quite simply, civil war. It is a country immoral in a very different way from the way in which the Soviet Union is immoral, but in so far as both are unchangeable, both are really very immoral indeed.

PLAYBOY: Do you envisage a spontaneous move to the right in America to the point where the rulers don't wait for revolution to come, but pre-empt it with force and repression?

TYNAN: I think there will always be enough men in positions of power in the United States who do not want to kill large numbers of people. I would hesitate to believe that it was a country that would condone the wholesale slaughter in the streets or in concentration camps of thousands of Americans who had not fired the first shot. But I think that the over-reaction of the authorities to those first shots could be an extreme and terrible thing.

PLAYBOY: Aren't they already over-reacting to the violence of the black man? Hasn't the killing of the thirty-odd Panthers been fairly systematic?

TYNAN: Yes, but numbers are important. I think if the tally were to reach twenty thousand, say, then something would be done to bring the killing to an abrupt halt. But I genuinely believe it would take that many deaths. The Pinkville massacre, for example, was received in the States with only a fraction of the shock sustained by Europeans. But we're talking of events that will alter the motion of society. Perhaps the only way of doing that effectively would be to split the U.S. up into fifty sovereign states. I think if Norman Mailer had succeeded in making New York a separate sovereign state, one would have seen a little hope, a new dynamic. The smaller the units into which the U.S. might divide itself, the happier I should be. Of course, there'd be some states I should hate even to visit, but there would be some I should find immensely sympathetic, far more so than this great monolith we have now.

PLAYBOY: It's curious how few years it is since 'American isolationism' was a dirty phrase to intelligent Europeans. Until very recently, they wanted America to be deeply concerned in the affairs of the entire free world; but wouldn't most thinking Europeans now be only too happy to see America retire peacefully behind her own frontiers?

TYNAN: I'm sure they'd prefer as complete an American withdrawal as possible. They didn't mind sheltering under America's nuclear umbrella while it looked like a reasonable safeguard, but one could hardly blame them for thinking differently now. I think they fear implication in America's mistakes more than they want her ambiguous protection. I was listening to a TV programme about 'Men Of The Decade' the other night, in which Alistair Cooke chose John Kennedy. And he illustrated his choice of this emblematic figure, this embodiment of all the liberal virtues, with newsreel extracts. And we saw Kennedy sending seventeen thousand men into Vietnam, we saw the Bay of Pigs invasion, we saw Kennedy at the Berlin Wall declaiming 'Ich bin ein Berliner!', and suddenly, and against the tenor of Cooke's argument, Kennedy emerged as one of the most aggressive figures imaginable. Especially when we saw his Cuba confrontation speech to Khrushchev on TV, where he committed the cardinal diplomatic sin of issuing a public challenge before he'd issued a private one. Seeing it in context, that was a very bellicose act. Khrushchev climbed down—a splendid moment for him and for all of us; but Kennedy, in retrospect, seemed at that moment not entirely distinguishable from John Foster Dulles.

PLAYBOY: Could you summarize what you've called the 'movement' of American society, under its present administration?

TYNAN: What I feel about any large industrial society in the West is that steps will be taken to see that the majority of its people will be clothed, housed and fed, in order that they can afford to buy the goods which the economy produces. They will also be kept healthy enough to earn the money to buy the national product at profit-making prices. The taking of these steps is known as politics. Steps will also be taken to see that the overseas areas on which the American economy depends for its profitability will remain under the control of the American government and economy, either by business interests on the spot, by C.I.A. machinations, or by direct military intervention.

This is also called politics. And another set of steps will be taken to provide reading matter and entertainment, in order to draw the people's attention to the advertisements that proclaim the merits of the goods. The provision of this material is called journalism or television production. Now that, at its most pessimistic, is my view of the United States: the politicians, the diplomats, the soldiers, the writers are all servants of the profit motive.

PLAYBOY: But isn't it a fantasy to envisage a world made up of small, soft-socialist countries run by sympathetic rulers, non-expansionist in politics, non-profit-making in industry, all this providing a favourable climate for self-expression and the arts, where people living fulfilled and happy lives free of sexual hang-ups and other urban neuroses all get the books and theatre and cinema and intellectual life they deserve?

TYNAN: Well, it's a dream, if you like, to imagine the whole world behaving in this way, but how can you call it a fantasy when certain countries have achieved this, or something close to it? Czechoslovakia is the classic example. The big argument going on in my mind is whether this state of things can be achieved without a social earthquake. Czechoslovakia had, when it evolved into a free socialist country, already become a state where the means of production were in public hands: without that basis, I don't think they would ever have arrived at the free socialism they eventually had. Because, for the first time, you had authors, actors, directors, free to do exactly as they wanted without for one moment selling themselves or even having to think of selling themselves. The mind was operating free of that fetter, that enslaving incentive, and it showed when one talked to them—there was a collective glow, a feeling of their competing with one another as creators, but not as commodities, as best-sellers, as Big Names, for some sort of spurious status and money. That sort of situation, I'm sure, is only possible in a small country with a socialist economy. If there's one credo of Marx that is more important and changeless than any other, it's the notion that who owns what is the basic determinant of the nature of human relationships. The private ownership of one's labour and the dictation for private profit of one's wage and therefore way of life deforms one's existence. And you do not know what a man or a society is capable of until you have removed that deformity. As Brecht said, it is not Communism that is radical: it is capitalism.

PLAYBOY: And the question of how efficiently the economy is run is therefore irrelevant?

TYNAN: Totally irrelevant. Firstly, it must be *fair*. Initially, this may mean that it would be less profitable, less productive. But why not take the thing to its extreme? I think I would say that until we've all achieved an equal chance of *unhappiness*, no one is really entitled to be happy. Ecstasy is a luxury. But ecstasy was there in Prague, during those short years, an experience that we in the West seem only able to find through drugs. It was a time when the human possibility seemed infinite. Much of our journey up from all fours has been a series of experiments like the Czech one, which was stamped on and destroyed through no fault of its own. The Cuban experiment was another, though different. America in 1776 was another, and that, too, has failed.

PLAYBOY: Would you say, then, that the United States is a great idealistic country which has now fallen short of its ideals, or a great cynical country which for a long time cloaked its cynicism in idealism, only to have the truth come out now?

TYNAN: I'd say it's an idealistic country that really didn't know that the economic system to which it was committed would prevent its ideals from being realized. And cynicism is the only human defence against that disappointment. That's why the greatest sense of humour, and the typical American sense of humour, is the Jewish sense of humour: the humour of a people who have had a history of disappointment.

PLAYBOY: How optimistic can one be about the United States and its future? If you were twenty, and an American, would you feel despair about what your adulthood would be?

TYNAN: If I were twenty and American, and felt as militant as I probably should, I'd emigrate with a group of like-minded chums, and try to form some sort of overseas socialist battalion, a kind of Lincoln Brigade of the 1970s. Then we'd go and join the guerrillas who are fighting for liberation in one of the South American countries.

There's a sound political reason for this. If we were winning, the government would ask Washington to send troops in, and I think Washington would hesitate if the troops were going to be used against American boys.

PLAYBOY: Would you fight for liberation if you were an American Negro?

TYNAN: It would be presumptuous of me even to attempt to identify with the Negroes; I've never been through the hell of it, and I don't know how angry or homicidal I would feel. I remember the first inkling I had of the real complexity of the black/white situation in America was when Floyd Patterson regained the heavyweight title from Ingemar Johannsen. I was at a party in Harlem after the fight; it was mostly black, with a few white liberals, including a lady from Long Island who was a professional liberal hostess of the type that Lenny Bruce used to send up so unmercifully, the sort who would touch a Negro and congratulate herself for a month. I was talking to her, and a very hip black actor called Roscoe Lee Brown—he'd be the perfect black Algernon Moncrieff in *The Importance of Being Earnest* —came up to us, and this very gracious lady turned to him and said, "Well, Mr Brown, it's been a wonderful night for your people, hasn't it?" And he said, "No." So she said, "What do you mean, Mr Brown? Your Mr Patterson won, didn't he? Isn't that a wonderful night for your people?" And he said, "No, ma'am, I'm Swedish." Long, long silence. Which Brown finally broke by saying, "I think you meant a wonderful night for the *American* people, didn't you?" And she said, "Oh, yes, yes, of course! I *did* mean a wonderful night for the American people!" And he looked at her, and he said, "Well, don't be too sure, ma'am. Next time, *we* may beat *you*." Leaving her in a marvellous state of pole-axed confusion.

PLAYBOY: Your dumb liberal lady makes me wonder whether we haven't now passed the point of meaningful communication with the black man. Is there any chance left of mutual understanding?

TYNAN: I think the possibility of understanding and contact exists more strikingly in England than in America. There must be a difference for the Negro between a country to which you have come of your own accord, and a country to which your ancestors were brought in chains as slaves, and, similarly, there must be a difference for the whites of the former country: they are bound to feel less guilt and responsibility, and the situation must carry less danger of explosion. Because there is not, in England, a backlog of resentment going back three hundred years. How I would feel as an American white, I don't know. I don't know how one would free oneself from the past. I certainly think the Negro is perfectly entitled to expect *every* American white to bear the burden of contemporary guilt, if not the burden of past beastliness.

PLAYBOY: You're always very careful to insist that you can't speak for Americans; and there's clearly a lot about the States that is anathema to you. But you've been involved for a long time in an inside-outside relationship with the country and the people. Have you taken anything from it and them?

TYNAN: My sense of humour. I've no sense of humour that isn't American, both of the *New Yorker* kind and the Jewish kind. The first is essentially cool, relaxed and urbane, the latter is warmer and more emotional; and I've drawn my entire sense of humour from these two sources—from people like Thurber, Benchley, Ring Lardner on the one hand, and people like Jack Benny, Bert Lahr, George Burns, Phil Silvers on the other. I'd say my sense of humour comes from the funniest country in the world. When I first discovered W. C. Fields, it was a new universe! So was Lenny Bruce: meeting Bruce and knowing him was, for me, to be in a state of apoplectic veneration. In fact, *all* my influences—apart from certain general ideas taken from Zen Buddhism and modernized Marxism—have been people whom I adore or imitate, or would like to imitate. So that it's very difficult for me to analyse influences—I'm a rag-bag of other people's bits, and a lot of those people have been Americans whom I've liked or admired. Terry Southern, Mike Nichols, Mort Sahl—and, of course, Orson Welles. Always Orson Welles. Orson coming into a room is like the sunrise. For me, and for a lot of people of my age, Orson is the man who tried it all: and every time he tried a medium, it capitulated. For the free flexing of a personality in full public view, there were no artistic rivals for Orson in the '40s and '50s.

PLAYBOY: It seems, from that and from what you were saying earlier, that it will always be the great performers that you most admire.

TYNAN: Always. Anyone who is a great performer, who, that is, communicates his whole personality with the minimum of visible strain and the maximum of precision, entirely fascinates me. Even if I don't agree with his ideas. And this applies to bullfighters, conversationalists, ski-jumpers, footballers, cricketers, actors, playwrights, all those who communicate the essence of their gifts with the greatest conciseness. Those are the people I worship. I don't think any public performer in Europe has given me greater pleasure in my life than Antonio Ordóñez, the bullfighter. I've been more moved by him than by any actor — except Olivier — because he displays extreme relaxation and precision in the face of considerable danger, and has the genius to make out of that danger something quite effortless and quite perfect. I'd put him very, very high on my list of heroes. Who else? Gérard Philipe, Lennon and McCartney, Peter Ustinov, Bix Beiderbecke, Ethel Merman — all people doing their thing, if you like, but not just doing it: doing it with a total awareness of the audience and an instinctive sense of shape and form, and bringing it off without visible effort. What I once called 'high definition performance'.

PLAYBOY: Is there, has there ever been, a politician who fulfilled those requirements?

TYNAN: Much more difficult to find. Great performances must disclose the personality completely, and for that very reason, I doubt that any politician could ever meet my prerequisites. Perhaps in wartime: wartime offers a tighter focus than peacetime. One thinks of Churchill being totally Churchill for those six incredibly melodramatic years. And there was Dubček, not in wartime, but in a period of similarly heightened tension; he was certainly a very honest performer, perhaps too honest, too self-revealing, not skilled enough in the arts of self-concealment. Which was probably what encouraged the Russians to step in, knowing that he would not call the nation to arms against them, because he had revealed himself as a non-violent man.

PLAYBOY: You wouldn't include Castro?

TYNAN: Oh yes, I'd choose Castro without any doubt, although I haven't read any of his oratory for the past couple of years. But up until then, the speeches were astounding, and certainly—to return to my earlier specification—instruction with delight. Because to hear him speak is not to hear the demagogue, the yelling fanatic we see in TV excerpts: he's a very rational man, most of the long stretches of those speeches were patient, entertaining expositions of basic facts about the economy. Castro is not a screaming megalomaniac. He would certainly count as a high definition performer.

PLAYBOY: These, of course, are all performers working just with the raw material of themselves, engaged in a simpler act of self-realization than constructors are—conductors, choreographers, architects, producers, those who require others to assist in the realization. Is there, say, a director who produces the same intense pleasure in you?

TYNAN: Fellini is a director who totally revealed himself, with perfect control: just once, in $8\frac{1}{2}$. Since then, sadly, he's been repeating himself with increasing vulgarity and coarseness, and now, with his new film, *Satyricon*, he's disappeared up his own arsehole. Perhaps there should be a moratorium on all films made by guilt-ridden narcissists.

PLAYBOY: Television, presumably, isn't a medium favourable to the high definition performance?

TYNAN: Yes, in several cases. For instance, Johnny Carson has real style, very high definition; I have enormous admiration for him, not least because of his control of the camera, the way he can, by a single veiled look at the lens, convey a whole attitude towards the person he's interviewing. No presence has ever dominated a TV camera more completely than Carson's. In his case, it doesn't involve self-revelation, just total control of the medium. He's a grand master.

PLAYBOY: In general, wouldn't you comparatively evaluate the areas these different performers are operating in? Wouldn't you distinguish the quality of the thing done, as well as the doer?

TYNAN: Yes. I would say that a medium is limited if its emotional and intellectual range is limited. A bullfight has quite obvious limits—it cannot, for example, be satirical, or gentle, and there are whole areas of human experience that are cut off from it: therefore, it is a minor art. Cooking is a minor art: I can't imagine a hilarious soufflé, or a deeply moving stew. You might, I suppose, have a moving wine; but not a moving fried shrimp. But those areas which are concerned with every aspect of human experience, films, plays, books, are obviously superior art-forms, simply because their range is greater. Anyone who operates in a lesser art-form is necessarily a lesser artist.

PLAYBOY: So you don't really embrace the concept that it is in the perfect doing that the joy resides, irrespective of the measurable worth of the thing done?

TYNAN: Well, perhaps I do feel that, after all. Zen has been a big influence on my life, and perhaps I do subscribe to the idea that a whole philosophy can be packed into the shooting of an arrow from a bow: the way in which the arrow is released and flies, the relationship between the man and the arrow, is in itself a philosophical statement. Like a Zen flower arrangement. I've met one or two Zen masters, and I was impressed by their radiant calm, their perfectly contained movement: their entering a room was so extraordinary, their sitting down, their getting up. But I'm getting dangerously close to saying that everything one does is 'art'. Let's just say that there are certain varieties of human experience which are limited, and that bullfighting, baseball, cabinet-making are some of these experiences.

PLAYBOY: We've talked a lot about things experienced and things witnessed, and in that context one is always bound, today, to bring up the experience of drugs. Have you tried any?

TYNAN: I smoke grass whenever it's offered to me. I haven't tried L.S.D., but I have taken mescalin. This was in the very early days of drug-interest, and I took the mescalin with a girl who had taken every known form of narcotic. She terrified me by saying, 'I've taken everything, but mescalin is the boss.' And I'd taken nothing, and here was this really wild chick telling me that I was about to climb Everest. She said, 'Wait forty minutes. Nothing will happen before that, and then mescalin will tap you on the shoulder, and you'll follow.' There was a friend with me, an actor, also taking it for the first time; and we both turned on.

And what she said was true: after half an hour, there was this sense of being summoned by the drug, of being tapped on the psychic shoulder; and, immediately, all man-made things, like paintings, like the music coming out of the hi-fi, like books, all these things became monstrous deformities, they became so many wriggling worms. What was fascinating was that the frames of the paintings, the pure wood, became more important than the pictures themselves: the wood became a living tree, the painting a writhing squiggle. The only things that seemed real were trees, the sun, natural objects. The wallpaper had pictures of roses on it, and these roses became Charles Laughton as Henry VIII, whereupon they grew larger and filled the room. That made me laugh. And I knew that laughter felt like cotton-wool, and I knew what the sound of it tasted like; there was a cross-pollination of the senses. And then my friend said that we had to get rid of the girl, who was saying things like 'Groovy!' and 'Far out!' and shrieking all these cult cries, and they seemed just as unreal as the painting and the music and the books, and utterly irrelevant. So we pushed her rather rudely out of the door. Then I swept the laughter out with a broom, because by this time the room was embarrassingly full of cotton-wool. I swept all the laughter out, locked the door, and felt tremendously happy. And after about two years, my friend got hungry and went down to a snack bar, and he came back about, oh, eighteen months later, and he said: 'I've done a terrible thing. I went into this snack bar and I looked at this old man standing there staring at a sausage with congealed fat around it, and I went up to him and kissed him and said "You poor bugger!" and he hit me.' So I commiserated with him, and we decided to drive around for a bit, and we ended up at a party. The place was full of people in expensive clothes, intelligent, fashionable liberals, and all we could hear was this strange twittering, like an aviary full of parakeets, and I said to my friend, 'What's that noise?' and he said, 'That's intelligent conversation.' So we thought about that for a couple of months, and then he said, 'Let's go and look at a loaf of bread.' So we went into the kitchen and we both looked at a loaf of bread for about four years. And it was a lovely thing. Next morning, I had a terrible come-down; I couldn't, in fact, get down from the high for a long time, and I had a date at, of all places, Scotland Yard. Someone had arranged for me to go to look at the Black Museum, this collection of grisly horrors, the relics of violent crimes of the last hundred years, that the Criminal Investigation Department keeps — all the nooses that have hanged all the killers, all the most grotesque souvenirs, and to go round those sickening rooms, blissfully high and staring at the horrors, was a shattering experience. I had to go to bed for twenty-four hours after that. Because I'd been looking with deep and passionate involvement at things which should inspire revulsion. They had, in a jar of surgical spirit, the arm of a murderer whom they'd caught because his victim had scratched his elbow and they'd found traces of her nail varnish in the wounds. And I think I started singing when I saw it.

PLAYBOY: You didn't try mescalin again?

TYNAN: No. I smoke pot, but all that pot does for me is suspend the tyranny of time: it doesn't seem important to go to bed by twelve in order to get up at eight. Time seems flexible. The moment spreads itself: instead of being over with the next tick, it goes on and on, centrifugal and elastic. In a way, it restores one to childhood, because in childhood time seems longer — you're aware of more sensual experiences per minute than at any subsequent time. As you grow older, you grow less sensitive to those experiences; and pot restores that sensitivity. That's why I support pot: because it's so restorative. It makes a hand stroked feel like the first hand you ever stroked, rather than the thousandth. And I do find that it's good to make love after pot — even the next day, there's a total relaxation. Which makes for easy concentration and enjoyment without effort.

PLAYBOY: What would you say it is about pot that most horrifies people?

TYNAN: I've always suspected that it's because pot is the arch-enemy of capitalism: it makes one less willing to work hard. It may increase absenteeism in industry, it may make men care less about being productive. It's the antithesis of the Protestant ethic: pot tells you that it's not bad to be supine, to be a lotus-eater. I talked earlier about the increasing irrelevance of the word 'art'; the next thing to talk about is the increasing irrelevance of the word 'work'. The next big problem we'll have to face, if the affluent society survives, is how to learn to live with leisure. How shall we replace the infinite solace of work, the self-forgetfulness of work, the idea of work as tired Nature's sweet restorer, in which you can forget yourself and why you're alive and what it should mean to be human? How shall we replace this 9-to-5 narcotic that prevents you from worrying about what your identity is, that tells you only that you are a function of a factory or an office? When the time comes that the most potent drug of all—work—is no longer available, how will mankind learn to live without it?

PLAYBOY: How would you cope with the withdrawal? How would you treat addicts trying to kick the work habit?

TYNAN: The very rich have always known how to do it. They do, of course, issue occasional propaganda bulletins to the effect that money and leisure don't bring happiness, and occasionally one of them, a token rich person, commits suicide or goes mad through drugs or drink or something, as if to prove that it isn't all milk and honey; but for the mass of the rich, worklessness is not only possible but delightful. You must never forget this about the rich: they do an awful lot of fucking and drinking and drugging, and they enjoy themselves enormously. We must never forget what a very nice time the really rich have, and what superlative medical care they receive, and how very long many of them live. The time may be coming, especially in the West, when large numbers of people will have as much spare time as they do; and the difficulty will be to make people use it for pleasure, real pleasure, instead of just for staring at a box or sleeping. My guess is that as soon as automation and computerization reduce the time needed for human labour to a tiny fraction of the week, a lot of men will start going out and looking for hard, unpleasant physical tasks: they'll start chopping logs and digging ditches just to feel good, to acquire virtue.

PLAYBOY: Then what's the best lesson the rich can teach us?

TYNAN: How to understand play. For me, as soon as my work ceases to be a form of play, I lose interest in it. In order to utilize our spare time we're going to have to learn much more about the nature of play. Anthropologists have written books about *homo ludens*; *any* competitive human activity which takes place within a limited space of time in a specified geographical area, with rules acceptable to both sides, is a form of play. Parliament is a form of play, law courts are a form of play, just as plays themselves are; and democracy is probably the best form of play—there are equal chances of winning, and any number can take part. As soon as you limit the numbers, it becomes a less good game. And as soon as work diminishes, we'll have to learn how to take up the time with play. So let's find ways of using play creatively; if I had to endow a chair at a university, it would be a Chair of Play.

PLAYBOY: Won't people still demand play with a demonstrable end? In order to make it a surrogate-drug for work, won't men require evidence that play is making them better, giving them more things, improving their lives and status?

TYNAN: Yes, many people will, of course, find forms of play which *are* in fact work, which do produce concrete benefits. They'll also find ways of relating income to play. Not everyone nowadays can accept the dole without guilt or shame, but in future many of us will have to learn to accept remuneration without work. It's interesting that among the richest writers who have existed in the last fifty years were the Hollywood screenwriters of the '30s; and they spent much of their spare time inventing and playing the most complex, convoluted and ferociously competitive party games.

PLAYBOY: And would that satisfy you? A life that was merely a protracted game, or series of games?

TYNAN: Well, I've been a games-player all my life, and, with the right competition, success in really challenging games can give unbelievable satisfaction. But, of course, if I dream of a leisured world, a workless world, a world as a great and endless game, if you like, I also dream of something larger. There's a concept known as the Golden Age; it is the period you look back to, the period you dreamt about in childhood, or heard about somewhere in the distant past, the ideal community where all men were equal, inhabiting a pastoral paradise, and all goods were held in common. It's the place for which we are all nostalgic, though, in fact, we never lived there. This is a theme that runs right through literature, the great pastoral dream:

the Greeks, the Romans, the Elizabethans, the Augustans, they all had it, everyone had it. Christians say it's a premonition of heaven; non-Christians like me might see it in the form of an island-dream. *Island* was the name of Aldous Huxley's last and to my mind most human novel. In it he envisaged an island set between the spheres of influence of East and West, somewhere in the Indian Ocean, a sort of surrogate Eden. He drew a portrait of an ideal state: it was non-industrialized, of course, like all these dreams, and it embraced the best of liberal socialism and the best of Buddhism. It was a very good dream and it attracted me a lot. Or did, when the book first appeared. One's immediate thought *now* is that such a society would be annexed immediately by one or other of the large powers. So one has to find an Eden even smaller. I therefore have an alternative dream — and I don't think there can be many men who haven't had it at one time or another in their lives — of picking a group of friends, say about twenty-five of them, and going off to a small island. To raise one's own food, build one's own shelter, all that. I doubt that I'll ever have either the resources or the guts to do it, but I should like to. It would be wonderful to put one's own social theories to the test like that, on a small scale, on an island somewhere not too far from the Mediterranean.

PLAYBOY: Why there?

TYNAN: Because it means the Middle Earth, and stands for the middle way; gently changing seasons, no outrageous natural phenomena, no typhoons, no hurricanes, few earthquakes, no terrible extremes of heat and cold. That is the climate in which to experiment with a new way of living.

PLAYBOY: Hasn't a book like *Lord of The Flies* taken your Eden-myth and exposed its inherent flaws?

TYNAN: That's a very potent piece of iconoclasm, yes, the very opposite of the Utopian myth, claiming that if people are left alone to develop by instinct, they will plump for evil, and destroy one another. But I do not subscribe to that thesis. The ideal community *can* be constructed, and Caliban *can* be pacified. The least we can do is try. As Byron says in Tennessee Williams's play *Camino Real*: '*Make voyages — Attempt them!* — there's nothing else!'

Section Four

In Praise of Hard Core

It's always pleasant to see prudery knocked, and whenever I read articles by fellow-intellectuals in defence of pornography, I do my best to summon up a cheer. Lately, however, the heart has gone out of my hurrahs. The old adrenalin glow has waned. And now that I've analysed a number of recent anti-censorship tracts, I think I know why. *The writers are cheating*. A whiff of evasiveness, even of outright hypocrisy, clings to their prose: too much is left unspoken, or unadmitted. Their arguments, when you look at them closely, shift on the quicksands of timidity. On the surface, a fearless libertarian has come forth to do battle with the forces of reaction. But between the lines he is usually saying something like this:

(a) I hate censorship in all its forms, but that doesn't mean that I actually like pornography.

(b) In fact, I don't even approve of it, except when I can call it 'erotic writing' and pass it off as literature.

(c) I wouldn't go into a witness box to defend it unless it had educational, artistic or psychiatric value to make it respectable.

(d) I read it only in the line of duty, and feel nothing but pity for those who read it for pleasure.

(e) Needless to say, I never masturbate.

Such—once you've stripped off the rhetoric—is the accepted liberal viewpoint; and safer than that you can hardly play. At best, it adds up to a vaguely progressive gesture that could never endanger the author's moral standing or give his wife a moment's worry. From first to last he remains socially stainless and—to me, anyway—utterly unreal. He is like a man who loathes whorehouses in practice but doesn't mind defending them in principle, provided that they are designed by Mies van der Rohe and staffed by social workers in Balenciaga dresses.

At this point I had better offer a definition. By pornography I mean writing that is exclusively intended to cause sexual pleasure. I am not talking about novelists like D. H. Lawrence or Henry Miller; sex is often their theme, but titillation is never their main objective, and if they happen to arouse us, we keep ourselves resolutely zipped, aware that what we are feeling is only an incidental part of a large literary design. (This, of course, can be fairly frustrating at times. In *Lady Chatterley's Lover*, for instance, Lawrence has a teasing habit of getting the reader tumescent and suddenly changing the subject from sex to the dreadful side effects of the Industrial Revolution.) Nor am I concerned with the Anglo-Saxon exiles in Paris who used to concoct spare-time pornography under pseudonyms for the Olympia Press; straight smut wasn't their *métier*, and too often they strayed from the purpose at hand into irrelevant gags and other flights of asexual fancy. *Candy*, by Terry Southern and Mason Hoffenberg, is a brilliant example of pseudo-pornography, praised by the liberal critics precisely because it was too funny to be sexy. As the porter in *Macbeth* said of drink, 'It provokes the desire, but it takes away the performance.'

What we are discussing is something different—hard-core pornography, which is orgasmic in intent and untouched by the ulterior motives of traditional art. For men, it has a simple and localized purpose: to induce an erection. And the more skilfully the better. Contrary to popular myth, it takes discipline and devotion to be a first-rate pornographer, and only the subtlest command of rhythm and repetition will produce ideal results. These usually take the form of solo masturbation—usually, but not invariably, since vocal excerpts from bawdy books can often be employed to vary or intensify the customary fun of sexual coupling. In any case, the aim of pornography is physical enjoyment. Yet the liberals, at least, disdain it, and the public as a whole seems eager to burn it. I think it deserves a few words of exculpation and thanksgiving.

In 1962 John Osborne wrote a short and startling play called *Under Plain Cover*. It deals with a happily married suburban couple named Jenny and Tim, whose private life is entirely given up to the acting out of sexual fantasies. Sometimes she dresses up as a nurse, and he plays the apprehensive patient; in another version of the game he is a strict master threatening to punish a slovenly housemaid. They are both obsessed by

Victorian knickers, of which they have a unique collection. After one fetishistic session, they meditate as follows:

JENNY: Do you think there are many people like us?
TIM: No. Probably none at all, I expect.
JENNY: Oh, there must be some.
TIM: Well, yes, but probably not two together.
JENNY: You mean just one on their own?
TIM: Yes.
JENNY: How awful. We are lucky.

Pornography is expressly designed for those who are not, in Jenny's sense, 'lucky'. If your taste is for earrings or high heels or spanking or any of the other minority appetites, you may have trouble finding a like-minded bedfellow. You will be 'one on their own', and that can create a strangulating sense of guilt. Pornography loosens the stranglehold and assuages the solitude; you know, at least, that you are not alone. Having bought a book that matches your fantasy, you emerge from the store with a spring-heeled stride and a surge of elation. I have felt that radiant contentment, and so have you — *hypocrite lecteur, mon semblable, mon frère*. If chance denies you the right partner, that book and others like it will be your lifelong companions. Just as old habits die hard, old hards die habits.

The erotic minority man is not alone in needing the aid and comfort of pornography. Worse by far is the plight of those who are villainously ugly and unable to pay for the services of call girls. (If they are rich, their problem is negligible; beauty, after all, is in the eye of the stockholder.) To be poor and physically unappetizing is to be sexually condemned to solitary confinement, from which pornography offers the illusion of release. And we mustn't overlook its more commonplace uses. For men on long journeys, geographically cut off from wives and mistresses, pornography can act as a portable memory, a welcome shortcut to remembered bliss, relieving tension without involving disloyalty. And for uncommitted bachelors, arriving alone and short of cash in foreign cities where they don't speak the language, hard core is practically indispensable.

It's difficult to be an enemy of pornography without also disapproving of masturbation. In order to condemn the cause, it is logically necessary to deplore the effect. A century ago, when it was generally believed that self-stropping led to loss of hair, blindness and mental paralysis, I could have understood this attitude. Nowadays, I find it as baffling and repugnant as when I first encountered it, at the age of fourteen. The debating society at my school was discussing the motion 'That the present generation has lost the ability to entertain itself.' Rising to make my maiden speech, I said with shaky aplomb, 'Mr Chairman—as long as masturbation exists, no one can seriously maintain that we have lost the ability to entertain ourselves.' The teacher in charge immediately closed the meeting. Today his successor would probably take a more tolerant view. But the old prohibitions still persist.

In a recent letter to the *Sunday Times*, a respected liberal clergyman wrote: 'To be sexually hungry is the fate of thousands, both young and old. There is nothing evil in this hunger, but it is hard to bear. To have it stimulated when it cannot be honourably satisfied is to make control more difficult.'

Here, in three short sentences, all the puritan assumptions are on parade—that sexual deprivation is the normal state of affairs, that it is morally desirable to grin and bear it, and that masturbation is a dishonourable alternative.

Because hard core performs an obvious physical function, literary critics have traditionally refused to consider it a form of art. By their standards, art is something that appeals to such intangibles as the soul and the imagination; anything that appeals to the genitals belongs in the category of massage. What they forget is that language can be used in many delicate and complex ways to enliven the penis. It isn't just a matter of bombarding the reader with four-letter words. As Lionel Trilling said in a memorably sane essay on the subject:

> I see no reason in morality (or in aesthetic theory) why literature should not have as one of its intentions the arousing of thoughts of lust. It is one of the effects, perhaps one of the functions, of literature to arouse desire, and I can discover no ground for saying that sexual pleasure should not be among the objects of desire which literature presents to us, along with heroism, virtue, peace, death, food, wisdom, God, etc.

That is the nutshell case for pornography as art. It could hardly be stated more concisely, and I have yet to hear it convincingly refuted. If a writer uses literary craft to provoke sexual delight, he is doing an artist's job. It is for him to decide whether four-letter words will help or hinder his design. C. S. Lewis, a great literary critic and Christian apologist, once jolted me by saying that he objected to venereal monosyllables mainly because they were anti-aphrodisiac; from antiquity onward, the best writers had found that the oblique approach to sex paid higher erotic dividends. ('The direct approach', he told me, 'means that you have to resort to the language of the nursery, the gutter or the medical textbook. And these may not be the associations you wish to evoke.') But that is a question of taste. Whatever technique the writer employs, we are entitled to judge the end product as a work of art. And the basic criterion, in the case of pornography, is whether or not it succeeds in exciting us. If it doesn't, we can write it off as an artistic failure.

Lawyers, as I discovered a couple of years ago, are not impressed by the Trilling doctrine. The English distributors of *Fanny Hill* were being prosecuted for obscenity, and the publishers' legal advisers asked me whether I would appear as a witness for the defence. I said I'd be delighted. And what form (they inquired) would my evidence take? I replied by pointing out that under English law obscenity is permissible as long as it has redeeming artistic merits. I considered erotic titillation a legitimate function of art, and therefore proposed to defend *Fanny Hill* on the ground that it was expertly titillating. The lawyers' professional smiles froze on their faces. They didn't exactly throw me out, but they made it arctically clear that I would not be called on to testify. In terms of courtroom tactics, they may have been right; it's just conceivable, however, that they missed a chance of establishing (or at least of testing) a new legal precedent. In any event, they lost the case.

But I mustn't lurch into the trap of suggesting that pornography is defensible only when it qualifies as art. It is defensible in its own right and for its own sake, no matter whether it is art or not, and whether it is well or badly written. Freedom to write about sex must include the freedom to write about it badly. Some of the younger critics — guerrillas at the gates of the literary Establishment — would go further and argue that pornography is not only different from art but in some respects more important. A reviewer in the *International Times*, London's underground newspaper, recently declared:

In the brave new world of sexuality, perhaps we can forget about art, and read Henry Miller as he was meant to be read: as the writer whose craft describes intercourse better than anybody else's. If we have learned nothing else from Genet, we can be sure of this: his result may have been art, but that's not as important as his intention, which was pornography.

Very few critics, even today, can write about hard core without tremors of prejudice and preconception. You can sense them worrying all the time about what their readers will think of them; it mustn't be suspected that they enjoy it, because that would imply that they masturbate. So they get defensively jocose, or wearily condescending. They indulge in squirms of pity for those who actually go out and buy the stuff—the sort of pity that is twin brother of contempt. Of course, the hellfire preachers of popular reviewing don't bother with such petty qualms; for them, all pornography is subversive filth and ought to be destroyed unread. It's only in the work of intelligent critics that you hear the special tone of veiled liberal distaste, which is rather like that of a lecturer on toxicology who feels compelled to reassure us, every few seconds, that he has never actually poisoned anyone. This tone is audible, even in *The Other Victorians* by Steven Marcus, a much-praised and often perceptive study of pornography in nineteenth-century England. The author is an Associate Professor of English at Columbia. Let me list some of the errors, ambiguities and critical confusions that I detect in his book:

(1) Overdependence on Freudian dogma. Professor Marcus prefaces his text with the famous quotation in which Freud proclaims that 'the grandest cultural achievements ... are brought to birth by ever greater sublimation of the components of the sexual instinct'. In other words, the less energy you invest in sex, the more likely you are to produce a work of art. This is a hypothesis with no scientific basis of any kind. It is rather like saying that if you hoard enough milk, it may somehow turn into wine. The whole theory reeks of hidden puritanism, not to say magic.

(2) Overaddiction to Freudian symbolism. Describing a Victorian handbook on pornography, Professor Marcus points out that its author often hangs a page of footnotes on to a single

line of text. He adds that 'one is tempted' to see in this 'an unconscious iconography: beneath a very small head there is attached a very large appendage'. Resist the temptation, Marcus: this is sub-Freudian tittering at its coyest. Later on, the professor quotes from a pornographer who casually—and to avoid repeating himself—uses the word 'evacuation' to mean ejaculation. 'If one expands the metaphor,' Marcus comments with pole-axing pedantry, 'one begins to see that the penis then might be either a fecal column or the lower end of the alimentary tract out of which fecal matter is to be expelled, the woman's body, particularly her genitals, becomes a toilet, etc.' Watch out for expanding metaphors, Marcus, especially if they're anal. Again, when a hard-core hero, busily undressing a girl, says that he 'unveiled beauties enough to bring the dead to life', the professor insists that the phrase is an unconscious reference to the author and his readers: *they* are the dead who need to be brought to life. If clichés can legitimately yield interpretations like that, we enter a minefield every time we uncover our typewriters.

(3) Verbal snobbery, i.e., the assumption that the sexual act is inherently too ignoble to be described in noble words. When a pornographer writes about 'that inner sovereignty or force, within my balls', Marcus gets witheringly scornful: 'An "inner sovereignty" that is yet "within my balls" is hopeless and impossible. Sovereignty is toppled from its throne by being so located—there is nothing majestic about such an urgency.' This reminds me of a telling exchange at the Old Bailey in 1960, when *Lady Chatterley's Lover* was being tried for obscenity. Counsel for the prosecution, an Old Etonian and veteran of the Coldstream Guards, read a passage from the novel in tones of frigid derision and then asked Richard Hoggart, a young scholar giving evidence for the defence, whether he seriously contended that it was possible to feel 'reverence for a man's balls'. 'Indeed, yes,' said Hoggart, with quiet compassion for the fellow's obtuseness. He made it seem so obvious; and as he spoke you could feel the case swinging in Lawrence's favour.

(4) Facile generalization, based on sloppy research. This crops up in the brief, disdainful chapter that Marcus devotes to the vast Victorian literature of flagellation. In books of this genre, he says, 'what goes on is always the same. A person is accused of some wrongdoing. This person is most often a boy ... The

accuser is almost invariably some surrogate for his mother ... An adult male figure, father or schoolmaster, occurs very infrequently.' In fact, the victim is usually a girl, and male accusers are just as common as female. The professor's reading list must have been curiously selective.

(5) Moral censure masquerading as stylistic disapproval. Marcus has a habit of attacking pornography in particular on grounds that apply to literature in general. At one point, for instance, he quotes a sentence that makes cloudy use of epithets such as 'voluptuous', 'amorous' and 'tumultuous'. He goes on to say that, because they are vague and unspecific, 'they express an important tendency in pornography'. Nothing of the sort: what they express is a tendency that exists in bad writing of any kind. Foggy prose is no more abhorrent in pornography than in Norman Vincent Peale.

But for all his lapses, Marcus is at least trying to be an objective witness, and often he succeeds. The roughest frontal assault on hard core in recent years has come from George Steiner, a sprightly American don who teaches at Churchill College, Cambridge. It was launched in an essay called 'Night Words', which Steiner contributed to the English magazine *Encounter*. He begins by contending that, since the number of sexual positions and combinations is limited, pornography is doomed to ultimate monotony. To which one replies that dawn and sunset are likewise limited, but that only a limited man would find them monotonous.

Already, quite early in the piece, there are signs that Steiner is easily bored. With a stoic yawn, he says that after any kind of sexual fulfilment 'there is the grey of morning and the sour knowledge that things have remained fairly generally the same since man first met goat and woman'. (Why grey instead of flesh-pink? Why sour rather than sweet? Why goats anyway?) Hereabouts he takes a sudden swerve that brings him into head-on collision with Professor Marcus, who is approaching from the opposite direction. According to Steiner, one of the definitions of abstract art is 'that it cannot be pornographic'. According to Marcus, pornography is 'in reality very abstract'.

Steiner now zeros in on his target. Reasonably enough, he maintains that there is no essential difference between 'erotic writing' and hard core except in the matter of verbal sophistication. But from this he argues that neither category 'adds anything new to the potential of human emotion; both add to the waste'. An assumption is buried here, and I trust you dig it: what Steiner means by waste is masturbation. A long passage follows in which he easily demolishes the pretensions of Maurice Girodias, founder of the Olympia Press, who is for ever protesting that what he published was not pornography but art. (My own complaint would be that although it was sometimes good art, it was always lousy pornography.) This section is dotted with words like 'bore', 'boredom', 'repetitive' and 'dull', just in case you are in any doubt about Steiner's attitude towards the desirability of writing about physical lovemaking. For what he is leading up to is nothing less than a blanket condemnation of all attempts to put the sexual act into words. He asserts that the best novelists leave sex in the wings; they stop at the bedroom door. To support his case he cites Tolstoy and George Eliot, both of whom lived at a time when it was forbidden to go further. As for modern outspokenness: 'There is no real freedom whatever in the compulsive physiological exactitudes of present "high pornography", because there is no respect for the reader whose imaginative means are set at nil.' Sex is a private citadel to be jealously guarded, an experience in which two human beings must find for themselves the mental images that will set their blood to racing in dark and wonder ever-renewed. (I am compressing, but not all that much.) 'The new pornographers', Steiner warns us dourly, 'subvert this last, vital privacy; they do our imagining for us.'

They do our imagining for us. It sounds like a fearful affront, a chilling premonition of 1984; but in fact it is exactly what all good writers have done since the birth of literature. The measure of their talent has immemorially been their ability to make us see the world through their eyes. If they can heighten our perceptions, we should thank them, not resent them. And on the matter of privacy: I don't think Steiner is seriously suggesting that commando groups of scribbling voyeurs are going to burst into our bedrooms and take notes. We can always keep our sex lives to ourselves if we wish. But that doesn't mean (why should it?) that we must shrink from reading about other people's.

Steiner's climactic point is that hard core has no respect for 'the sanctity of autonomous life' as far as its characters are concerned. They don't exist in their own right, independent and self-sustaining, like people in Stendhal and Henry James. Pornographers, he says, 'shout at their personages: strip, fornicate, perform this or that act of sexual perversion.' The error here is one we have already noted in Marcus: Steiner is damning bad pornography for a crime that it shares with all bad fiction. Incompetent writers *always* shout at their characters: drink, take dope, perform this or that act of psychological perversion. In good pornography, as in good writing of any kind, the characters need no such external prompting. But Steiner goes on to compare pornographers with S.S. guards, who barked their orders at living men and women: 'The total attitudes are not, I think, entirely distinct. There may be deeper affinities than we as yet understand between the "total freedom" of the uncensored erotic imagination and the total freedom of the sadist. That these two freedoms have emerged in close historical proximity may not be coincidence.'

But have they? History refutes the argument. Sadists were indulging their grisly whims centuries before the modern era of sadistic pornography. Slaughter for fun is not a recent invention. Gilles de Rais was exploiting it to the full long before the Marquis de Sade began his missionary activities; like all enthusiasts of his kind, in whatever period, Gilles needed sadistic books to inflame him about as much as a Madras curry needs a pepper mill.

The question of banning de Sade has been urgently debated in England ever since the Moors Murder trial in 1966, at which a neofascistic Scot named Ian Brady and his mistress, Myra Hindley, were sentenced to life imprisonment for a series of explicitly sadistic killings. Their victims were a seventeen-year-old youth and two children aged ten and twelve. Among the books found in Brady's lodgings was a study of the life and ideas of the Marquis de Sade. Did it supply him with fantasy scenarios which he later enacted in reality? Was this a case of life imitating art? Pamela Hansford Johnson, the novelist and wife of C. P. Snow, suspects that it might have been, and has poured her qualms into an agitated little book called *On Iniquity*. In it she comes out strongly against the free dissemination of pornography. 'There is a tyranny of libertarianism as well as of restriction,' she says, 'and we can already hear its baying, and the rolling of its tumbrils.' Miss Hansford Johnson is no professional bigot; she is a decent liberal in a state of sincere unease;

but a cool survey of the facts suggests that her natural horror at the Brady-Hindley crimes has carried her to irrational extremes. Brady's record shows that he was cutting up live cats with a flick knife at the age of ten; and around the same time he tied up a school friend and tried to burn him to death. He was a practising sadist before he ever heard of de Sade.

To my mind, the really evil books about physical cruelty are those which give it a moral justification. I am thinking, for example, of those Catholic tracts that appeared at the bloody high noon of the Inquisition, telling true believers that it was necessary to maim and incinerate unrepentant heretics for the good of their souls. I think, too, of military manuals on the use of bayonets and small arms, which teach you how to inflict the most refined and crippling pain for the greater good of your country. I despise such books and regret that there are people who like to read them. But I would not ban them.

One inalienable right binds all mankind together—the right of self-abuse. That—and not the abuse of others—is what distinguishes the true lover of pornography. We should encourage him to seek his literary pleasure as and where he finds it. To deny him that privilege is to invade the deepest privacy of all.

Eros Belied

Pensioning off euphemisms like 'visual hymns to Pan' and 'joyous celebrations of Eros', let us agree that the aim of erotic art is erotic arousal. Not perhaps the only aim, but certainly a primary one, and to my mind very philanthropic. For as long as I can remember, I have enjoyed having erections, and I have always been keenly grateful to all those people—whether artists, writers, performers or private individuals—to whose exertions I owe them. This strikes me as a courteous and civil response, and I mention it merely because it differs so sharply from that of the Longfordians, whose reaction in similar circumstances is one of apoplectic rage, followed by a ferocious determination to round up those responsible and fling them in jail. The trouble with the new Weidenfeld anthology*—opulently produced, with an elegant text by Robert Melville—is that it will provoke few spasms of Longfordian fury, or, to put it another way, few of the scrotal stirrings that herald tumescence.

For one thing, it contains work by too many great artists, and the work of great artists rarely succeeds in being erotic, mainly because it is trying to be so much else—e.g. fit to be publicly exhibited, acceptable to the taste of posh patrons, psychologically profound, formally beautiful, etc. Pure eroticism demands the discipline of a strictly limited vision, a genuine respect for banality of subject-matter, and total indifference to public acceptance; and these are qualities seldom found together in first-rate artists. It also presupposes a moral climate capable of tolerating explicitly sexual images—a climate unknown in Europe between the rise of Christianity and the dawn of the twentieth century. Simon Wilson, who prefaces the book with a capsule history of Western erotic art, points out that in Christian

* *Erotic Art of the West*, by Robert Melville.

iconography 'the body had ceased to be ... a mirror of divine perfection and had largely become an object of humiliation and shame.' (In this view he is stoutly supported by Kenneth Clark, who wrote in 1956 that under the influence of Christianity 'the body ... ceased to be the mirror of divine perfection and became an object of humiliation and shame.') In general, it is the minor artists in Mr Melville's index who are the sexiest — unpretentious masturbation-fantasists like Michael Zichy and Félicien Rops; Viennese voyeurs like Klimt and Schiele (when the latter is not being too bleakly bony); fetishist image-makers like Allen Jones; priapic surrealists like Balthus and Dali, the latter hauntingly represented by 'Young Virgin Auto-Sodomized by her own Chastity', which features a stupendously cloven bottom; and a page of illustrations from Victorian pornography, which are titillating precisely because they seek no other justification for their existence. (The *Concise Oxford* says that titillate means 'tickle, excite pleasantly', which seems to me a very agreeable and not at all demeaning task for an artist to perform.) But the book as a whole betrays a fatal hankering after respectability, a desperate regard for human dignity; whereas sex is essentially undignified, an act of reciprocal abandon in which poise and solemnity and 'what other people will think' are forgotten. If an agnostic is an atheist with aspirations to the Royal Enclosure, 'erotic art' is pornography with aspirations to the coffee-table. We never encounter in Mr Melville's pages the Dionysiac ecstasy of which Kenneth Clark writes in *The Nude* — 'that antique religion of sensuality from which, in the end, the female nude derives its authority and momentum'. Lord Clark illustrates the cult of Dionysus by means of sculpture, a tactile, inherently sensual art of which Mr Melville shows us only three examples from the whole range of Western art. Instead, he spends a lot of time toiling to impregnate sexually neutral paintings with erotic significance. These include Renoir's 'Dance at Bourgival', in which a fully-clad couple soberly waltz; Bosch's 'St John the Baptist' (the monstrous plant that proliferates beside the saint is apparently a penis symbol, if that is what grabs you); Correggio's design for a fountain into which three coy *putti* are peeing; Longhi's 'Meeting of Dominoes', which shows a masked couple sedately promenading; Artemisia's 'Judith and Holofernes', fancifully described as 'a decapitation and a castration in a single act';

7

Da Messina's 'St Sebastian' ('the trickle of blood running into the waistcloth from the arrow in his stomach is a ravishing glimpse of his interior life'); Veronese's 'Death of Lucrece', in which the suicide's *décolletage* is as discreet as the Queen Mother's; Max Ernst's 'Garden Aeroplane Trap', a landscape littered with strips of metal that are, we're implausibly told, 'exhausted by love-making'; and Holman Hunt's 'The Hireling Shepherd', a glib genre work in which a yokel puts his arm round a girl to catch an insect — 'a situation', Mr Melville says gravely, 'that gives the death's head moth the significance of a winged phallus'.

And there are far too many familiar faces: Titian's Bacchus comes hurdling out of his chariot to embrace Ariadne, Giorgione's Dresden Venus sleepily wanks. The impact of one pair of familiar *fesses* — those of Boucher's Miss O'Murphy — is ruined by loony layout: the lady gets a double-page spread, but the fold brutally bisects her bum, which is the focal point of the picture. Homage to the female bottom — 'that living altar', as James Joyce called it, 'where the back changes name' — is scanty and tepid throughout. Mr Melville devotes only two pages to it, taking as his epigraph a cryptic and unconvincing statement by Sartre: 'Many women loathe their backside, that blind and public mass which belongs to everyone before belonging to them.' (Blind? What about Chaucer's 'nether ëye'?) This cursory account of the holy hemispheres is accompanied by only four plates, of which one is mislabelled in the text (the Jordaens painting is of Candaules's wife, not Bathsheba) and three depict bottoms whose grotesque corpulence makes Rubens's Three Graces look like a triptych of Twiggys. Pygophilia may be, in Mr Melville's phrase, 'an infantile condition', but it is by several months less infantile than the curious obsession with breasts that plays so dominant a role in modern *machismo*. Mr Melville deals even more dismissively with flagellation than with its customary target; and none of the miserly three plates he devotes to it covers what is known in the porn trade as 'soft fladge' — i.e. spanking — which, apart from homosexuality, is easily the most popular erotic variation in the Western world. (A humanist, it has been said, can be defined as someone who remembers the faces of the people he spanks; and I am nothing if not a humanist.) In a book of this kind, I would swop a dozen Botticellis and Tintorettos for a single work—possibly 'Le Supplice de l'Attente'—by Malteste, the great French master of soft-fladge lithography. Apropos of buttock-fixations, I congratulate Mr Melville on quoting from 'Don Leon' the persuasive and eloquent stanzas in which it is alleged that Byron buggered his wife and that this was the cause of his subsequent ostracism. (How appropriate, by the way, that nineteenth-century English literature should be enclosed within the parentheses of two tremendous anal scandals!) But far from being 'a rather sad poem', as Mr Melville describes it, 'Don Leon' is one of the most brilliant and audacious satires on official morality in the English language. For Mr Melville's further information, it was published in 1866, not 1856, and the author was George Colman the younger.

If I sound self-indulgent, it is because self-indulgence is the *raison d'être* of erotic art. I suspect, however, that my carnal response to the livelier nudes in Mr Melville's book might not meet with the approval of John Berger. In his dazzling TV series, *Ways of Seeing*, Mr Berger challenged Lord Clark's distinction between nakedness, which is merely the state of being unclothed, and nudity, which is the basis of an art form. In Mr Berger's words:

> To be naked is to be oneself. To be nude is to be seen naked by others ... A naked body has to be seen as an object in order to become a nude.

Where a male lover is present in a painting as well as a nude woman, the latter usually directs her gaze not at him but at her 'spectator-owner', the man who has bought the picture. The rare exceptions are what Mr Berger prizes: paintings in which the onlooker is an outsider and the true relationship is between the artist and his subject—e.g. Rubens's portrait of his beloved second wife, Hélène Fourment. My own view is that works of this kind (like Rembrandt's studies of Hendrickje) can never be erotic. They belong in a special category, perhaps best described as monogamous art. Looking at them, I feel like a Peeping Tom: I would much rather be an honest voyeur. At least an artist's model is fully aware that she is going to be looked at; and voyeurism, after all, is implicit in all activities where one group of human beings observes another. (All sports fans, for example, are voyeurs.) As for being 'seen as an object'—well, the human body is by definition a material object, and the foundation of happy fucking, I would have thought, is to accept it as such, which is much less easy, in our shame-ridden society, than it sounds. If two people regard each other as desirable sexual objects, they are halfway to mutual fulfilment: it is the pre-condition from which all else flows. (I have, incidentally, my own rather different objection to obsessive eroticism: namely, that it is extremely time-consuming. This is true not only by day but also when we are asleep. Perhaps it would help if one of Lord Longford's disciples were to compose a letter on the subject to *The Times*:

Dear Sir,

I hope I am not a prude, but I feel compelled to lodge a protest against the ever-increasing flood of obscenity in dreams. Many of my friends have been as shocked and sickened as myself by the filth that is poured out nightly as soon as our eyes are closed. It is certainly not my idea of 'home entertainment'.

Night after night, the most disgraceful scenes of perversion and bestiality are perpetrated behind my eyelids. In the past week alone, I counted six rapes, one of them involving a woman old enough to be my mother (indeed, I thought at the time it *was* my mother), and four sadistic orgies, during which appalling liberties were taken with members of the Royal family.

Things have come to a pretty pass when a law-abiding citizen cannot drop off for a few minutes without being forced to witness such edifying spectacles as last night's episode, in which a senior Palace official was seen ravishing the elderly lady I mentioned before—and wearing my old school blazer to do it. I presume that this is what our hippie students would call 'social comment'. It looked to me more like the work of a three-year-old sex maniac.

It is imperative that official action should be taken to curb these exhibitions of smut. Could the government not consider imposing—at least for a trial period—a three-night sleeping week?

Yours sincerely,

'TREAD SOFTLY')

What is the future of erotic art? It lies, I believe, not in easel painting at all, but in full-length animated cartoons that show human beings in sexually provocative situations. Because Disney concentrated on exploiting the comic possibilities of clothed animals, and because he failed to make Snow White more than a sugar-coated puppet, it has been taken for granted that his limitations were those of the medium itself. Nothing of the sort: true eroticism, unconfined by the physical inhibitions of live actors, will hit the screen only when artists learn to make figurative drawings (and paintings) move on celluloid. The Japanese are already experimenting in this field (witness the voluptuous cartoons of Osamu Tesuka and Eiichi Yamamoto). It's time that Western animators shook off the Disney mantle and, drawing on the rich heritage of European decadence, evolved a tradition of their own.

Section Five

The Fiesta Route

Our subject isn't arts festivals, or trade fairs, or charity galas or sporting events. We are talking about fiestas, by which I mean explosions of communal gaiety that recur on prescribed dates in specific places for locally significant reasons.

Somewhere in Europe, on almost every day of the year, a village or a city or a whole district is embarking on a phase of riot. For a spell, people will wear unaccustomed and fanciful dress, and find themselves dancing in the streets, greeting strangers as friends and everyone as equals. The cycle of work-sleep-work is temporarily suspended; play takes over from work and annihilates sleep. The spasm is usually annual. It may last a day, a week, or even — in certain stalwart regions — a month or more. Sometimes it is tied to the Christian calendar, sometimes it is a pagan festival. (Often it is a combination of both. Over the centuries, the Church has showed itself extremely adroit at annexing pagan celebrations and claiming them for Christianity.) Whatever its roots, the yearly flower is a period of licensed uproar, of officially sanctioned whoopee.

Some fiestas are commercialized tourist-traps, which needn't mean that they aren't exciting. Others are simple and unspoiled, which needn't mean that they aren't dull. What follows is a consumer report on four of the major European jamborees — *Fasching* in the Rhineland and Munich, Midsummer Eve in Sweden, and the great Spanish ferias of Sevilla and Pamplona. The order of events is chronological, and the point of view personal.

Fasching

This is the pre-Lenten carnival season that rampages through south-west Germany from New Year's Eve to Shrove Tuesday — a matter of two months or so, mounting to a climax in the final week, when there are half a dozen enormous costume balls every night in the big *Fasching* centres: Cologne, Mainz and Munich. Rumour has it that adulteries committed during this period cannot be used as evidence in German divorces. As as often, rumour has it wrong; but it's easy to see how the idea got about. The atmosphere is distinctly orgiastic, and when Germans go in for orgies, they do so with dedicated zeal, barring few holds. People really do rush up to you in broad daylight and kiss you smack on the lips. This can be a messy experience if you are a lovely-looking fellow and often accosted, because the girls will probably be wearing clown make-up, Masai war-paint or gigantic blobs of false freckle. Nothing as prosaic as work is allowed to interrupt the revelry. In Cologne I went into a jewellery store to look at some watches. The place was deserted, or so I thought until a hand crept up from behind the counter and deposited an empty champagne glass under my nose. Peering over, I saw at least three members of the staff locked together in horizontal enjoyment.

I didn't go to Mainz. They tell me that the carnival in Mainz is highly intellectual, bristling with subtle cabaret wit: if so, it differs wildly from what happens in Cologne. Carnival there is folkloric, robustly medieval, full of local patriotism, and above all *massive*. It's as if two thousand conventions were being held simultaneously in the same place. About a million people turn out on Rose Monday (Lent minus two) to watch the procession of bands, *papier-mâché* giants and expensively decorated floats, from which 40,000 mini-bottles of *eau de Cologne* are tossed into the crowd. The final float carries a traditional trio in antique attire—the Prince, the Peasant and the Virgin. All three are impersonated by middle-aged men, elected by the business community. It costs them a lot of time and money to assume these roles for a couple of months, in the course of which they are expected to give and attend a great many parties; but it seems that the publicity justifies the outlay. When I was there, the Virgin (symbolizing the unconquerable spirit of Cologne) was played by the Vice-President of an insurance company in flaxen pigtails.

In fact, the tradition is not very old. The tourist officials explain that the festival derives from pagan times, when ships were sent floating down the Rhine from Cologne to celebrate the annual rebirth of the goddess of fertility; but they admit, if pressed, that the carnival in its present form dates back no further than the early nineteenth century, when Napoleon withdrew his occupying army from Cologne and left behind him a city disposed to rejoice. The festival committee, first convened in 1823, laid down the rules for the fiesta we see today.

It is rough and gross, and not even a cloud-burst can damp it. The soaring black bulk of the cathedral, scarred with war-time shrapnel, reminds you that this is Catholic territory, where sensual indulgence must be followed by penitential fasting. While it lasts, however, the indulgence is extreme. I arrived a week before Shrove Tuesday. Already the bars and beer-gardens were full from 10 a.m. onward, their tables jammed with family groups, swaying from side to side and chorally singing. Typical song-titles: 'Kiss me for three days but never ask my name', and 'Who in hell has enough money to pay for all this?' Favourite disguises for both sexes: convict, sailor, circus clown and hula-dancer. Outside (in the rain) an officially appointed comic in a three-cornered hat gets off anti-officialdom gags to a drenched but receptive mob. The irreverence of his act is proudly stressed by my eager young guide. 'In Cologne,' he says, 'we mock everything. We were never militarists.' As he speaks, a military band goes by. Catching a look of scepticism in my eye, he continues, 'You must remember that German oom-pah music is part of American jazz. Bix Beiderbecke came from German immigrant stock—you can hear it in his playing. I am making a joke, of course, but would it not be possible to say that white Dixieland music came down the Rhine from Cologne?'

The rule at night is to shun nightclubs. Squalid even when crowded, they are smoke-filled deserted bunkers during the last weekend of carnival. The correct procedure for tourists is easily defined. After checking in at your hotel (the Excelsior for long-established opulence, the Eden or the Mondial for modernity), you buy tickets from the concierge for the best of the evening's balls. You then go up to your room and change: jeans and a tropical T-shirt will do for either sex—though the less you can wear, the closer you are to the carnival wavelength. Cat-suits and grass skirts are perfectly acceptable, even for males, and Tarzan and Jane make an ideal twosome. Dining *en déshabille* comes next. You can choose between the Hanse-Stube (superb for venison), the Bastei (a saucer-shaped place with 1930s decor, jutting out on stilts over the Rhine) and the Wiesel, where I found the best food in the city. Just across the road from the cathedral, the Wiesel is a sumptuous room with a black doorman who wears one golden earring. He is conceivably the most *avant-garde* sight in Cologne.

Having eaten, you ball-hop—preferably by taxi, and taking care not to start before 10 p.m. By then every dance-hall in town is thronged and throbbing. At the Rock 'n' Roll Ball, the crowd is young, brash and sardine-packed; at the Artists' Ball, the music is cooler and the girls are more imaginatively undressed—I notice Victorian corsets and 1920s bathing-suits. 'Western European people', shouts my guide, swinging past me with a girl disguised as a chained cheetah, 'are basically very much aware of their limited time on earth. Don't you think I am right?' I move on to the Gürzenich, the city's most ancient palace of festivities, where six bands are playing in six rooms for the pleasure of several thousand dancers. Many of the girls are skimpily clad, and what makes them particularly appealing is that they look naked rather than nude. Nobody is drunk, partly because of all the leaping about, and partly because you can't buy anything more potent than beer by the bottle and wine by the glass. The action tapers off around dawn. To get full value, it's wise to come in a party of four or more, of whom at least one speaks German.

On the Saturday before Shrove Tuesday, I recommend travelling to Munich, where the tone is more elegant and worldly, as befits a southern, quasi-Mediterranean city. Take the Trans-European express from Cologne: for six and a half hours, you slide smoothly up the Rhine valley as if on the gentlest of ski-lifts. The restaurant car feeds you well, and the view from the observation dome is gorgeous. The trip bridges the gap between the regional gusto of Cologne and the less parochial sophistication of Munich.

Fasching in Munich is a playground for individualists. This is the Latin quarter of Germany, with a colony of artists whose taste is reflected in the bizarre and inventive frolics of the carnival season. It's a point of honour to design your own costume. I can sum up the ambience in a single image. A fiftyish man enters a cigar-store at high noon, wearing magenta leotards and a Viking helmet. On top of the helmet is a tiny model of an opera house, with clockwork ballerinas twirling on the stage; and on top of the opera house an electrically operated sputnik revolves, emitting a beeping sound and alternate flashes of red and green light. The shopkeeper sells the man a packet of cigarettes without raising an eyebrow.

The Vier Jahreszeiten is the smartest hotel, but I wouldn't advise you to stay there. For reasons of snobbism, they won't let you into the restaurant in fancy dress—which, considering that fancy dress is indispensable for *Fasching*, is an absurdly inconvenient taboo. The Bayerischer Hof (grand and glossy) is more tolerant, and therefore to be preferred. But wherever you stay, don't expect impeccable service: the staff are hung-over too.

The gaiety is far more varied and outlandish than in Cologne. The art students spread themselves at the Jungle Ball, where you shuffle and sweat amid décor that ranges from mock-Rubens to Op and Pop. In every corner there's a wriggling pile-up of close friends in togas, leopard-skin bikinis and fishnet stockings. The hunting, shooting and beer-swigging aspect of Teutonic fun is represented by the Ball of the Foolish Knights, for which everyone dresses up like something out of *Alexander Nevsky*, with mops for wigs and chamber-pots for helmets. It was here that I met a former Carnival Prince (Munich has neither Peasant nor Virgin) who told me that his term of office had cost him more than £4,000. 'But I was lucky,' he said. 'I was subsidized jointly by a tape-recorder company and a firm of champagne exporters.' For sheer visual exuberance, the best of the balls are those held in the Deutsches Theater. For two months before Lent, plays are banished from the auditorium, which is transformed into a glowing cavern of silver and gold, of pendent gondolas and harvest moons. The seats are ripped out of the orchestra stalls, making way for a dance-floor alive with feathers, flowers, yashmaks, burnouses, Kabuki masks and Mephistophelean horns.

Sunday (Lent minus three) is the day of the big parade, which is two miles long and makes up in quantity for what it lacks in fantasy. Have an early lunch at Humplmayer's restaurant, and then push your way on to the pavement to watch the procession. Cannons filled with confetti are fired at the crowd; last year, one of them was aimed by a girl wearing nothing but a Prussian helmet and frayed cami-knickers. There are cowboy floats, pirate floats, pop-music floats, anti-nuclear floats and frankly commercial floats, interspersed with striding bands and gyrating drum-majorettes. I froze for a moment when a smiling child marched into view holding a sign that read 'The Dachau Boys' Orchestra'; but the war had ended before he was born, and Dachau — a dormitory suburb just outside Munich — is a word that carries few emotive connotations for Germans under twenty.

On Monday all traffic is banned from the central streets and squares, and dance music is piped in from loudspeakers attached to every lamp-post. Weather permitting, the whole of Munich is out of doors. This is the night when nobody sleeps, and you stumble into the Café Donisl at dawn to look for the people you started out with. Here you fortify yourself with sausages and beer for the last day of orgy before the Lenten clamp-down. Emerging into the streets, I am startled by fireworks and pelted with bucketfuls of confetti. A man reclining on the brink of a sixth-floor balcony points a trumpet at the sky and plays 'Summertime'. Below on the pavement, a recumbent tot, aged about two, sips at a discarded bottle of champagne. At the Hofbräuhaus — the largest pub in the world — I am bought a drink by an Austrian dressed as an Arab and carrying a pair of skis.

To escape from the tumult, I hail a cab and ask to be taken to Dachau, where the concentration camp is preserved by international subscription as a monument to the dead and a reminder to the living. The driver is reluctant. 'Today is Crazy Day', he says, 'and everybody is fooling around in the streets. I expect Dachau will be closed.' He also claims not to know the way. When at length we reach the camp, it is open, but deserted. After spending an hour in this haunted place, I am in no mood for further junketing, and we drive on to the airport, stopping off at the hotel to pick up my baggage.

Fasching in Munich is a marvellously elating experience, but Lent begins at Dachau.

The Sevilla Feria

A Spanish city in the grip of penitential ardour is an extremely gaudy sight, and tourists arriving in Sevilla during holy week — when towering, gem-encrusted statues of the Virgin are borne glittering through the streets — often get the mistaken impression that this is the Feria. In fact, there is no connexion

between the two events, which are under quite separate manage-
ments—respectively, God and Mammon. Only when the
saviour is safely risen does Sevilla prepare for its secular eruption. The Feria (which lasts for seven days) officially starts on
April 18th, but if the opening date falls close to—or during—
the moveable feast of Easter, the whole affair is postponed
until the following week. The Spanish feel that a decent interval
should elapse between spiritual and sensual incontinence.

As fiestas go, the Sevilla Feria is not particularly ancient:
it was inaugurated in 1847. It began as a fair to which Andalusian ranchers brought their horse-flesh for sale or barter, and
although it is no longer a market-place, it remains in spirit
intensely local and exclusively Spanish. Foreigners tend to
feel outsiders, unless they are rich, famous or aristocratic. In
1966 the featured guests were Jacqueline Kennedy and Princess
Grace of Monaco, each trying to outsmile the other at every
bullfight and charity ball. Astride high-stepping Spanish
horses and clad in Andalusian riding kit (Cordoban sombrero,
short velvet jacket and intricately embroidered chaps), both
girls made daily appearances in the park of San Sebastian,
which is the heartland of the Feria. It's a large rectangular
field, occupied during the Feria week by row upon row of
candy-striped, cheek-by-jowl canvas huts, known as *casetas*.
Some are open to the public, but the great majority are private,
owned by wealthy Spaniards or run by Sevillian clubs. It's
in the private *casetas* that the best food and wine are served, and
the best *flamenco* parties take place. Unless somebody up there
likes you (enough to ask you in), your quest for gaiety is likely
to be confined to hot-dog stands, street bars, sordid and minus-
cule dance-halls, and the rackety attractions of the adjoining
fairground. Not to put too fine a point on it, the Feria of
Sevilla is snobbish.

The poshest hotel is the Alfonso XIII, Victorian and very
formal. 'Staying there', said a recent guest, 'is like turning up
for a coronation fifty years late.' The graceful eighteenth-
century building next door, now a centre for higher education,
was formerly the tobacco factory where Carmen rolled cigars.
Opposite the Alfonso XIII is the Reina Cristina, number two
in the social rating: it overlooks the Guadalquivir river, where
top people moor their yachts during Feria week. My advice
is to ignore the pecking order and go for the only hotel in

Sevilla that is modern and air-conditioned: the Luz-Palacio, on the other side of town.

A typical Feria day has a strictly predestined shape. Between 1 p.m. and 4 p.m. you patrol the park of San Sebastian, preferably riding but at least in a horse-drawn carriage. You are jostled by the pride of Andalusian cavalry—hundreds of gleaming horses with impassively arrogant riders. Inside the *casetas* the children dance, whirling like tiny dodgem cars in frills and miraculously failing to collide. Even babes in arms wear *flamenco* dresses, with flowers Sellotaped to their hairless skulls. If a rich Sevillian chum calls you over for a drink ask for a glass of San Patricio—the most delicate of sherries—and make sure that you haven't committed the supreme sartorial gaffe of wearing a Cordoban hat *and* a necktie. (One or the other is fine: both together are not.) Lacking local friends, you might as well stay in bed. Orson Welles, an adopted *Sevillano* of thirty-five years' standing, explains the midday ceremonial as follows: 'Sevilla is the Christmas of Spain—and who wants strangers at Christmas? It's a tremendously bourgeois Feria. The *casetas* are like shop-windows where you show off your marriageable daughters.'

Fasching is a carnival with plenty of room for intruders from other nations: Sevilla is emphatically not. Welles continues, 'This is the kind of Feria that a hundred rich foreigners can ruin. Already a lot of the best Spaniards have stopped coming. There's talk of moving the Feria next year to a larger park, to accommodate the tourists. That would kill it altogether.'

Lunch is taken between 4 p.m. and 5.30 p.m. The favoured spots are La Riviera (where the speciality is Chop de Ávila—a medallion of baby lamb wrapped in bacon) and the Bodegon Torre de Oro, a noisy, oak-beamed tavern which I commend for its low prices, its chicken fried with garlic (*pollo al ajillo*) and its nearness to the bullring. While eating, you can bet on the results of the afternoon's bullfight. The principle is simple. Six bulls are to be killed, which means that the total number of trophies awarded to the matadors can range from no ears to twelve. Everyone at the lunch table picks a different number and stakes a hundred pesetas (or more, if it's an affluent group) on his choice. After the fight, the winner scoops the pool. If nobody wins, the stake money is carried over to the next afternoon. When I invented this gambling method several years ago, my *aficionado* friends shuddered at the blasphemy of it; but you'd be surprised how useful it can be in sustaining one's flagging interest in an otherwise flaccid *corrida*.

Sevilla holds bullfights daily during the Feria. The audience is the best informed in Spain, living as it does in the region that traditionally produces the best toreros and the best bulls. (If you can arrange an introduction to a breeder, it's uniquely thrilling to travel out of Sevilla and spend a day on the range, just surveying a herd of great black beauties. The noblest and fiercest belong to the ranch of Isaias and Tulio Vazquez, who raise animals so powerful that they are hardly ever fought: they offer a challenge to which star matadors no longer care to be exposed. Appreciative of art and effort, intolerant only of apathy and incompetence, the Sevilla crowd is unswervingly fair. Unfortunately, the April *corridas* are seldom worthy of its intelligence. The top matadors dutifully appear, but they have already signed contracts for the more important May Feria in Madrid, and are therefore inclined to take as few risks as possible.

After the bulls, you drink in the bar of the Hotel Colón, where the bullfighters stay. (Alternative oases: Los Corales and La Traga for loud local colour, and the Alfonso XIII for social mountaineering.) If stirred by the *corrida*, you may plan for the next day a respectful trip to the cemetery of San Fernando, on the outskirts of Sevilla, where Joselito and Belmonte—the golden pair of a golden age—are buried, together with many other toreros of note. When you go out to dine, you could do worse than head for the Casa Senra, a rowdy little bistro near the church that houses the Virgin of the Macarena, patron saint of all bullfighters. The red mullet is beautifully cooked, and you may find a matador sharing your table, along with his mink-coated mistress. Custom then dictates that you return to the Feria—canopied by now with avenues of lanterns that make a blaze in the sky. Having toured the *casetas*, you should wander out into the narrow, crepuscular streets of the Barrio Santa Cruz. Here you will probably wind up in a costly but authentic *flamenco* joint called Los Gallos. The smoke is dense and there's a persistent noise of clashing glasses at the bar, but away at the end of the room a stolid middle-aged man, seated on a chair, will be singing his blue-serge heart out.

In Arab countries, the *muezzin* calls the faithful to prayer; this *muezzin* bewails infidelity, and calls the faithless one to dance. Which she does, her body arched and imperious as the neck of a swan. In what he sings there is great emotion, but never a hint of comedy. Alone among popular art forms, *flamenco* is totally dedicated to tragedy.

Those who are immensely rich or immensely Spanish are best equipped to enjoy the Feria of Sevilla. For the rest of us, it is—on balance—dispensable. As far as sexual recreation is concerned, I should perhaps add that this clannish horse-fair is held in a city where, until quite recently, ballroom dancing was considered a sin.

Midsummer Eve in Sweden

Real pagan stuff at last. What the Swedes enact on June 23rd is a genuine fertility rite, older than any written records. Long before I visited Sweden for the first time, I had built up a composite portrait of the average Swede. He was withdrawn and spasmodic, reserved on the surface but explosive beneath it, veering between troughs of depression and fits of abandon. He was a pacifist, a Socialist, an alcoholic and a hiker. He swam nude and tended to commit suicide during the long winters. Like many other popular preconceptions (e.g. that the French are greedy and the Spanish stoical), this turned out to be fairly close to the truth.

I had another mental picture—just as detailed but rather more romantic—of the Midsummer Eve celebrations. It was vaguely based on movies like Ingmar Bergman's *Smiles of a Summer Night*, and plays like Strindberg's *Miss Julie*, in which the aristocratic heroine, giddy with midsummer madness, dives into bed with her father's valet. My image of June 24th centred on a sort of peasant orgy, set in the grounds of a baronial house. On all sides, huge bonfires were flaming, around which troops of naked virgins cavorted, menstruating freely. If you ever had a similar image, erase it at once. Times have changed, and what happens in Sweden on Midsummer Eve has less in common with *Miss Julie* than it has with *The Wild One*.

To see the merrymaking at its most typical (as the Swedish tourist people put it), you must go to the province of Dalarna in central Sweden. It's a place of great lakes and low hills, covered with forests of spruce and pine, and dotted with wooden homesteads, nearly all of which are painted the colour of congealed ox-blood. In every back yard there's a white flag-pole, from which the national banner flies on feast days. The focal point of festivity is the village of Leksand, 170 miles to the north-west of Stockholm. (Whatever you do, don't linger in Stockholm: during the summer months it's a ghost city, with no theatre and no night-life. It's also wickedly expensive.)

Leksand is a dainty little riverside community with a popu-lation of 2,000, an onion-dome church dating back to the thirteenth century and a superb ice-hockey team. It has about 1,500 beds available for the flood of tourists—estimated at 40,000—who converge to take part in the midsummer jollity. Either book well in advance or bring a tent. The principal hotels (i.e. boarding-houses with gardens) are the Tre Kullor and the Furuliden. My vote goes to the latter, which is managed by a pair of fastidious and mutually affectionate males. They care about simple food, well prepared, and their smorgasbord is just what it should be—the culinary equivalent of democracy in action, presenting a choice of two dozen dishes that range from haughty smoked salmon to humble (but home-made) meat-loaf.

I took the train from Stockholm and arrived in Leksand the day before Midsummer Eve. The place was alive with mosquitoes and little else. It looked fatally suburban, like an Englishman's idea of Canada, and I wasn't surprised to find a Salvation Army band playing at a street corner. I drove out to a nearby hamlet where a warming-up dance was being held on a hill-top. A pop group was singing, and there, swivelling in sweaters and ski-pants, were the sulky blonde girls I had expected to see—the darling daughters of affluent farming folk. Many of them speak English, which renders them helpfully vulnerable to Anglo-Saxon predators. Their horizon is utterly parochial. 'Were you born in this district?' I asked a girl in scarlet jeans. 'Oh, no!' she said. 'My parents didn't move here until I was eight. I was born nearly seven miles away.' She spoke as if that made her practically Polynesian.

Next day nothing happens in the morning, apart from a few marriages and christenings—the Swedes like to have the sexual highlights of their lives solemnized at Midsummer. I set out to explore the village, stopping now and then to buy a warm Coca-Cola: the mighty thrust of refrigeration has not yet penetrated throughout Leksand. Sweden, of course, is a dry country, where beer and wine can be publicly consumed only in restaurants, and hard liquor (outside hotel bars in the major cities) not at all.

Around noon, the invasion began. Cars of all sizes started to roll into town, their bonnets adorned with traditional sprigs of birch. Many of the drivers were young and visibly sloshed. Brandishing bottles of Scotch as bait, they enlisted recruits from the squads of hitch-hiking girls who had suddenly materialized on the pavements. Transistors brayed through the streets; motorcycles roared in; and I had a powerful sense of impending mayhem. (Not without cause—during a recent midsummer outburst at Leksand, a policeman was killed.) Two notes on Swedish teenagers: if male, they resemble queer Germans, smile anxiously and seldom laugh. If female, they laugh quite a lot, which causes the males to smile even more anxiously.

By mid-afternoon, the temperature was in the low seventies, which is about as high as it gets in this part of Sweden. Already people were moving in a steady trickle towards the *Sammilsdal*—a deep amphitheatre of grass near the river—in the middle of which lay an outsize maypole, at least eighty feet in length. By 8 p.m., the sun had almost stopped setting (this is the whitest of Sweden's white nights), and the mob in the enormous dale numbered approximately 20,000. Two ancient long-boats, propelled by eighteen oarsmen apiece, now pulled up at the river-bank, piled high with garlands of birch-leaves and wreaths of daisies. These were carried in procession through the crowd, with an escort of fiddlers in peasant costume, and gravely fastened to the recumbent totem of fertility.

A priest addressed the multitude through a mike, urging us to pray for a good harvest. He described the pole as a symbol of national liberty. Though we listened politely, I think many of us recognized his speech for what it was—another Christian take-over bid for a controlling interest in a pagan ritual. (Example of an earlier and more successful bid: Christmas.) What was happening in the great bowl of greensward was a ceremony of tree-worship. Despite the planes that towed advertising signs overhead, submerged memories of gods far older than the Christian one were stirring in our veins.

The fiddlers played and a choir sang folk-songs during the

weary, hour-long process of raising the maypole by means of wooden props until it was fully erect. Each tremendous heave was urged on by a unified shout — 'Aaaahhh — *huh!*' — from the assembled votaries. When at last the totem, leafily bedecked, reached the upright position, I could not help thinking of the scene in D. H. Lawrence's novel where Lady Chatterley adorns the gamekeeper's prick with flowers. The Leksand bard — a stout and bespectacled middle-aged man — then declaimed an ode to international friendship. It exuded good liberal sentiments, but this was an occasion that needed the passion of an Allen Ginsberg.* When the poet had finished, the people nearest the maypole held hands, and began — a few of them at first — to trot around it. Soon others joined in, and before long 20,000 temporary heathens were whirling in a vast, expanding spiral of jubilation. It looked like the fulfilment of Busby Berkeley's wildest choreographic dream.

At 11 p.m., the light was still milky, and you could photograph wild life on the glassy expanse of Lake Siljan. Knut Hamsun, the Norwegian novelist, has an apt description of what happened next: 'The sun barely dips his face into the water, and then comes up again, red, refreshed, as if he had been down to drink.' For a while, just before and after midnight, the forests grew darker. At 2 a.m., a pink halo appeared through the mist, and bird-song began to be heard. (I must here append my explanation of the dawn chorus, which is that birds are fools with absurdly short memories. Because they can't remember what happened yesterday, dawn always takes them by surprise. 'What the hell is that?' they pipe in panic. 'Look at the white light. Something crazy going on up there. Stay home and take cover.' They aren't greeting King Sol, they are merely spreading alarmist gossip.) Soon after 2.30 a.m., the sun rose at breakneck speed, and golden lances went shooting across the lakes and woods.

Midsummer in Sweden is a fiesta with prehistoric roots and plenty of opportunities for modern frolicking. Its major drawbacks are that it takes place an awfully long way off and lasts for only one night. Unless, of course, you choose to spend a whole summer boating, swimming, fishing and painting in the neighbourhood of Leksand: which might not be such a bad idea.

* Or perhaps — just as appropriately — Allen Ginsberg's father, himself a poet, who once observed to me: 'Two pints make one cavort.'

The Feria of San Fermin in Pamplona

It begins at 7 a.m. on the seventh morning of the seventh month, and it goes on for seven days. A little history—and slightly less geography—before we plunge into the annual tumult. Famous as the setting of Hemingway's *The Sun Also Rises*, Pamplona is the capital of Navarre, a province of northern Spain. It is also the background of Shakespeare's *Love's Labour's Lost*, the hero of which is Ferdinand, king of Navarre. Taurine festivals have been a regional speciality since the thirteenth century, and conservative guessers reckon that the *encierro*—the running of bulls through the streets—is at least three hundred years old. San Fermin, after whom the fiesta is named, was the Christian son of a Roman consul who served in Navarre; but there was a Feria in Pamplona long before there was a saint to dignify it.

The city lies in the foothills of the Pyrenees, fifty-five miles inland from the yellow sands of San Sebastian. It has 110,000 inhabitants, whose number is more than quintupled during this running, jumping and falling-down Feria. In the entire province there are fewer than 2,000 hotel beds, so it's essential to book a year ahead. The Tres Reyes, spacious and new, is the most comfortable place to stay. Traditionalists go for the Perla, which is older but much noisier, since it overlooks the central square; and many of the matadors favour the Yoldi. Ask for full *pension* when writing for a room, because otherwise you won't get one. On arrival, however, explain that you've changed your mind and would rather eat out. (In the chaotic swirl of the Feria, you won't want to check in for meals.) If the manager objects, remind him that it's illegal in Spain for a hotel-keeper to insist on full *pension* rates, and threaten to report him to the Ministry of Tourism. He will always cave in. Another sneaky tip: although the *concierge* can get you tickets for the bullfights, he will add a 50 per cent mark-up. It's more sensible to write direct—and many months in advance—to the Santa Casa de Misericordia of Pamplona, the charitable organization that runs the Feria. There's no other way to avoid being brutally overcharged.

'Prudencia' beseeches a road-sign just outside the city. It's a vain plea in Feria time, when everyone in sight is committed to a week-long binge of total imprudence. Sleep is indefinitely postponed as hordes of dancing people pursue a dozen marching bands through the streets. This is the most democratic of fiestas, and also the most inordinate. Every year more tourists get drunker, and the place moves closer to riot. Here's a dawn-to-dusk account of a Pamplonican day, as lived through by me in the summer of 1966:

6 a.m. Wake up to attend *encierro*, remembering to leave no valuables lying about room. This is the time when everyone knows you're out. Streets grey, but already full of people, scurrying towards the wooden palisades that keep the bulls on course as they run from the corrals outside the city wall to the bullring at the centre. Stop off at café for reviving cup of coffee and *anis*. Shoving through the mob near the approach to the bullring, I observe a big change since my last trip to Pamplona, four years ago: there are now *two* rows of barricades between the spectators and the dare-devils sprinting in front of the bulls. The onlookers' view is blocked by lines of cops and photo-graphers, and everyone battles for a vantage-point. 'This', sighs a fellow-struggler, 'is the worst of Fascism combined with the worst of democracy.' A public-address system (another novelty) blares out folksy music and snippets from the tourist handbook.

7 a.m. A rocket is fired, and six bulls start their three-minute canter to the bullring, escorted by steers and preceded by thousands of runners. The whole spectacle goes by in a flash, virtually unseen. In the old, single-barricade days, non-running cowards like myself could at least get close to the bulls: nowa-days, all we see are the rear views of policemen and photo-graphers taking shots that will attract other tourists, who in turn will be prevented from seeing the *encierro* by other photo-graphers and other policemen. (Note: for runners who start out well ahead and aren't incapably drunk, the *encierro* is as safe as crossing the road. But a slip can be perilous: in 1966 a 75-year-old native of Pamplona was severely injured, and mortal gorings are not infrequent.) Dashing into the bullring—every seat of which is packed—I watch the arena filling like an hour-glass as the runners pelt in through the main gate. The bulls follow them, scampering across the ring and out through another door to the corrals beyond. Afterwards, a couple of calves with padded horns are let in for the crowd to play with. They are soon brought to their knees by sheer weight of numbers: it isn't an edifying sight. There are too many people here. In some ways the Feria is tamer than it used to be; in others, more barbarous.

9 a.m. Breakfast in the main square, the Plaza del Castillo. It is lined with cafés, of which only two are socially acceptable – the Choko (for artists, hippies and *aficionados*) and the Perla (for the same groups plus Darryl Zanuck, who hasn't missed a Pamplona since he produced the movie of *The Sun Also Rises*). At this hour, the *ambiente* is predominantly male – which is true of the Feria as a whole. Only in recent years have girls been allowed to dance in the streets, and they're still forbidden to run with the bulls. American tourists who have survived the *encierro* toast each other with a glow of wartime solidarity. ('You guys see me this morning? I ran like a *mother*!') At the next table, I hear a description of a pretentious loudmouth who suffers from Spanish stomach: 'He doesn't run with the bulls – he bulls with the runs.' A mixed foursome is ideal for a visit to Pamplona: the men can suffer through the *encierro* while the girls sleep in.

9.30–11.00 a.m. The traditional siesta. Ear-plugs and thick blinds are desirable, since bands are still parading the streets and the sun tends to glare. Alternative activity: skip the *encierro* and drive out to lunch at the Pantano de Yesa, a huge, man-made lake thirty miles to the east, where you can swim, water-ski and bask in escapist solitude. This is the perfect antidote to Pamplona. The place to eat is the Club Náutico.

12 noon. Beginning of the daily Bloody-Mary party held by the hard core of Anglo-Saxon Pamplona addicts in the sleazy *pension* they take over every year. (I'll conceal its name, but it's on the Calle San Nicolas, which is known to initiates as Death Alley.) The hard core consists mostly of vagabond Britons and American exiles. Among its members are novelists, poets, teachers, artists, male models, female models, jazz singers, journalists and assorted junkies. They have two things in common: their average age is over thirty, and they rarely meet outside Pamplona. Each has a special Feria nickname – e.g. Mickey the Loser, Nutty Ed and Dirty Old Man – and they wear 'I'm Doing All I Can For Regis Toomey' buttons. Although they drink hard, they are astonishingly brave, and it is their habit to refer to the *encierro* as 'the milk-run'. Sample of hard-core conversation: 'I am the most *tranquilo* cat,' says a bearded writer with his nose pouring blood. (He's a pacifist, and has scars on his knuckles to prove it.) Another sample: 'I had my *barmitzvah* in Pamplona. That means I have *chutzpah*.'

And you know what *chutzpah* means? It means I have seventeen-minute ejaculations.' The speaker pulls up his shirt, revealing a chest like a rug. 'How's that for a hairy man? *Hair is blood!* Did you know that?' A third excerpt: 'Mickey the Loser just went blind for three hours. He shacked up with this Danish doll in the Pamplona football stadium. She gave him crabs in his eyelashes, so he poured the lotion into his eyes.' Finally, overheard in the hotel corridor:

NUTTY ED (*outside the loo*): Dirty Old Man, what are you doing in there?

DIRTY OLD MAN (*a sorrowful George Sanders voice from within*): I'm deceiving myself.

NUTTY ED: What is that—some esoteric term for jerking off?

Administered to groups, alcohol notoriously cements male unity. Pamplona is an alcoholic Feria.

3.00–5.00 p.m. Lunch, eaten in a rising hubbub. Wherever you slice it, the cuisine is crudely provincial. There's little to choose between La Maitena, Las Pocholas and Marceliano's (which was Hemingway's haunt), and beyond these three, there's little worth eating.

5.30 p.m. Bullfight time. 13,000 people fill the ring. Next year, when plans for expansion have been carried out, it will seat 4,000 more. Eleven bands—each waving its special banner—play simultaneously throughout the *corrida*. The din is overpowering: this is acoustical rape. Priests crowd to the top of a nearby church tower to get a free view.

What they (and the paying customers) see is unlikely to be a true bullfight. North of Madrid, the fighting of serious, fully-grown bulls has virtually ceased. Another spectacle has usurped its name—the cynical assassination of juvenile bulls, so hastily fattened up to make the official minimum weight that they fall down at every step. The 1966 *corridas* in Pamplona were the most corrupt and disgraceful in memory. Even Antonio Ordoñez, the greatest of living matadors, was bitterly disappointing—so much so that I hired a plane to write in the sky, just before his final appearance in the Feria, four simple words: 'Ordoñez is a fink.' I was even willing to pay extra for the wiggle over the 'n', but at the last moment the pilot (a former Luftwaffe ace) copped out.

A footnote on bullfight behaviour: during a thunderstorm so violent that everyone—including the toreros—rushes for shelter,

Zanuck does not budge from his front-row seat. He sits there coatless for thirty minutes, alone in the downpour. Yet throughout it all, his cigar remains alight. Moral: God does not rain on Darryl Zanuck.

8 p.m.–10.30 p.m. Cocktails at the Hotel Yoldi, followed by dinner (same restricted choice as for lunch), followed by fireworks of middling extravagance in the Plaza del Castillo. The city by now is thronged and full of liquor. Half a dozen Pamplonican boys, posing as customs officials, successfully halt and search all cars entering the square. Orson Welles rolls into the Choko bar and gives me a lecture on the racial origins of Pamplona: 'These people are Basques, and the Basques are the aborigines of Europe. No one knows where they came from. They invented whaling, but they have no word in their dialect for the wheel. They are unique.'

10.30 p.m. onward. Apart from a dance-hall called 'El Night-Club', there are no nightclubs. Nor is there a brothel. Between spells indoors, I join the leaping, untiring, ecstatic mob in the open air. Two members of the hard-core set drag me off to a repulsive alley which they describe as 'the Street of Broken Taverns'. It contains the cheapest, filthiest, most turbulent bars in Pamplona. In one of them, they improvise a dialogue between an interviewer and a wounded bullfighter:

Q. What did you do this morning, matador?

A. I started on a five-year plan to stop hurting.

Q. How did you feel when you fought Miura bulls for the first time?

A. (expressive shrug) Bleeding is bleeding ...

Outside, the streets are clamorous with music. Behind every band there's a prancing multitude of boys, each bearing a lighted candle. At sunrise, the last candle is blown out, and the Feria is over. Other fiestas may be more inventive or sophisticated, more folkloric or lyrical, but for me the convulsion that shakes Pamplona is the archetype, still the peak of them all.

Beyond Freedom and Dignity
and Running Hot Water

The Omar Khayyam Hotel in Cairo, after a short stay in which I am now convalescent, is a converted palace that was built to house the Empress Eugénie when she visited Egypt in 1869 for the opening of the Suez Canal. Whether it has in fact been converted into a *hotel* is the subject I want to discuss. It certainly looks as a hotel ought to look—i.e. like a palace built to house the Empress Eugénie in 1869. It has numbers on the doors and a reception desk and a rapacious concierge and it charges (a great deal) for the use of its rooms. But it does not, as I shall soon demonstrate, *behave* like a hotel. My own theory, based on deduction and hunch, is that since being nationalized by the government of the United Arab Republic, it has been converted from a converted palace into a rehabilitation centre for backsliders who still yearn for a privileged way of life—a sort of crazy house for unreformed bourgeois sympathizers. It operates, I believe, on the behaviourist principle of aversion therapy. 'If this is the splendour you long for,' it implies, 'you must be out of your unreconstructed mind.'

I say 'implies' because the message steals up on you with great subtlety. Nobody clubs you over the head and tells you to go back to work on the High Dam. Let me describe how the process works. My wife and I began our two-day visit by dining in the 'hotel' restaurant. An ashtray no bigger than a man's hand was placed on the table before us. On it were written the words SHEPHEARD'S HOTEL. This, the first hint that all was not well, provoked the first faint tremor of displacement. My wife then ordered pea soup from the table d'hôte. Bright red tomato soup was instantly and enthusiastically poured out for her. The concept of serving the wrong thing with the right efficiency proved to be typical of the 'hotel's' approach to its job. Instead of the advertised *poulet en cocotte*, my wife was proudly given a little grey steak. (*Médaillon de chameau*, perhaps.) When she made an inquiry, she was told there was no more chicken, but it was not explained why the only alternative should be a little grey steak, nor why no warning had been given of the change.

Meanwhile I had looked at the wine list and been enraptured. Among its clarets were an Haut Brion '45, a Lafite '42 and a Mouton-Rothschild '49, all at less than the equivalent of £3 a bottle: dirt cheap by English standards. Salivating at the prospect of such a bargain, I ordered the Haut Brion. Fifteen minutes later the waiter told me there was none left. A pity, I felt; but no matter; the Lafite—of a year with which I was unfamiliar—might well be an even more exciting choice. The waiter grinned knowingly and left. Ten minutes later he was back: the Lafite too was finished. It was the work of not much more than half an hour to establish that not one of the 17 clarets on the list still existed in the cellar. Having made this report, the waiter withdrew, but he seemed to have been moved by my dismay, for he soon reappeared with a dusty bottle of Burgundy, labelled 'Volnay-Santenots 1945', which did not figure on the wine list. Would I like to try it? It was ominously ullaged, but its credentials looked very promising, so I said yes.

What followed was a classic example of Khayyam therapy. At the first touch of the corkscrew, before any pressure had been applied, the cork disintegrated completely and crumbled into the wine. The waiter immediately poured the obligatory thimbleful for me to taste through a tea-strainer *which he already had in his pocket*. If you have never tasted cork-sprinkled wine from an Egyptian cellar (or boiler-room, to judge from its condition) served through a tea-strainer, you do not know what it is like to drink warm Ribena mixed with rock salt and ammonia. The experience had, of course, the intended effect of making me wonder why I had ever liked wine. Shaking my head (and, more jovially, my fist), I sent the bottle back. The waiter nodded and said he was sure I would enjoy some proper Egyptian wine more. 'Egyptian wine', he said with the air of a kindly man educating halfwits, 'is *fresh*.' The technique behind this whole episode was flawless. First, the promise of great treats, which are dangled and then removed. Next, the promise of an unscheduled treat, a special privilege. Finally, the revelation

that the special treat is a peculiarly revolting penalty. Hitchcock himself could not have played on one's nerves with more
inventive sadism.

My main dish was an extremely virulent but none the less
palatable curry. I wondered how this could have happened.
Was some saboteur at large in the kitchen, preparing edible
dishes in bold defiance of official policy? I learned the answer
an hour or so later, when my wife and I had gone up to our
room. The lavatory, of which by then I stood in some need,
did not work. The edibility of the curry was no more an accident
than its virulence. No sooner had I realized this than my wife
made two other discoveries. There was no hot water in the
wash-basin, and none in the bath. 'So much for your filthy
revisionist whims!' I imagined the head of the Gyppu (the
Cairo Security Police) sneering as he peered at us through a
spyhole in the fake Gobelin tapestry. The bedroom was vast,
genuinely palatial in aspect and set about with ornate standard
lamps; but shaving, hot baths and the flushing of the toilet
were precluded. I sourly reflected that package tourists from
Uzbekistan (of whom there had been dozens in the restaurant)
would probably be too overwhelmed by the mere sight of
taps to be upset when no hot water emerged—even from the
cold tap, its traditional source in Egypt.

At this point my wife, letting out the little yelp of the dis-
oriented, dashed into the bedroom with a towel. The words
printed on it were SEMIRAMIS HOTEL. Where the hell were
we? And what were *our* names? Controlling my panic, I called
the front desk and extracted a promise that someone would at
least come to mend the loo. An hour and two phone calls
later, a man did indeed arrive. When my wife answered the
door, he gave her a bouquet *of dead flowers*, bowed and departed.
We both agreed that this macabre piece of business showed a
poetic flair that Buñuel, let alone Hitchcock, might have
envied.

We turned in. The double bed, which looked innocuous
enough, proved to have been resourcefully booby-trapped.
Perhaps because its solitary occupant in the old Mameluke
days had been an obese eunuch, it sloped so precipitously towards the middle that one had to hang on to the edge of the
mattress with both hands to avoid rolling on to one's partner
like a runaway boulder. My wife now asked me to turn off the

lights. (I have mentioned that the room was set about with standard lamps.) Since they did not respond to any of the wall-switches by the bed, I hauled myself out to deal with them separately. Now came the touch of sheer genius. *None of them could be switched off.* We have all heard (or had experience) of hotel lights that will not turn *on*. But here was something far more baleful—a permanent blaze, as if at any moment the interrogation were about to begin. It finally became necessary in two cases to remove the plugs from their wall-sockets, in one to unscrew three red-hot bulbs, and in one to actually wrench the wire out of the wainscoting.

That was undoubtedly the Omar Khayyam's masterstroke, although throughout the next day small events took place that kept us on our toes. In response to an order of coffee for two, room service sent us two coffee-cups with a dwarf pot that held slightly less than enough for one. My pleas for a hot bath were answered by a waiter who escorted me 500 yards across the windswept grounds in my dressing-gown to a bungalow-type chalet containing a shower with a trickle of lukewarm water and no soap. When I asked for soap, he vanished altogether. Half an hour passed before I found out that he had delivered the soap to the chalet next door, apparently failing to observe that I was not in it.

As my wife and I lowered ourselves into bed for our second and last night, she pointed out a stump of wire protruding from the ceiling just over our heads, and wondered what it might be, or have been. All I could guess was that on some previous occasion a guest had so far failed to respond to the Khayyam treatment that he had actually *enjoyed* his exposure to the horrors of bourgeois life and showed no disposition to leave. 'Very well,' I pictured the Gyppu man saying on the fourth day. 'The time has come for sterner measures. *Loosen the chandelier in Room 6 …* '

The Judicious Observer will be Disgusted

While not eliminating the personal touch, I shall try in what follows to preserve a decent objectivity. This is especially necessary because my subject is one that arouses either high passions or, more often, none at all.

Testimony of the Author's Friends and Acquaintances (c. 1953–68)
In 1968, at the invitation of my wife and myself, Mr and Mrs John Barry Ryan III left their New York home to attend the July Feria in Valencia, a populous industrial port on the Mediterranean coast of Spain. (With approximately 600,000 inhabitants, it is in fact Spain's third largest city, after Madrid and Barcelona.) The experience subjected the Ryans to considerable strain at first, but they buckled down, entering into the fantasies and embarking on the voyages of self-discovery that this curious town provokes, and ended up by diverting themselves greatly. During a visit to the Botanical Gardens, Mr Ryan lost his watch-fob (a small silver stirrup) under or near a banyan tree that was planted a month before Columbus set sail for the New World.

Mrs Ryan, a woman whose lion-hearted chic nothing can daunt, offered one or two comments on the place. 'Valencia', she said, 'lets you make your own choices. It preserves its own pride and lets you preserve yours. Also it doesn't matter what you wear because God knows you aren't going to *meet* anyone.' She can still mime what she describes as 'that special, unforgettable *look* you get from Spanish friends when you tell them you're going on vacation to Valencia'. It is a look of stunned, incredulous grief.

Talking to people about foreign cities you have visited is not the easiest way of enjoying yourself or of being enjoyed. If they have been to the place you want to tell them about, they may know more about it than you do, which is infuriating for you. (E.g.: 'Then we went to Modena—a lot of people skip it, but the cathedral is amazing.' 'Yes, and I hope you didn't skip the pigs'-feet at Fini's restaurant.') On the other hand, if they have not, they are apt to feel envious, which is infuriating for them. With Valencia these problems scarcely arise. Hardly anyone tops you, because hardly anyone has been there; and nobody envies you, because nobody wants to go.

Before explaining why Valencia is my favourite city on the whole Mediterranean seaboard ('the wart on the Mediterranean lip', as it is sometimes called) and why I regard it as a supreme test of identity, I shall list a few other foreign reactions. John P. Marquand, Jr, son of the late novelist and an author in his own right under the name of John Phillips, went there in the early 1950s and told me in a letter: 'I have travelled around the world and seen many wonders, but of all the water resorts of the Atlantic and Mediterranean that lugubrious city is for me the queen.' He recalled with particular relish the incontinent fireworks (very much more of these later) and the therapeutic fun-fair booths 'where you pay for the simple satisfaction of destroying clay plates—no kewpie dolls or Mickey Mouse watches for your reward, just a dun-coloured shambles of crockery.' Mr Marquand also had a warm word for the ubiquitous bats of the region, one of which appears on the city's coat of arms; like him, I do not know whether this merely reflects the fact that there *are* bats or whether it is a tribute to some brave individual bat, which flittered its way through the sleeping Moorish army with a message for the Cid clenched between its little teeth. Luis M. Stumer, an American archaeologist and *aficionado* who has been going to the bullfights in Valencia for over a decade, frankly detests the steaming humidity of its summer climate ('so reminiscent of a paper factory') but feels more affectionately towards the people: 'They are about as stupid as you will find anywhere, except Murcia, but unlike the Murcians, who are so stupid they are sullen, the Valencians are amiable.'

As for Tennessee Williams, the playwright, he went to the July Feria at my prompting some fifteen years ago. The day he arrived the water supply for the entire city was abruptly cut off, a state of affairs that lasted a week and was never referred to, let alone explained, in the local press. There was also a power-cut every evening between 7 p.m. and midnight. Although he is a man of immense physical fastidiousness, Mr Williams did not complain. Like the rest of our party, he bathed by candlelight in mineral water and *eau de Cologne*. The majority of Valencians could not afford such luxuries, and by the third day the air in the bullring was distinctly fetid. On the fourth day, we heard rumours that a plague of some kind was quietly raging near the docks. Next morning the playwright packed and left. He did not say what he thought of Valencia in so many words, and as we disinfected our hands and shook them, he looked more bewildered than angry.

Dame Margot Fonteyn, who visited the city in 1968 with the Royal Ballet, departed with what I took to be similar feelings. The company gave two open-air performances on a creaking trestle platform in the municipal park, and Dame Margot later spoke with awe of the conditions under which they had worked. It seemed that whenever anyone hit the boards after a leap, half a dozen nails would spring from their sockets, so that by the end of the evening they might have been dancing on a fakir's bed. She said she had never known anything like it, anywhere, and I had no trouble believing her.

The Verdict of the Past
There is an almost spooky unanimity about most of the published accounts of visits to Valencia in the past. In many cases the tone goes so far beyond mere distaste as to border on the vengeful. Few cities, either in the Mediterranean area or anywhere else, can have had such a consistently terrible press. The English traveller Henry Swinburne, great-grand-uncle of the poet, passed through in 1775 and wrote:

Various and overpowering are the stinks that rise up in every corner ... The houses are filthy, ill-built and ruinous; and most of the churches are tawdry, and loaded with barbarous ornaments both without and within ... In all, the judicious observer will be disgusted with loads of garlands, pyramids, broken pediments, and monstrous cornices — a taste too Gothic and trifling for any thing but the fruit of a mountebank's booth, or a puppet-show in a fair.

Understandably, he was glad to get away:
8

We shall leave Valencia tomorrow, being heartily tired of our quarters ... Every thing we eat is insipid and void of substance ... Here a man may labour for an hour at a piece of mutton, and when he has tired his jaws, find he has been only chewing the idea of a dinner ... The vegetables, with the finest outward show imaginable, taste of nothing but water. This washy quality seems also to infect the bodies and minds of the Valencians. They are largely built and personable men, but flabby and inanimate ... Low amours often consume the best part of their fortunes.

Josiah Conder, who quotes Swinburne with approval in his *Spain and Portugal* (1830), makes polite use of litotes when summing up his own impressions. Valencia, he says, is 'far from being an amusing town'. Writing a decade later, Théophile Gautier found the city 'flat, sprawling and confused in plan':

Its streets are narrow, flanked by lofty houses of surly aspect, on some of which one can still make out worn and mutilated escutcheons ... fragments of eroded sculpture, chimeras without claws, noseless women, armless knights.

He thought the cathedral a big yawn after the marvels of Burgos and Sevilla, and, like Swinburne, he was sickened by the ornamentation of the other churches: 'Surveying these extravagances, one can only bewail the total loss of so much squandered wit and talent.' He disposed of the cuisine and the citizens by quoting a single traditional couplet:

> En Valencia las legumbres son agua,
> Los hombres son mujeres y las mujeres nada.

> (In Valencia the vegetables are water,
> The men are women, and the women nothing.)

For a touch of the authentic Swinburnian rancour, we move on to *A Handbook for Travellers in Spain*, which appeared in 1845. Richard Ford, the author of this minor classic, describes the Valencians as 'perfidious, vindictive, sullen and mistrustful, fickle and treacherous':

Theirs is a sort of *tigre singe* character, of cruelty allied with frivolity; so blithe, so smooth, so gay, yet empty of all good: nor can their pleasantry be trusted, for, like the Devil's good humour, it depends on their being pleased;

at the least rub, they pass, like the laughing hyena, into a snarl and a bite: nowhere is assassination more common; they smile, and murder while they smile.

He has even less patience than Gautier with the cathedral of 'this unsubstantial city':

> The edifice is one of the least remarkable of Spanish capitals; it has also been modernised inside and outside, and in both cases without much taste ... The principal entrance is abominable, the concave form is in defiance of all architectural propriety. It was modernised by one Conrado Rodulfo, a German, and is a confused unsightly jumble of the Corinthian order.

1886 saw the arrival and rapid departure of one S. P. Scott, red in the face and wheezing ('The dust is choking, and the breeze like a whiff from a furnace'); and although Rose Macaulay admired much of the architecture when she stayed in Valencia shortly after the Second World War, her general verdict falls well short of ecstasy:

> ... it is, with its ill-assorted medley of old and new, its often tasteless modernisation surrounding (and too often engulfing) elegant seventeenth and eighteenth-century houses, its tendency to disintegrate into dusty squares that have the air of building lots, an untidy town.

For sheer bile, impartially sprayed in all directions, you can't improve on Augustus Hare, who published his findings in *Wanderings in Spain* (1906). Hare didn't even like the fertile farmland, known as the *huerta*, which extends around the city:

> The miasma from the stagnant waters ... is unwholesome, and combined with the frequent sirocco, fresh from African deserts, renders the climate very depressing.

But literature isn't wholly devoid of pro-Valencian feeling. *Melmoth the Wanderer* (1820), Charles Robert Maturin's celebrated Gothic horror story, contains a passage in which an Englishman named Stanton turns up near Valencia on a stormy evening in 1677:

> The sublime and yet softened beauty of the scenery around, had filled the soul of Stanton with delight, and he

enjoyed that delight as Englishmen generally do, silently. The magnificent remains of two dynasties that had passed away, the ruins of Roman palaces, and of Moorish fortresses, were around and above him; — the dark and heavy thunder-clouds that advanced slowly, seemed like the shrouds of these spectres of departed greatness; they approached, but did not yet overwhelm or conceal them, as if nature herself was for once awed by the power of man; and far below, the lovely valley of Valencia blushed and burned in all the glory of sunset, like a bride receiving the last glowing kiss of the bridegroom before the approach of night.

Which is very impressive until one remembers that Valencia is not in a valley and that Maturin never visited Spain. There is a parallel here with the bouncy marching song, played throughout the Latin world, by which the city is best known:

> Valencia
> Es la tierra de las flores, de la luz y del amor —
> Valencia
> Tus mujeres todas tienen de las rosas el color
>
> (Valencia
> Is the country of flowers, of light and of love —
> Valencia
> Your women all have the colour of roses)

The lyric was written by José A. Prada, a man who, like most people, went to his death without ever seeing Valencia.

Ernest Hemingway's portrait of the city in *For Whom the Bell Tolls* is sketchy and incomplete; nevertheless, it is the one to which, at this stage, I am happiest to draw your attention. Here, at least, some of the secret and eccentric flavour of the place comes through:

> 'Fernandito,' Maria said to him. 'Tell us of the time thee went to Valencia.'
> 'I did not like Valencia.'
> 'Why?' Maria asked ... 'Why did thee not like it?'
> 'The people had no manners and I could not understand them. All they did was shout *ché* at one another ... '
> 'Oh, get out of here, you old maid,' the woman of Pablo

said. 'Get out of here before you make me sick. In Valencia I had the best time of my life. *Vamos!* Valencia. Don't talk to me of Valencia.'

'What did thee there?' Maria asked ...

'We ate in pavilions on the sand ... Prawns fresh from the sea sprinkled with lime juice. They were pink and sweet and there were four bites to a prawn. Of these we ate many. Then we ate *paella* with fresh sea food, clams in their shells, mussels, crayfish, and small eels. Then we ate even smaller eels alone cooked in oil and as tiny as bean sprouts and curled in all directions and so tender they disappeared in the mouth with chewing. All the time drinking a white wine, cold, light, and good at thirty centimos the bottle ... '

'And what did thee do when not eating nor drinking?'

'We made love in the room with the strip blinds hanging over the balcony ... and from the streets there was the scent of the flower market and the smell of burned powder from the firecrackers of the *traca* that ran through the streets exploding each noon during the Feria. It was a line of fireworks that ran through all the city, the firecrackers linked together and the explosions running along on poles and wires of the tramways, exploding with great noise and a jumping from pole to pole with a sharpness and a cracking of explosion you could not believe ... '

'We have done things together,' Pablo said.

'Yes,' the woman said. 'Why not? ... But never did we go to Valencia. Never did we lie in bed together and hear a band pass in Valencia.'

Tourism on the Decline: Anti-Tourism Defined. Valencia's Virtues Adumbrated: You Wander Lonely in a Crowd.

By the standards of conventional tourism, the travellers of the past were right to sniff at Valencia. Artistically, it doesn't belong on the Grand Tour. At the same time it lacks many of the attributes that modern travellers expect of a holiday resort: 'Pittsburgh without the air pollution' is how a visiting American recently described it. But I suspect that a new kind of Mediterranean tourism, with new standards, will have to be developed—a necessary alternative since the old kind is becoming more of a penance every year. *Mare Nostrum* today is

Europe's cesspool. Much of it is an undrained tank, noxiously brimming with human waste-matter, oil and garbage. High-rise apartments and assembly-line hotels, which already infest the Spanish coast from Gibraltar to the eastern end of the Pyrenees, will soon spread until they cover the entire Mediterranean littoral. If we want solitude, translucent sea and virgin landscape, we shall have to wait for the first jumbo jet services to Madagascar or Mauritius. There are still a few Mediterranean outposts where these things are available, but their days are numbered, like the Swiss bank accounts of the property tycoons who are buying them up.

The tourist explosion, I believe, is already creating a new breed of European tourist—the anti-tourist, with appetites quite different from those of his predecessors. The traditional holiday-maker goes abroad in search of sun, sea, famous works of art, picturesque scenery and people of his own nationality and kind. The new tourism, of which I am a charter member, is more selective. Of course we insist on sun; but, for the reasons mentioned above, we are chary of sea. We quickly tire of landscape that lacks evidence of continuing human habitation, but we do not want the human beings in question to be fellow-tourists: hence we avoid popular beauty-spots and cultural centres. *Above all, we seek to escape the company of our compatriots, apart from any we may happen to be travelling with.* Valencia, where a noisy and majestic ugliness stands sentinel, ever ready to repel outsiders, is one of the few places that come close to fulfilling all our demands. We enjoy being idle in bright sunlight in a large Mediterranean city: here we can loaf, not so much solitary as truly alone, contemplative and detached while the rest of the world is visibly at work. Some people go on vacation in order to meet strangers. Others go to meet themselves. For this group Valencia, world hub of anti-tourism, is the predestined haven and hiding-place.

First Impressions: Hotels And Other Amenities, or the Lack of Them
Approached from the sea, it hits you first with dockyard squalor and clamour: a great deal of rusting and riveting is going on. Streetcars grind inland from the waterfront, past bars without character and bankrupt-looking small businesses, possibly derelict dust factories. Next, taking your choice of a dozen bridges, one or two of them very elegant, you cross a broad, litter-

spattered bed of rubble through which a dribble of yellow water runs. Such, for most of the year, is the appearance of Valencia's river, the Turia: in the autumn it has been known to rise in devastating flood. You are now in the city proper, and almost everything you see is a bank, a neon sign, a department store, a supermarket, a cinema, a snack-bar, a bristling municipal façade, or another bank. Architecturally, the twentieth century seems to be locked in mortal conflict with the late nineteenth. Spiritually, you would think that the native past had lost the battle against the Coca-Cola future without a blow being struck, without even being paid to lie down.

Both these impressions are false, but you do not realize it at first glance, or even at second. What you immediately recognize, if you are a genuine anti-tourist, is that this is a town where you can create your own private myths and live cocooned in your own emotional climate. It is obsessively unsmart, an alien nullity peopled with busy Spaniards who will ignore your presence, a blank slate upon which you (and your companions, if any) can freely doodle. This makes it a remorseless touchstone of personal relationships. And also, of course, a potential tombstone for them; because it throws you back on yourself, offering no familiar landmarks to reassure you, no peace to act as a sedative, and a bare minimum of beauty as a distraction. If a relationship can survive Valencia, it can survive anything. My own record is: one marriage and one affair laid in ruins there, and one marriage cemented. It should by now be clear that if you shun risks and love beaten paths, this is not your town. Yet it has its rewards, as we shall see, for those who grit their teeth, hold their noses, and persevere—the odd baroque doorway or belfry, glimpsed between fly-blown cafés and prematurely crumbling apartment blocks; and two astonishing art forms, one of them peculiar to the city, both of them ancient precursors of the instantly obsolescent, destructible art that the Anglo-Saxons have just discovered and made fashionable.

Not being a tourist haunt, Valencia has never learned the techniques of ingratiation or self-salesmanship. The Astoria Palace, glassy and glossy, is the only hotel with air-conditioned rooms, and although its prices are remarkably low, there are occasional lapses that may explain why the management hesitates to raise them. The last time I stayed there, for example, scalding water poured out of both bath-taps, so I had to cool my tub with the shower. And the dining-room is best ignored. I remember a meal that consisted of green paint soup, followed by a generous slice of braised eraser, served with turquoise-blue *haricots verts*. The most extraordinary hotel in the Valencia area is twelve miles outside the city—the Hostal Monte Picayo, a gargantuan architectural folly that cascades down a hill overlooking the coast road to Sagunto. It opened its doors ('lowered its drawbridge' might be a better phrase) in 1966, and its decorative style is somewhere between early *Prisoner of Zenda* and late *Late, Late Show*. The entrance hall looks like a multi-level medieval banqueting chamber, and some of the staircases seem to have been hewn out of the living rock. Stalactites of stucco festoon the ceilings; the bedrooms have television sets in frames of gilded wrought iron; and if anyone ever wants to remake *The Old Dark House* in costumes left over from *Ivanhoe*, I would guess that this must be the place. It would also be an ideal setting for a really advanced game of Murder. The lobby, as you enter, cries out for Basil Rathbone to come strolling in from behind a tapestry with a foaming mastiff on leash. 'To what', he would silkily ask, 'do we owe this unexpected pleasure? I fear I must ask you not to move. Caravaggio here is a little—shall we say?—impetuous.' Inexplicably, but characteristically, the Hostal has four swimming pools. Its other selling-points include a miniature bullring, where guests can pit their wits against an experienced and thoroughly ignoble little calf.

Hotel situation poor; golf courses in short supply; surrounding countryside undramatic; beaches not pretty and too full of local Spanish—these, according to a former U.S. consul in Valencia, are the main reasons why the city is unlikely ever to make it touristically. 'On the Spanish coast,' he says, 'Barcelona and Málaga draw the foreigners. Valencia falls right between the two. Anything it can do, they can do better.' With or without tourists, however, it is doing all right economically: local industries such as furniture and footwear are booming, and the province can always rely on its two staple exports, rice and oranges. (Valencia, mysteriously, sells rice to *the Japanese*.) What upsets the ex-consul is that the place could be even more prosperous were it not for a certain lack of vision and get-up-and-go on the part of the inhabitants: 'This is the smallest big city in Spain. You'll get three bakeries on the same block, two upholsterers across the street from one another, things like that. Somehow they can't think in larger units than small family businesses.' He shakes his head.

Instances of Tourist-Repellence

There are times when it seems as if the Valencians were going out of their way to discourage tourism. This may even be a tradition. Among the few architectural features that early Victorian travellers praised were the fourteenth-century walls that encircled the city. 'Very perfect' and 'very picturesque', Richard Ford called them. In 1871 they were torn down to provide work for the poor during a spell of severe unemployment. (Project for a sociologist: balance the social service rendered by this piece of vandalism against the historical disservice.) For a more recent example of disregard for the past, take a look at the Taurine Museum, which is one of the nastiest sights you can pay to see anywhere. Bullring photographs, buckled and discoloured, hang behind broken glass in splintering frames. Costumes worn by the illustrious dead rot on their hooks, and fungus sprouts from the stuffed bulls' heads on the walls. There is talk of moving the collection to a new home; a smarter move would be to start assembling a new collection.

A classic case of tourist-repellence is the monastery of Porta-Celi, twenty miles out of town and probably the best-known architectural landmark in the neighbourhood of Valencia. Founded in 1272, it sits on a little hill amid pine forests that have been the setting for many poems of frustrated love. Inside the walls, which at present enclose a community of only thirteen monks, there are two cloisters (one Gothic, one Renaissance), a baroque church, and spacious terraces on which white peacocks walk. Rose Macaulay wrote passionately of Porta-Celi, and for Sacheverell Sitwell it was 'one of the most beautiful of all the old Spanish abbeys'. But they both went there a long time ago. Today, as it has been for the past twenty-five years, Porta-Celi is completely closed to visitors.

Culture and Life After Dark: The Valencian Underworld Explored in a True Story

Artistically, Valencia cannot be said to have shaken the world, or even Spain, in modern times, although volumes have been written by local zealots about the 'Valencian Renaissance' that is alleged to have burgeoned in the early part of this century, producing such peripheral figures as Vicente Blasco Ibáñez, the author of *Blood and Sand*, and the pianist José Iturbi. Nor is the city terribly efficient when it comes to more frivolous forms of urban diversion, such as night-life. I don't mean that there are no nightclubs. On the contrary, there are literally dozens. In this field, at least, Valencia is going to be handily placed if the tourist invasion should ever materialize. The trouble is that most of the *boîtes* are empty most of the time, and this occasionally drives the proprietors to adopt some fairly greedy practices. By way of illustration, here is an extract from a Valencian journal I kept in the spring of 1969:

March 22: Leaving tomorrow, so determine to make last attempt to enjoy night-life of city. Select club named 'El Peep-Hole': Kathleen [my wife] is tired after week of Feria, so go alone. Arrive at midnight, doorman having assured me that floorshow begins at that hour. Descend stairs into flashily upholstered vault, deserted but for self, barman and 28 hostesses. No band, just tapes of ten-year-old hits. I order *anis*, cheapest Spanish liqueur, at bar. Fat little hostess with thick Catalan accent and hair like steel wool tells me story of her life; seems she used to be top model until photographer molested her. Buy her Scotch and ask what became of floorshow, since it's almost 1 a.m.? Barman says not long now. Order second drink for self and hostess, who continues memoirs, revealing that bitter experience has taught her to despise vulgarity in men. 1.45: still no other customers, no sign of floorshow, so call for check. Get it in spades: little matter of 1700 pesetas (well over £10). For 4 minidrinks and no cabaret, this seems outlandish. Send for boss and, filled with crusading fervour on behalf of clipped tourists everywhere, announce refusal to pay unless police officer assures me bill is correct. Boss mimes fury and disgust but finally goes in search of cop. Alone (hostess having fled at hint of trouble), calmly await vindication.

Boss returns with three uniformed cops who drag me from bar stool into alley outside, make me lean forward with hands on wall and frisk me. Even shoes are removed and searched, presumably for drugs. I ask what the hell is going on, I'm not the accused, it's me who's accusing the club, and — Cop cuts in: boss has reported me not only for declining to pay tab but for vilifying General Franco, abusing the Spanish people and calling the Valencian police force corrupt pigs. Am therefore under arrest. Blood leaves head.

Am driven in squad car to concrete blockhouse on outskirts of town, ideal for work involving glowing cigar-ends and electrodes. Hear boss dictating account of my alleged diatribes. As subversion piles on obscenity, reflect that if he is opponent of system, this must be highly therapeutic exercise. Ask permission to phone wife and lawyer. Head guard (played by late Pedro Armendariz, chewing cigar, neck bulging over collar) snarls no. Shrug and smile wryly. Bad move: Pedro swaggers over, bends till head within inches of mine, then bellows: 'Why do you smile? You are not in England now.' He can say that again, and does. (Can see London newspapers now: 'Writer seized in Spanish nightclub. Charged with insulting behaviour.' Had always assumed people in such stories were drunk. *Am not drunk, goddammit.* Steady now.) Plain-clothes detective darts out of office and demands passport. Explain that I haven't got it on me. 'Uneducated as well as a slanderer!' he sneers, and we drive to hotel to get it, sirens wailing. Am marched through lobby between cops, one of them swinging handcuffs. Then back to H.Q., followed by horrified Kathleen in taxi.

Detective reads charge to me. On sudden inspiration, feign ignorance of Spanish even greater than is actually the case, and claim that I thought check was 7000 pesetas, not 1700. Would be overjoyed, naturally, to pay 1700, most reasonable, practically a steal ... Am reaching for cash when detective interrupts: the other charges, of course, must stand until answered in court. Am vaguely aware that crime of knocking regime carries with it prison term of several years. It will be my word against boss's, and boss is Spanish. Am also, not at all vaguely, aware that accused can spend months or years in gaol awaiting trial. Mouth extraordinarily dry, ask if detective has any idea when case might come to court. In (he consults watch) about ten minutes, says this man of men, this model of non-piggish probity.

Kathleen and I are driven to courthouse with boss, latter looking rather sulky. It is now 5 a.m.: iron door of echoing fortress-like building is opened by janitor with absurdly outsize key-ring. Court consists of thin-lipped young judge who has dressed in great hurry, unless he normally wears pyjama jacket under suit. He accepts my plea that whole thing big mistake and

236 THE SOUND OF TWO HANDS CLAPPING

orders grumbling boss (who by now believes his own story) to grab my 1700 pesetas and go. Thus I walk out into new dawn and liberty, having been taught enormous unwisdom of hollering copper in a dictatorship. But: suppose I had been staying in fleabag instead of Astoria Palace, and suppose I had been bearded and bejeaned instead of shaven and suited, would the court have been convened? and would I have been believed? Answer: would I hell.

Un Peu D'Histoire: Valencia Dreams of Being a Movie Star
The known history of Valencia begins in 138 B.C., when it was settled by the Romans. What followed in the annals of the city of the brave — *la valiente ciudad*, whence its name — has been deftly compressed by Rose Macaulay:

> ... under the Romans Valencia prospered greatly, was sacked by Pompey, revived again, prospered more, was occupied by Visigoths for three centuries, by Moors for five, except for a short interval of five years at the end of the eleventh century when it was seized by that enterprising, ferocious and perfidious mercenary, the Cid. Then the conquering James of Aragon annexed it from the Moors, and presently the Catholic Kings annexed it for Castile.

In 1960 Samuel Bronston annexed it for the movies. *El Cid*, a Bronston production directed by Anthony Mann, showed the great warrior hero raising the Moorish yoke from Valencia, whose citizens were seen brandishing triumphal cabbages to hail his passage through their gates. Rodrigo Diaz de Vivar, nicknamed the Cid (from the Arabic word for 'lord'), was born in Castile around 1043. He won a high reputation for his skill in generalship and his valour in single combat, and died at Valencia in 1099: this is probably the most famous thing that ever happened there. As played by Charlton Heston, he was a muscular paradigm of magnanimity in victory and stoicism in defeat. The result was an honourable and often quite beautiful film, which might have ranked among Valencia's happiest souvenirs. It turned out to be a source of profound embarrassment. For the director, after seeing a few tests, decided that the city was not presentable enough to be allowed to play itself.

In consequence, the part was given to Peñíscola, a more photogenic spot, some eighty miles up the coast.

Vestiges of Conventional Tourism in Valencia

Despite its overwhelming attractiveness to the anti-tourist (and I haven't yet mentioned the smell in the streets, which on warm days conjures up an image of several thousand veteran turbot trapped in an avalanche of guano), I cannot deny that Valencia has one or two features that orthodox tourism would not scorn. For the most part, it keeps them well hidden and carefully under-publicized. It would be difficult, though, for even the most cursory visitor to miss the massive architectural grouping that clusters around the Plaza de la Virgen, made up of the heteromorphic cathedral, the basilica of Our Lady of the Helpless, and the sombre, four-square Palacio de la Generalidad. Juxtaposed by chance, these three diverse structures chime together in a formal congruence seldom achieved by design. But you could easily tour the cathedral without noticing, among its treasures, a small goblet of black agate, mounted on a gold stand in a simple glass case. Which would be a pity, because this chalice is supposed to be the Holy Grail itself, as used by Christ at the Last Supper. I cannot judge whether its credentials are in order, or how they match up against those of its challenger at the Cloisters in New York; but I have heard Valencians claim that on it you can still see traces of Judas's slipstick.

Similarly, the fifteenth-century Silk Exchange ('perhaps the most beautiful building in the city': Rose Macaulay) is obvious picture-postcard material: but it was not until my sixth trip to Valencia that I turned a corner behind it, crossed the Plaza Lope de Vega—a model of unplanned intimacy, with the slender bell-tower of Santa Catalina dominating one exit—and walked through an archway into the Plaza Redonda, a unique ensemble of eighteenth-century houses whose façade forms an unbroken circle, like a domesticated bullring, with a covered street-market thriving in the middle. This is a place of wonderful convenience and civility—one of the city's best-kept secrets.

The Fine Arts Museum has the usual morose contributions from Murillo, Ribera and Ribalta, and lays heavy stress on works by regional artists: some minor Goyas and a Velázquez self-portrait briefly threaten to relieve the monotony. A note more stridently Valencian is struck by the Paleontological Museum, which, unpredictably, houses the world's most extensive collection of extinct South American fauna, and by the National Ceramics Museum, which contains—in addition to tiles and pots of many periods, from the Middle Ages to Picasso —a baffling chaos of bric-à-brac, including dolls, sedan chairs, playing-cards, four-poster beds and theatre placards of the 1920s. This bizarre assembly of *objets trouvés* (many still look *perdus*) is laid out in the opulent salons of the Palacio del Marqués de Dos Aguas, and you approach it through what, for me, is Valencia's greatest monument. Most people come upon it for the first time by accident. Passing the Hotel Inglés, they glance down a sidestreet, and what they see often stops them in their tracks. There, reeling and writhing in marble coils, prefiguring *art nouveau* in its convoluted whorls of ornamentation, is the doorway of the Dos Aguas palace, carved in the 1740s from designs by the Valencian painter Hipolito Rovira, who died mad. This is baroque at its most ecstatic which is how Valencia likes it and how the last century loathed it—a disparity of taste that may account for some of the revulsion Victorian writers felt towards the place. Richard Ford found the portal 'grotesque ... a fricassée of palm trees, Indians, serpents and absurd forms'. Sacheverell Sitwell spoke for an era less aesthetically constricted when he said: ' ... it is in the style to which we must become accustomed if any pleasure is to be had from the highest expression of gay exuberance there has ever been in architecture.' He admitted that it had 'a distinct likeness in texture to almond paste', but this did not worry him. In a good light, he pointed out, many fine marble buildings look 'nicely edible'.

Who is This Man?

He declared that a league of nations was the only means whereby wars of aggression could be prevented. He said that the causes of poverty were war, a continuously expanding population, inadequate educational opportunities and an economic system based on false priorities. He insisted that public welfare was the primary aim of all government. He attacked inquisitions that employed fear to investigate men's private beliefs, and recommended introspection and self-assessment as the best guides to spiritual health. He is described in a modern history of medical psychology as 'the first true forerunner of Freud', and by a recent biographer as an undoubted Socialist. Who is he? An eighteenth-century Encyclopedist? A nineteenth-century liberal? Neither: he is Juan Luis Vives, born in Valencia in 1492 and educated at its university. He died in Bruges at the age of forty-eight, having spent the last thirty years of his life outside Spain. Here are some snippings from the voluminous work of this remarkable man, friend and equal of Erasmus and Sir Thomas More. On insanity:

> Treatment suited to each individual case should be tried; for some, gentle care; for some, teaching; others may require coercion or bonds, but everything should be done in a way likely to pacify and lead to recovery.

On education for the poor:

> It were better to strive to turn beggars into good citizens than to punish them when it is too late.

On economic inequality:

> Indeed, it is not to be tolerated in a city, I will not say in a Christian community alone but in any other as well, so long as it is a community of human beings, that some should be so wealthy that they can lavish thousands of pounds on their tombs, or on a tower, or pretentious buildings, or on a banquet, or public gifts, while for the matter of fifty or a hundred florins others are forced to endanger a girl's chastity, or an honest man's life and health, or to desert their wife and young children.

On freedom (remember, we are speaking of the early sixteenth century):

> Among all nations men are springing up, of clear, excellent and free intellects, impatient of servitude, determined to throw off the yoke of tyranny from their necks. They are calling their fellow citizens to liberty.

You cannot accuse Valencia of over-selling its most prophetic son. A bad Victorian statue in the university courtyard is the only external evidence that he ever lived there.

But What's in it for my Palate?
Good food exists in the city, but great pains are taken to conceal

it. On view beneath the vast tiled dome of the central market there is so much vegetable wealth, such an amplitude of meat and fish, that you wonder at the ingenuity with which the cooks of Valencia contrive to ruin them. Most of the hotels offer an anaemic, anonymous diet that passes for international cuisine, and the expensive restaurants tend to specialize in botched versions of renowned regional dishes. As Luis M. Stumer points out: 'Probably the worst *paella Valenciana* in the world is served in Valencia, where all the ingredients are fried after being boiled, until their texture is that of roasted peanuts and their flavour less.' The best food in the centre of town is sold at Casa Olano, a plain Basque restaurant-and-bar just behind the bull-ring. It seats only thirty, has no décor to speak of, and is always packed with Valencianos: the *patron*, a stolid patriarch in a beret, looks after the bar while perspiring middle-aged women bustle in the kitchen. Last spring I had a meal there that I would not have exchanged for anything in the Michelin galaxy. First, *almejas marinera*, on which I append my wife's notes:

Baby clams baked in an earthenware dish with oil, bread, pepper, garlic and parsley. The ingredients give nothing away. I expect the secret is the temperature at which they're cooked: low to start off with so that nothing burns or fries: removed from the fire when the oil begins to bubble. The sweet baby clams remain sweet and tender. So far from frying, the crumbled bread has the pulverised consistency of semolina. The oil is pale as if just poured from the cask. Even the chopped parsley retains its colour. You won't find this dish anywhere in the great eating capitals, and certainly not outside the Mediterranean. You won't find those clams; olive oil doesn't travel; *and above all, what self-respecting tourist restaurant would dare such simplicity?*

My italics. Next: stuffed pimentoes, sharply flavoured with basil. Next: a rack of lamb, grilled over charcoal, with a salad of sweet, tart, baseball-sized Valencian tomatoes. Finally: a perfect *crème caramel*, sleek yet not too bland. Casa Olano does not serve coffee and presents no bill: you are simply told the price, it being assumed that you will not doubt the proprietor's honesty. In this case it was his sanity, not his honesty, that seemed open to question. Four courses for two people, together with two jugs of wine, had run up a grand total of five dollars and eighty-seven cents.

Down by the dingy, overcrowded beach, alongside the docks, there is a row of low-priced hotels and restaurants. One of the latter—the biggest, cleanest and noisiest, its walls and ceiling of coal periwinkle blue—is La Pepica, which may be the best place in the world to eat before or after a bullfight. This, I imagine, is where the woman of Pablo had her prawns and eels; certainly Hemingway himself went there often, and during Feria weeks it becomes the social centre of the taurine world, the tables and Van Gogh chairs spilling out on to the sand, the sound level rising to that assertive, classless uproar you hear in so many of the finest Spanish restaurants. Not the murmur-and-giggle of jet-settery: just dukes, truck-drivers, matadors, cobblers and scholars, eating side by side. In England or France, so much more democratic in other respects, this would be inconceivable; and if Valencia ever ceases to be an anti-tourist town, no doubt La Pepica will learn how class distinctions operate in the catering game.

You enter by way of the kitchen: beyond the heaps of lobsters, clams, crayfish, shrimps, prawns and octopus, the clients sit in silhouette against the tonic blaze of sky and sea. The food is aggressively fresh and spicy, from the mussels in tomato-and-garlic sauce to the home-made *turrón*, a marvellous local dessert compounded of honey, brown sugar, crushed almonds and coffee ice-cream. The family that started La Pepica in 1890 still runs it, and Pepe Rubio, the dapper head waiter, has worked there since 1935. On bullfight days, lunch having ended at the traditional hour of five in the afternoon, Señor Rubio would leave for the *plaza de toros*, where for more than three decades, a dedicated moonlighter, he was employed as a *monosabio*, or bullring attendant, under the nickname of Pepet. It was his job to follow the picadors round the ring, keeping their horses in position with a discreetly prodding stick, and to use his own body, whenever necessary, to distract the bull's attention from an endangered colleague. After the *corrida* he would dash back and get his black tie on just in time to greet the first diners, and it could be a strange experience to have your fish soup immaculately ladled out by a man you had seen, less than an hour before, being chased by a Miura bull. Still under fifty, he retired from the ring in

1969, and the national press paid homage. 'With the departure of Pepet, Valencia loses one of its supreme attractions,' a bullfight critic wrote, going on to praise his serenity in the plaza, his skill at soothing nervous horses, his valour when drawing the bull's charge away from fallen toreros. Pepet, who has photos of himself being embraced by the likes of Hemingway, Antonio Ordoñez, El Cordobés and Orson Welles (the last-named in his capacity as *aficionado*, not as movie celebrity), sees no pressing reason for any more people to visit Valencia. 'This is a rich province,' he says. 'We work hard, and we do not need tourists. There are other ways of making money. A tourist is someone who thinks Spain is the first big city he sees when he crosses the border—San Sebastian or Barcelona if he comes from France, Málaga or Sevilla if he comes from Gibraltar. But Valencia has no frontier, so tourists do not think it is Spain. We are a city of artisans. The Moors who occupied us were magnificent artisans, and from them I think we get our love of explosives, too. These things are in our blood. We breed artisans, and we also breed artists.' Like most Valencians, Pepet sees no great difference between the two.

Summer Feria: (1) The Bulls and their Followers
This is not only a place where you can eat well, survey a few droll monuments and wander lonely in a crowd. Even if it were no more than that, I would still have gone back; but perhaps not quite so often. It is also (and this is a clue to my recidivism) a place where you can be alone in a Feria. Unlike Pamplona, which sucks you into its annual allowance of riot, Valencia retains its identity and respects yours. Pamplona *en fête* resembles a city under foreign occupation (except that it is the invaders who are being looted); but when Valencia rejoices, you will seldom see anyone non-Spanish, apart from a handful of Anglo-Saxon bullfight fans.

Moreover, not content with one Feria each year, the Valencians demand and get two. As a French observer, Alexandre Laborde, said of them in 1809:

> ... they are swayed by the love of pleasure ... they are fond
> of singing, dancing, banqueting, and all kinds of feasting ...
> these are perpetually running in their head, at work or at
> prayer, abroad or at home, in the streets or in company.

The summer Feria, held in honour of San Jaime, happens in the last week of July and features at least seven *corridas* on consecutive days. Outside the spring fair in Sevilla, this is generally the best and most representative programme of serious bullfights in the Spanish season. Experts complain that the public in Valencia is *torerista* rather than *torista*, meaning that it venerates the matador more than the bull, who should be the protagonist. The criticism is just, and it's also true that the Valencians tend to discard their idols as swiftly and rabidly as they enthrone them. Hemingway cites the case of a local hero called Chaves, who gave a few bad performances in the ring and then had a public urinal named after him. However, the rule is not invariable. Antonio Ordoñez, the reigning maestro of Spanish tauromachy, was born in 1932, and his art, now in late autumnal bloom, must soon resign itself to fading. Yet Valencia has always cherished him, even through times of eclipse; and after last year's Feria of San Jaime he was moved to give one of his most authoritative interviews. In it he coolly demolished the sacred theory that bullfighting represents the triumph of mind over matter:

Q. How does your intelligence compare with the bull's?
A. The bull is much more intelligent than I am.
Q. But it is always said that the torero dominates the brute strength of the bull by virtue of his intelligence?
A. No. Bullfighting consists of doing with the bull what he wants you to do.
Q. In that case, how can the bull's intelligence ever be controlled by the matador's?
A. *Hombre*, by collaboration.

The hard-core American *aficionados*, who turn up year after year, are better informed about the bullfight than most Valencians. Their queen-mother is Alice Hall, a retired school-teacher from Georgia who conducts herself with the elaborate gentility, though not the insobriety, of Birdie in *The Little Foxes*. One afternoon in 1968, to her surprise and joy, the matador Diego Puerta dedicated a bull to her and was awarded an ear, which he threw to her seat in the stands. I saw her that night at La Pepica, wearing a white picture hat, beaming and blushing as she clutched the blood-stained trophy to her bosom, preparatory to having it stuffed. Not all Americans who follow the bulls are as beguiling as Miss Hall. There used to be an American library in Valencia, and I recall a plump mid-Westerner who marched into it during the McCarthy era, pulled off the shelves copies of *Death in the Afternoon* and the works of Tom Paine, and jumped up and down on them, shouting to the unnerved borrowers and librarians, 'Me gusta mucho la corrida de toros, pero estas son obras Comunistas!' He was killed several years later in Torremolinos by a gust of wind that blew him into a swimming pool beside which he was practising a difficult pass with the cape.

Summer Feria: (2) The Artificial Fires
After the bullfight you shower, eat and amble off to the Feria grounds, a crowded avenue of open-air dancehalls, fun-fair rides and ornate Victorian pleasure-domes, spread out for a mile or more alongside the river. Dozens of dance bands competitively blare, and the sound of *flamenco*, rare in Valencia, may even be heard. It is apt to be brutally unauthentic: I doubt if many more Valencians can play the castanets than can play the sousaphone. The whole city seems to be out of doors, strolling *en famille*, absorbed in a purely local festival and utterly incurious about the activities of outsiders like oneself. The sense of mutually uninvaded privacies is very strong. To test the reality of this, I used to make a habit of walking expressionlessly through the Feria mob with a helium-filled balloon on a twenty-foot string tied to my left ear. Apart from a few impressionable infants, nobody ever paid the slightest attention.

Around 1 a.m., the lights dim and the people settle down, wives rocking sleeping babies, everyone patiently gazing upwards, waiting for the spectacle to begin, this thing the Valencians do better than anyone else: which is to paint the sky. It was at a summer Feria that I first saw the more lyrically short-lived of the two great transient arts of Valencia—*fuegos artificiales*, artificial fires, fireworks, the art that dies in the act of being born, 'like the lightning, which doth cease to be/ Ere one can say: "It lightens".' These displays, nightly events during the Feria, are carefully, even symphonically planned: statement of theme, development, militant movement, pastoral digression and apocalyptic conclusion is a common sequence:

and considerations of form, just as much as sheer awe, dictate the amount of applause at the end.

Three giant bangs, like the *trois coups* that precede the rise of the curtain in French theatres, announce that the volcano is about to erupt; and the movements are punctuated by single detonations. But these are niceties you do not notice until familiarity sets in, four or five displays later. What you notice the first time is quite simply one of the greatest free entertainments on earth: a prolonged spasm of organized fire, animating the night sky in streaks and splashes, so that it looks like an indigo sea reflecting sunlight at noon. There are the solo heavyweight missiles, blown into the air from mortars and descending in quintuple tiers of expanding colour, prodigally scattering bracelets of emerald fire, ruby pendants and vast drooping sapphire chandeliers; the salvoes of elemental noise, rising to a percussive crescendo of violence like Philly Jo Jones run amok in your ear; the flaring swarms of marsh-lights that whistle, or fizz in circles, or dart laterally like mayflies, or even float down by parachute, illuminating the whole townscape; and always the rockets in their regiments, thrown into battle regardless of casualties, rushing upwards to re-enact in multiple form the big-bang theory of cosmogony—initial flash, bright centrifugal spray, and final decline into darkness. They are images, on the way up, of individual birth, so many spermatozoa squirming for survival; on the way down, of cosmic death, so many cooling stars. You realize that an art superficially childish can be emotionally overwhelming, touching some very resonant chords indeed. Thanksgiving by fire, the element that warms us and cooks our food, must be one of the oldest and most appropriate means of human celebration. Three more explosions signal the end of the show, and the spectators clap their approval (or, more rarely, hiss their disdain) of the pyrotechnics manufacturer who provided it. If it has been a good night, you will observe, as they disperse, that their eyes are shining. So are your own, and strangers look at you in recognition. You have shared with them a glittering, shimmering, shattering, zooming-every-which-way experience; and when the celestial gang-bang is over, and you walk home through night air that is dense with cordite, along avenues strewn with the sticks of rockets, it is not uncommon to feel a momentary glow of communal bliss.

There are daytime fireworks, too, beginning at 1.30 p.m. in the main square, and watched with the same critical intentness. Since even a Valencian might baulk at attempting to outshine the sun, the emphasis by day is on unaccompanied sound: if they cannot dazzle you, by God they will deafen you. Puff-flash-boom, multiplied several thousand times, is the outcome: conversation ceases, windows shake, and late-sleeping strangers shoot bolt upright in their hotel beds, wondering why anyone would choose Valencia for a pre-emptive strike. When the barrage is over, applause breaks out, the audience having taken rhythm as well as volume into account. Until a few years ago the streets radiating from the plaza were hung on Feria days with cables of fire-crackers, as described by Hemingway, and only when they had all exploded, like fuses leading to a keg of gunpowder, did the big bombardment begin. But so much damage was done *en route* (John Marquand, Jr, writes nostalgically of 'waiters dousing smouldering awnings with pitchers of water'), and so much inconvenience caused by squibs plopping into the drinks at sidewalk cafés, that this extra refinement has been abolished. The latest development is the use of coloured powders mixed with the explosives, so that puffs of violet, primrose, royal blue and vermilion smoke fleck the sky, producing a *pointilliste* effect in contrast to the bold dripping brush-strokes of the evening performances. Drifting on the wind, these specks intermingle to make fugitive patterns—a thin carpet of abstraction floating over the city, advertising nothing but its own dissolving prettiness.

Spring Feria: (1) Fireworks at Closer Range
The other Valencian Feria, and the first big one of the Spanish year, is Las Fallas, which takes place in the douce weather of mid-March, less oppressive than the blasting heat of July. Las Fallas is even more intensely provincial than the summer fair: the city fills with peasants from the *huerta*, little brass bands from neighbouring townships strut through the streets, and there are endless processions of tiny children in traditional costume, looking like mobile nosegays. Valencia becomes an extended family unit, an inflated village. It is as if you had wandered into somebody else's dream—a private world with its own calendar, ceremonies and obsessions, discordantly co-existing with the public world of streetcars, lottery tickets and

the Banco de España. The Fallas bullfights are less numerous (there are rarely more than four or five) and as a rule less exciting than the summer ones, mainly because the season has hardly begun and the matadors are still out of touch; but the fireworks are even more glorious. There is an international competition, carrying with it immense prestige and a first prize of 50,000 pesetas for the best *castillo*, or display. Last year, entries came from France, Portugal, Italy, Japan and the top three Spanish pyrotechnical factories, all of which, by a coincidence that hardened long ago into a tradition, are situated in the province of Valencia.

To watch at close quarters a really large *castillo* being prepared for detonation calls up several confused emotions, including not only mild apprehension but a fair amount of contempt for gentlemen in England now abed who will live to kick themselves for not having been with you and the rest of the happy few upon Saint Crispin's *Da-a-a-ay!* In the middle of the central plaza, what looks like a battlefield is laid out behind a high wire fence, enclosing an area roughly a hundred yards long and seventy wide. There they stand, an army awaiting the order to charge—the formations of rockets, lined up like infantry; then the small mortars, or light artillery; and then the big guns, the heavy stuff, nearly twelve inches in diameter and over three feet high, each ready to launch a missile that can spawn up to thirty separate explosions. These latter are solidly sandbagged to hold them in position: like all the other devices, they are chain-fused. The whole complex arsenal, worth roughly £1,000 (paid out of civic funds) and weeks in the planning, has been expressly designed to be blown to cinders inside twenty minutes. Silent figures in goggles and orange helmets now begin to pass among the fireworks with flares, lighting the fuses. Soon they are barely visible through the holocaust, like attendant demons in a benign inferno, or torch-bearers at a funeral pyre raised up in honour of disposable art.

The Pirotecnia Brunchu, one of the ruling triumvirate in Spanish fireworks, is a family concern that has operated in the same ratty suburb of Valencia since it was founded in 1809. The present owner is Luis Brunchu, a burly, calmly domineering man in his mid-forties. Fireworks are not big business: there are only thirty workers in Don Luis's factory, and he dresses more like a farmer than a member of the managerial class. He is a craftsman, taciturn and pragmatic, with a quasi-mystical faith in his product. 'Fireworks', he says, 'are an art on their own. They speak to the soul through the eyes. We are more than painters because our canvas is God's sky, and our pictures are alive — *they move*.' Don Luis's office is full of diplomas, silver cups and other trophies, and he carries on a brisk export trade: the King of Morocco, for example, never lets a major state occasion go by without ordering a *castillo* from Brunchu. (Definition of a big *castillo*: one consisting of not less than 10,000 explosions.) 'Fireworks came to Spain from China, by way of Italy,' Don Luis says. 'Today, we Valencians, with perhaps some Italians and Portuguese, are the best firework designers in the world. This is a very ancient art. We build on classical traditions, but we are always experimenting with new forms, always trying to improve.' (How many matadors have I heard describing their work in exactly the same terms!) 'Look at midday fireworks,' he adds, 'I was the first to add colour to sound.' And as for night-time shows: not long ago Brunchu's technicians perfected a device that rises, then comes down, then shoots up again, flaming all the time until it vanishes into the sky. Called *una corona de subir y bajar* — a rising and falling crown — it is a firework with a built-in helicopter.

Fire has its own vocabulary, venerable and pleasantly fanciful. Don Luis helped me to compile this glossary:

carcasas: big mortars
tracas: strings of fire-crackers
luzes fugaces: fugitive lights (flying in all directions)
estrellas: stars (shooting)
lagrimas de colores: tears of colour
cabelleras: comets' tails
palmeras: palm-trees (with explosions shaped like palm-leaves)
paracaidas: parachute flares
fuentes luminosas: luminous fountains
bombas japoneses: Japanese bombs (which explode to look like dandelion clocks)
ramilletes: bouquets of flowers
serpentinas de colores: coloured twirlers (with spiral trajectory)
mariposas oscillantes: flickering butterflies

Spring Feria: (2) The Art of Cremation and the Cremation of Art
Valencia's second impermanent art is considerably weirder.

Falla means bonfire in Valencian dialect, and the festival to which it gives its name is certainly an ordeal by fire, but the word has come by extension to mean the object that is burned. There may be over two hundred of these objects in any given year, and it is not easy even to describe them, far less to account for them. *Fallas* are exuberant, satirical, semi-symbolic, semi-realistic, garishly painted groups of statuary, made of *papier-mâché*, wood and wax, and executed in a visual style of gross and stupendous flamboyance, combining elements borrowed from surrealism, comic strip, decadent baroque and mature Walt Disney. Some are relatively small, not more than a dozen feet high, but many are gigantic, towering above four- and even five-storey buildings to heights that sometimes top eighty feet. They are transported in sections to street-corners, cross-roads and plazas all over the city: throughout the night of March 16th they are laboriously erected, under arc-lights set up for the benefit of Spanish television. Each may cost as much as a million pesetas. None survives longer than three days. Shortly after midnight on March 19th, the feast-day of San José, all the *fallas* are simultaneously incinerated in a con-flagration beyond anything seen elsewhere in Europe since the last fire-storms of the Second World War.

Looking back on that paragraph, I see how miserably it fails to convey what a *falla* is like. Let me be more circumstantial. Walk along any Valencian street where fairy-lights are hung. (In Feria time the grimy old hag of a city puts on all her tiaras.) At the next corner, you will find that a crowd has gathered. Some of its members are carrying one or other of the many little booklets you can buy, containing maps, sketches and descriptive interpretations of the current crop of *fallas*. What stands before them may be a model of the crescent moon, with the face and hair of Brigitte Bardot, peering through an outsize microscope at a group of pigs who are rolling about in an orgiastic frenzy. That is by no means all that is happening, but you will begin to understand why the explanatory booklets have such a wide sale. From one of them you learn that this *falla*, entitled 'Malevolent Germs', shows the moon surveying with dismay the ill-behaved human beings who are about to explore and contaminate her. (My examples are drawn from the 1969 Feria.) A block further on, three predatory fish, each about thirty feet in length, pursue a terrified minnow through a marine forest of pink coral. Solution: the U.S., Russia and China are competing to gobble up the world. Most *fallas*, you are dimly aware by now, follow the same general pattern: a dominant theme is expressed in a large central object (e.g. the helmeted head of a scowling Viking, symbolizing 'Invasions') and illustrated in life-size vignettes, laid out around the base. Quite often, the symbolism goes mad, and the *falla* becomes a fantastic welter of visual puns, local references and grandiose philosophical meditations. In 1969 the Plaza de la Merced came up with one of this kind, a cautionary mish-mash whose targets ranged from the theory of natural selection to the unreasonable number of holes in the streets of Valencia. It was called, with simple finality, 'Life', and the handbook described it thus:

On top, the hunted deer, with the wormy apple of the world impaled on its antlers, represents the weaker members of the human race, always persecuted by the ravenous hounds of the powerful. Nearby, the four horsemen of the Apocalypse ride out of the cauldron of the future in a thick cloud of smoke. A witch manufactures synthetic foods which are poisonous. Life inverted: the blacks lament because they are not white, the whites go to the beaches to become black. Those who work and cannot earn enough to live are contrasted with those who speculate and live richly without working. A poor old man is besieged by vultures, relatives waiting to make off with his savings The tablets of God's law are erased by the law of the survival of the fittest. A small businessman in a little boat is drowned by the rival waves of big business. Some young hippies in a paper dinghy run aground on a reef of guitars and amplifiers. Satan welcomes the wedding of the year: Jacqueline and Onassis. Excess of bureaucracy: the public service companies spend too much time and money digging up the roads. To pay for the studies of his children, a father tightens his belt. A man who has had a heart transplant suffers a heart attack on seeing the bill. A rabbit joins the queue of stupid women who are waiting to buy the pill.

Only a Latin could conceive and create an object like that. It reminds me of an exalted passage in Peter Fleming's book,

Brazilian Adventure. He is writing about a monumental piece of civic sculpture he saw in Rio de Janeiro:

Victory has got a half-nelson on Liberty from behind. Liberty is giving away about half a ton, and also carrying weight in the shape of a dying President and a brace of cherubs. (One of the cherubs is doing a cartwheel on the dying President's head, while the other, scarcely less considerate, attempts to pull his trousers off.) Meanwhile an unclothed male figure, probably symbolical, unquestionably winged, and carrying in one hand a model railway, is in the very act of delivering a running kick at the two struggling ladies, from whose drapery on the opposite side an eagle is escaping, apparently unnoticed. Around the feet of these gigantic principals all is bustle and confusion. Cavalry are charging, aboriginals are being emancipated, and liners launched. Farmers, liberators, nuns, firemen and a poet pick their ways with benign insouciance over a sub-soil thickly carpeted with corpses, cannon-balls, and scrolls. So vehement a confusion of thought, so arbitrary an alliance of ideas, takes the reason captive and paralyses criticism.

So it is with the *fallas*. Whether or not they are art is a topic much debated in Valencia. The men who invent them are called *artistas falleros*, and some become famous enough to have books written about them. A successful *falla* artist has a squad of assistants and may spend a third of his year designing and executing three or four commissions. In addition to his fee, he may receive one of the prizes for imaginative achievement that are awarded to *fallas* in various categories of expensiveness: the winner in the top group picks up around £700. On the outskirts of Valencia there is a district known as the *Falla* Artists' City, mainly occupied by workshops in which some twenty thousand people are employed all the year round on the building of these mighty absurdities. Critics anxiously study the annual output for trends: is there a movement towards neo-classicism? Are modernist tendencies growing or waning? Is it still correct to speak of the *fallas* as a late and low offshoot of baroque? But these are scholarly quibbles. The main point is that we have here that rarity in contemporary Europe, a thriving and popular primitive art, able to assimilate ancient myths and yesterday's headlines without the least hint of self-consciousness.

The late Mariano Benlliure, a notable Valencian sculptor, used to insist that any connexion between *fallas* and true art (such as proper sculpture) was coincidental. 'There are *fallas* that look like monuments,' he said, 'and monuments that look like *fallas*.' Spain still makes a rigid distinction between High Art and Pop Culture. In 1949, Francisco Almela Vives, of the Royal Spanish Academy, published a history of the Valencian Spring Feria, in which he declared that although every *falla* needed a modicum of art, too much could lead to pretentiousness. 'One must avoid confusionism,' he wrote, 'which is hybridism and, in consequence, sterility.' Señor Vives would be amazed to learn how many Western critics nowadays regard 'hybridism' as a source of strength rather than weakness. It is precisely the crossbred *fallas*, amalgams of many styles and expressive on several different levels, that seem to us the most fertile.

In some respects the *falla* artist lacks the freedom we associate with modern art in the Western world. He works to order, inasmuch as the theme of each structure is decided by the district *falla* committee, which also raises from the local inhabitants the money to pay for it. But this limitation is inherent in all commissioned art. What is sadder is that under Franco's regime the Feria has lost much of the polemical zest that once made it, by all accounts, the most trustworthy political barometer in Spain. It began in the thirteenth century as a jamboree in praise of San José, patron saint of carpenters. With the coming of spring and more hours of sunlight, the members of the guild would burn the cheap wooden fixtures that held the candles by which they worked during the winter evenings. Soon the bonfire was fed with quaintly carved wooden figures, bearing recognizable faces, and the Feria became (to quote from Nina Epton's *Spanish Fiestas*) 'a displaced end-of-the-year festival, with its typical burning of the old year's vestiges and a public display of satire'. In its present form, involving large-scale symbolic constructions, it dates from the middle of the eighteenth century—the height of the baroque epoch from which so much that is profoundly Valencian derives. In 1789 somebody set up a *falla* with three moving dolls: one wonders why the idea of animation was allowed to die without issue. Now and then censorship was imposed, but always obliquely. If the authorities wanted to suppress a particular *falla*, they would do so on the grounds that the flames from its burning might endanger nearby buildings. Occasionally there would be an outbreak of female nudity in the statues, and the artists would be instructed to clothe the offending organs. It is noticeable that contemporary *falla* artists sneak in explicit erotic detail wherever they can, this being one of the few Spanish art forms in which they can get away with it.

Up to the end of the nineteenth century there were rarely more than twenty *fallas* on show. In 1927 there were fifty, and two years later the number had risen to a hundred. Today, as we have seen, there are twice as many; but with this proliferation has come a dilution of intensity, a faltering of purpose. A century ago the *fallas* were to Valencia what Aristophanic comedy was to Athens. It was said that by looking at them you could tell what had been happening in the world and in Spain during the preceding twelvemonth. This is still broadly true: in the work of certain *falla* artists, in their handling of arrogant or avaricious faces, you discern a harsh, splenetic power that would not have disgraced Daumier. What has vanished is radical dissent in the realm of ideas. Anti-clericalism has disappeared completely. The behaviour of authority in national (as opposed to municipal) affairs is no longer criticized, and political (as opposed to moral) comment is virtually non-existent.

Worse still, the social and ethical attitudes embodied in the *fallas* are rabidly and ferociously conservative—a ghastly fate to befall a popular art. They are in general xenophobic, anti-youth, anti-sexuality and anti-revolution. Among the images offered for general disapproval in the 1969 Feria were: workers who get above themselves (represented as pigs in finery), student rebels, young people who like rock (jiving donkeys), girls in miniskirts (pigs again), women who want emancipation, women who overspend at the hairdresser's, women who try to dominate their husbands, and women who take the Pill. The handbook says of one *falla*: 'On the left, a robust marriage fruitfully grows, bearing more and more children; while on the other side we see a pair of hairy, incontinent undesirables who have done nothing to increase the population of the world.' What other targets? Traffic congestion, abstract art, underdressed foreigners, hotel-keepers who batten on the Feria, and (repeatedly) Gibraltar, which is to right-thinking Spaniards what Cuba is to American hawks. This is a festival in which sour, admonitory themes are decked out in bright, unbridled colours and shapes. The most ribald feature is the voluptuous moulding, in *fallas* ostensibly meant to attack hippie immorality and the dreaded bikini, of female breasts and bottoms. Subversion is confined to *graffiti*. Painted slogans on the walls of tenements advocate worker power and 'España Socialista'. How seriously should they be taken? Probably not very; but we must not too quickly forget that in the Spanish civil war, Valencia was one of the last strongholds of anti-Franco resistance.

The Fire This Time

On March 19th, a red letter day in the pyromaniac's calendar, the Feria culminates by consuming itself. This is the Nit de Foc — Valencian dialect for 'night of fire' — and throughout the preceding twenty-four hours a rattle of what sounds like gunfire is heard in the streets, as if nests of snipers were being mopped up. People are letting off private explosions in readiness for the big show. Quite mature men in lounge-suits stroll up to you holding fizzing fire-crackers and genially toss them at your feet. This is a form of salutation, not intended to frighten: no Valencian can ever understand why anyone should be intimidated by noise. After dinner, you should drop in for a moment at the Parador de Foc, which is a nightclub specially set up for the Feria in the municipal park. *Le Tout-Valence* is there, jammed into a billowing tent made of canvas painted inside to simulate tapestry and lit by chandeliers. About four thousand people have come to hear an imported French pop group, and the startling thing is that *all the men are wearing dinner-jackets*. Where else in Europe would you find two thousand men wearing dinner-jackets in the same *building*, never mind the same tent? Having pondered this, you move on towards the main plaza. The climax is approaching and already the streets are filling up.

The next hour is a series of pictures inscribed by fire on the retina. Across the square the tower of Pisa is burning. (That was the official civic *falla* in 1969, an eighty-foot simulacrum with a sculpted group of brawny Valencian workers in the act of effortlessly restoring Pisa's folly to a vertical position.) At the ends of narrow alleys, at large intersections and in little squares only a few yards across, walls of white flame are going up. Two hundred and ten temporary art-works are being put to the torch as thousands cheer. They are burned, the Valencians tell you, in order to demonstrate that malice is mortal and that beauty, too, does not last for ever; rather a laborious way, one would have thought, of driving home two fairly uncontroversial points. It might be truer to say that they are spectacularly destroyed because spectacular destruction is the one sight on earth that fascinates everyone.

Jean Tinguely's self-destroying machines are petty sophistications, unserious toys, beside this basic, primordial sacrifice by fire. Inevitably, fireworks supplement the spectacle. The whores in the Barrio Chino sit through it all with extreme unconcern, looking like the models on the *fallas* themselves as their faces impassively take on the tints of the flashing rockets. The miraculous Valencian fire brigade meanwhile contrives, as discreetly as possible, to prevent private property and historic monuments from being damaged beyond repair: the crowd jeers the firemen as spoilsports. From some street-corners you can watch three or four cremations at the same time. Flying embers eat into your clothes, and every minute or so a crash of falling timber, greeted by a roar of applause, marks the collapse of yet another sky-scraping caprice. *'Precioso!'* I heard an old woman murmur, beaming through a haze of ash at a hundred-foot sheet of flame. High over her head she was holding a baby in a christening dress. I thought for a moment that she was going to throw it in.

The Spirit of Fiesta: Valencia Unmasked as Either an Integral Part of Civilization or a Well-baited Booby-Trap
The Feria has a modern urban setting, but it has not been uprooted from its past. This is not a freak-out, an acid high, a happening; a firework display in Central Park, accompanied by the ritual burning of a mountain of dummies from Macy's windows, would not produce the same exhilaration, because it would be out of context. Like all good fiestas, this is a celebration of something specific, channelled through an appropriate form. Its original content—the death of winter—is vividly present, but formalized, given a shape; and this is one of the secrets of deep enjoyment.

What is civilization? According to one judgment, it is a convenient and agreeable method of enjoying the resources of this planet which was perfected between the early fifteenth and late eighteenth centuries and has been practised by the occupants of a quadrilateral area whose four corners are Athens, Vienna, London and Sevilla. Valencia just scrapes in under the ropes of that admirable definition. It is, I hope, too perverse and unsightly a city ever to figure on the regular tourist route. I tell myself that people aren't ready for it. (It is definitely not ready for them.) But I could be wrong. It may even be that by the very act of claiming Valencia for anti-tourism, I am spoiling it for anti-tourists.

To guard against that possibility, let me stress that it really is something ultimate in pest-holes, and that anyone seduced by this love-letter into making reservations will be the victim of an epic put-on. I should also like to place on record a remark made by the present Lady Harlech—then Miss Pamela Colin, the bright young London editress of American *Vogue*—who joined Mr and Mrs Ryan in Valencia during the July Feria of 1968. She seemed chipper enough at the time but afterwards broke down and said: 'To be alone in Valencia is to be permanently twenty minutes this side of suicide.' Since she had never been alone in Valencia, I felt tempted to ask how she could be so sure, but her voice was trembling with conviction, and there would have been no point in arguing with her. I pass her reaction on, for what it is worth, as a warning to potential trespassers.